Beachcomber's Paradise

Beachcomber's Paradise

Selections from the writings of E. J. Banfield

edited by
James G. Porter

ANGUS & ROBERTSON PUBLISHERS

ANGUS & ROBERTSON PUBLISHERS
London . Sydney . Melbourne

First published in Australia by Angus & Robertson Publishers in 1983

Copyright © Text selection and introduction James G. Porter 1983
Copyright © Photograph selection Angus & Robertson Publishers 1983

National Library of Australia
Cataloguing-in-publication data.
Banfield, E. J. (Edmund James) 1852-1923.
  Beachcomber's Paradise
  ISBN 0 207 14756 6.

  1. Queensland — Description and travel.
  I. Porter, James, 1929-. II. Title.
919.43'0441

Typeset in 12pt Goudy Old Style by Graphicraft Typesetters Ltd, Hong Kong
Printed in Hong Kong

CONTENTS

Introduction 8

DREAMS TO REALITIES

Dreams to Realities 14

THE ISLAND

The Genius of the Isle 18
Habitation 20
Tropic Glory 22
Smiling Morn 24
Curious Crinkled Shadows 26
Beachcombing Instincts 28
A Bush Track 30
A Beach Almanac 33
Babbling Beaches 34
A Sailing Mishap 36
In the Making of a Chair 38

ON WEATHER

Worshipper of the Sun 40
Sorcery of the Sea 42
A "Temperate" Climate 44
The Scene-shifter 47
Wet Season Days 49
A Cyclone 51
Restoration 54
A Spinner of Sand 55
Refuse of Ages 56

SOUNDS, SILENCES AND SCENTS

Wooer of the Muses 58
A Tropic Night 59
Reading to Music 62
Sweet Airs 63
The Season of Scents 64

Neighbouring Isles and "Australia"

Isles Rediscovered 68
A Little Cove 71
Heights of Hinchinbrook 72
Isle of the Papaw 74
Silent Green River 76

The Plants which Crowd Each Other

Beach Plants 80
A Jungle Flower 84
The Conquering Tree 85
Silent Strangler 88
The Host 90
Mauve, Green and Grey 91
Tissue Paper and Spiced Honey 92
A Prickly Climbing Palm 93
A Lost Chord 95

Fruits

Dependent Upon Man 98
Mangoes and Mangoes 100
A Perfect Diet 101

Birds and their Rights

Daybreak Fugue 106
An Earthly Psalmist 107
Swift as Light — Silent as Dawn 108
The Sun-bird 110
Flight Soft as a Falling Leaf 112
Three Fishers 113
Smart Scrub Fowl 116
Nutmeg Pigeons 118
Terns 119
A Drongo — in Name and Deed 120
Socialistic Birds 122
Calloo-calloo 126

Butterflies and Lesser Insects

Lovers 128
Pilgrims of the Fence 130
Green-ant Cordial 132
An Actor 135
A Spider and a Bat 136
A Reasoning Wasp 137
Oo-boo-boo the Tarantula 138

OF FROGS, SNAKES AND FOUR-FOOTED CREATURES

Musical Frogs   142
A Death Adder and a Bird   143
Fight to a Finish   144
Coom-bee-yan the Echidna   146
Frugivorous Rats   147

LIFE OF THE SEA

Nature's Cruel Battlefield   150
Watery Meteors   154
Primordial Life   156
A Pearl in the Making   159
A Fantastic Patchwork   160
The Anemone and the Fish   161
A Sea-hare   163
Masquerading as a Spray of Seaweed   164
A Sand Crab and Bird Policemen   166
Sharks and Rays   168
Death Adder of the Sea   170
Four Thousand like One   172
Diet of Slush and Grit   173

THE FIRST MEN

Ancestral Shade   176
Art Studios   179
Fruits of the Earth   182
The Soul Within the Stone   184
To Paradise and Back   189

Photographic Credits   192

INTRODUCTION

Edmund James Banfield (1852-1923) has been called Australia's Thoreau. Certainly Banfield was an original thinker, a meticulous chronicler of natural history, and an untiring seeker of the essential truths of life. But whereas the American philosopher, who lived a half century earlier than Banfield, was an idealist reaching for what many consider unattainable heights, Banfield was a practician. Thoreau believed in simplifying one's life to the extreme, an idea he tried out for two years during his lone sojourn at Walden Pond. But if anyone on this earth ever put Thoreau's lofty ideals to the complete practical test, it was the Beachcomber of Coonanglebah, the aboriginal name for Dunk Island. Banfield lived that kind of life to the full, from the day of his commitment to his death on the island twenty-five years later.

It is interesting to note that at the very age when Thoreau's prolific literary career came to an end with his death at forty-five of tuberculosis, Banfield was just abandoning civilisation to begin what he would call his real life. Although Thoreau remained a bachelor all his life, Banfield's wife Bertha shared and enriched *his* island experience.

Alec Chisholm compared him to Gilbert White (1720-1793), the first notable English writer of natural history. Chisholm said of Banfield: ". . . his taste for natural history was unforced and sincere. He was, perhaps, a combination of Gilbert White and Thoreau, spiced and quickened by the sun of the tropics; so that he wrote engagingly of the wonder and beauty of his demesne — with an occasional excursion (as in *Tropic Days*) into the realm of Imagination — and accumulated a mass of valuable observations, including several discoveries new to science."

Edmund Banfield was born in England on 4 September 1852 and was only two years old when he accompanied his family on their migration to Australia. His father, J. W. Banfield, founded a newspaper in Maryborough, western Victoria, then took over a paper in Ararat, where Edmund later began a career in journalism which was to take him in 1882 to Townsville, North Queensland. He worked on the *Townsville Daily Bulletin* until 1897, when he and his wife Bertha went to live on Dunk Island. He wrote articles for the Townsville newspaper for the rest of his life, and in 1908 his first book, *Confessions of a Beachcomber*, was published in England. That was followed in 1911 by *My Tropic Isle*, and in 1918 by *Tropic Days*. Following Banfield's death in 1923, his remaining papers were collected together by Alec Chisholm and published in 1925 as *Last Leaves from Dunk Island*.

Banfield was a sick man when, at the age of forty-five, he decided upon a retreat to his Isle of Dreams. He was to write later: "When I landed feebly on September 28, 1897, and crawled up on the beach beyond the datum of the most recent high tide to throw myself prone on the consoling sand I was worn, world-weary, and pale, and weighed 8 st. 4 lb. Now my weight is 10 st. 2 lb., and my complexion uniformly sun-tinted."

It was no organic disease which had debilitated Edmund, but merely nervous exhaustion brought on by crowded years of newspaper work. He had been contemplating "a life of seclusion in the bush" for some time, and had long been fascinated by the islands dotted along the North Queensland coastline. Just a year before making the move, he and Bertha had sailed on a holiday cruise up the coast 160 kilometres north of Townsville. "In September of the year 1896 with a small party of friends we camped on the beach of this island — the most fascinating, the most desirable on the coast of North Queensland."

Coonanglebah: "From the sea, merely a range displaying the varied leafage of jungle and forest. A steep headland springing from a ledge of rock on the north . . . an obtruding sand-spit to the west, enclose a bay scarcely half a mile from one horn to the other, the sheet of water almost a perfect crescent, with the rocky islet of Purtaboi, plumed with trees, to indicate the circumference of a circle . . . Run the boat on the sand at high-water, and the first step is planted in primitive bush — fragrant, clean and undefiled."

The weary journalist had fallen hopelessly in love with an island, and had been so bold as to make a decision. Yet, when it came to the point of departure for the Isle, he was suddenly full of doubts. "We cannot always trust in ourselves and in the boldest of our illusions. There must be trial . . ." But everything had been arranged — a prefabricated cedar hut, tools, initial food supplies — and he had given up his job. So they sailed on the appointed day.

". . . it was an inauspicious landing. With September begin the north-east winds, and we had an average experience that afternoon. Was it not a farce — a great deal more than a farce: a saucy, flippant imposition on the tender mercies of Providence — for an individual who could not endure a few hours of tossing on the bosom of the ocean without becoming deadly sick, to imagine that he possessed the hardihood to establish a home even in this lovely wilderness? . . . They spread out tents and rugs for the weak mortal who had greatly dared, but who, thus early, was ready to faint from weariness and sickness. They made comforting and soothing drinks, and spoke of cheery things in cheery tones; but the sick man refused to be comforted. He wished himself back, a participator in the conflicts of civilisation, and was fain to cover his face — there was no wall to which to turn — and fancy that the most dismal sound in the universe was the surly monotone the north-easter harped on the beach. We reposed that night among the camp equipment, the sick man caring for naught in his physical collapse and disconsolation . . .

"But the first morning of the new life! A perfect combination of invigorating elements. The cloudless sky, the clear air, the shining sea, the green folded slopes of Tam O'Shanter Point opposite, the cleanliness of the sand, the sweet odours from the eucalypts and the dew-laden grass, the luminous purple of the islands to the south-east; the range of mountains to the west and north-west, and our own fair tract — awaiting and inviting, and all the mystery of petted illusions about to be solved! Physic was never so eagerly swallowed nor wrought a speedier or surer cure."

For the first couple of years Banfield took out a special lease of a small area of the island, ". . . only for the period during which our verdant sentiments were put to the test. That phase having passed without the destruction of a single illusion, no restraint was imposed upon the passion to possess the land." He then freeholded the equivalent of about 145 hectares.

Two months' provisions had been brought that first day, and arrangements made for mail and further supplies to be carried by the weekly coastal steamer. They set about clearing scrub and putting together the prefabricated, ceilingless, cedar hut, as well as building from scratch another "little shambling structure of rough slabs and iron walls — kitchen and dining-room . . . According to the formula neatly printed in official journals, the building of a slab hut is absurdly easy — quite a pastime for the settler eager to get a roof of bark or thatch over his head . . . When you have fallen your tree and sawn off a block of the required length, you have only to split off the slab. Ah! but suppose the timber does not split freely, and your heavy maul does; and the wedges instead of entering have the habit of bouncing out as if they were fitted with internal springs, and your maul wants renewal several times, until you find that the timber prescribed is of no account for such tools; and at best your slabs run off to nothing at half length, and several trees have to be cut down before you get a single decent slab, and everybody is peevish with weariness and disappointment, the rudest house in the bush will be a long time in the building."

Of course the ceilingless hut was an open invitation to the tropical wildlife. "Our desire to live in the open air became almost compulsory, for though you fly from civilisation and its thralls you cannot escape the social instincts of life. The hut became the focus of life other than human . . ." Beady-eyed geckoes, moths, beetles attracted by the kerosene lamp at night, buzzing wasps, bees and spiders, and in the end, bats and snakes. For a while the bats were tolerated because they were a check upon the mosquitoes, but when, eventually, snakes began to come in to gobble up the bats hanging from the rafters in early morning, the mosquito-

catchers were ejected. "So we lived, more out of the hut than in it, from October 1897, until Christmas Day 1903." After that they moved into a larger, more comfortable bungalow and there was room to accommodate Essie, the little Irish housekeeper who had been with the Banfields previously in Townsville. Essie was to remain on the island for the rest of Banfield's life — in fact, it was not until a year after his death that she and Bertha left.

Banfield, as one of Australia's earliest conservationists, was very conscious of having to disturb his pristine wilderness. "... this plot of the Garden of Eden, was not to be left entirely in its primitive state. It was firmly resolved that our interference should be considerate and slight; that there should be no rude and violent upsetting of the old order of things ... A certain acreage of land was to be cleared for the cultivation of tropical fruits; of vegetables for everyday use ... Bees were to be an ultimate source of profit ... from one of the cleanest, nicest, most entertaining and innoxious of pursuits ..." Unfortunately, after the original two hives had multiplied to a dozen, he found suddenly that his hives were being depleted. Two species of birds had begun to feast upon his bees — the rainbow-bird or bee-eater, and the white-rumped wood-swallow. He could have shot the raiders, but told himself that since he had declared the Isle to be a sanctuary, the birds had right of prior occupancy, that they were beautiful to look upon, of engaging habits, had become companionable and trustful, and were also extremely efficient in keeping down the rampant host of undesirable insects which breed in tropic climes. He made up his mind immediately to abandon the enterprise. Luckily, a friend relieved him of the hives.

Banfield had very obviously found his niche, in this place where he could "step to his own music" in peace and solitude. There is a very real sense of identification with his environment

in his writings. Chisholm said, "For all its charm, Dunk Island would have broken most men or wrapped them in the mantle of the misanthrope. With Banfield it did something very different. It stabilised the feeble frame and mercurial temperament; it crystallised and yet extended his interests and energies; and while withholding him from the sorry scheme of things known as civilisation, it gave him a definite and worthy part in the work of the world."

Though Banfield chose solitude, he was far from being a recluse. A warm welcome was extended to all who visited him in his paradise, be they Governor or cane-cutter. He soon became known along the coast for his unstinting friendliness and readiness to defend the rights of fellow North Queenslanders. Though his first love was Coonanglebah which was therefore the main subject of his writings, his pen did nevertheless speak for all North Queensland. The flora and fauna of his Isle was also that of the tropic mainland, and his nature observations are pertinent to both. Was it because he had lost one eye that he used the precious faculty of sight to its utmost? His powers of observation were amazing under the circumstances, as evidenced by the precise detail with which he wrote of everything that came under his attention, and he made several discoveries of species new to science.

Banfield was very fond of the "blacks" of his Isle. Did he not describe the Aboriginal as "a Lord of Creation . . . His bold front, fluent carriage, springy step, alert, confident, superior air proclaim him so, innocent though he be of the frailest insignia of civilisation. The monarch arrayed in seven colours ascends the steps of his throne with no prouder mien than that in which the naked child of the sun lords it over the empty spaces." But there, in that last line — his reference to "the naked child of the sun" — is contained the essence of prevailing attitudes of his time, and when reading his more condescending passages in relation to the dark people, one must make due allowance. As a keen naturalist himself, Banfield very much admired and gave due recognition to the greatest naturalists on earth.

Banfield wrote little *about* himself in his books, yet they reveal his essential self. In spite of that, one yearns for that little bit extra, the personal snippets such as Chisholm recorded: "The Beachcomber's step was brisk, his speech rapid (at times vehement), his enthusiasms as extensive and keen as those of any boy . . . Never was a tropic islander more charged with vitality. It was nervous energy that wrecked and brought him to Dunk Island in the beginning; it was this, largely, that sustained him in isolation. When he was past seventy it was a rare thing to see Banfield really resting, an unknown thing to see him idle."

The selections here have been drawn from Banfield's four books, and have been chosen in the main for their suitability for illustration. For although his writings are in themselves richly evocative visually, the accompanying photographs should serve to enhance this quality, as well as aiding those armchair travellers who perhaps have never visited North Queensland. Together, the writings and illustrations will hopefully bring to life the warmth of that bright sunshine on clinking coral beaches; the gentle breath of the sea-breeze which ripples those deep blue waters between the isles; the delicious cool and silence of shady jungle glades — and something too of the fury of a tropic cyclone; the cruelty in the dazzling coral reef; the sheer wonder in the unfolding of the life of an insect; the luxuriance of riotous bloom; the taste of tropical fruit; the melody of brilliant birds; and even a hint of that rare tropic fragrance of the Beachcomber's Isle of which he wrote: "Many a time, home-returning at night — when the black contours of the Island loomed up in the distance against the pure tropic sky tremulous with myriads of unsullied stars — has its tepid fragrance drifted across the water as a salutation and a greeting. It has long been a fancy of mine that the Island has a distinctive odour, soft and pliant, rich and vigorous. Other mixtures of forest and jungle may smell as strong, but none has the rare blend which I recognise and gloat over whensoever, after infrequent absences for a day or two, I return to accept of it in grateful sniffs."

James G. Porter

DREAMS TO REALITIES

"Small must be the Isle of Dreams, so small that possession is possible . . . Such is this delicious Isle — this unkempt, unrestrained garden where the centuries gaze upon perpetual summer."

DREAMS TO REALITIES

This — this was our life we were beginning to live — our very own life; not life hampered and restricted by the wills, wishes and whims of others; unencumbered by the domineering wisdom, unembarrassed by the formal courtesies of the crowd . . .

Here I came to my birthright — a heritage of nothing save the most glorious of all possessions: freedom — freedom beyond the dreams of most men in its comprehensiveness and exactitude. These few haphazard notes refer to the exercise of rare independence. They cannot be otherwise than trivial and dull, but they at least fulfil the purpose to which I was pledged. They reveal my puny efforts to be none other than myself. So tranquil, so uniform are our days, that but for the diary — the civilised substitute for the notched stick — count of them might be lost . . . One year, Good Friday passed, and Easter-time had progressed to the joyful Monday, ere cognisance of the season came.

. . . the obscure and minor part the writer plays in the tragi-comedy of life affords gratification. He does what he likes to do. He frankly confesses that he sought isolation because of the lack of those qualities which make for dutiful citizenship, because of indifference to the ordinary enchantments of the kaleidoscopic world, not because of any lack of appreciation of the wisdom of the majority. He has dared to be what he is, rather than submit to be pulled this way and that on the rack of fashion and custom . . .

"Some day ere I grow too old to think I trust to be able to throw away all pursuits, save natural history, and to die with my mind full of God's facts instead of men's lies."

Charles Kingsley

All is lovable . . . the dim jungle, the piled up rocks . . .

Small must be the Isle of Dreams, so small that possession is possible. A choice passion is not to be squandered on that which, owing to exasperating bigness, can never be fully possessed. An island of bold dimensions may be free to all — wanton and vagrant, unlovable. Such is not for the epicure — the lover of the subtle fascination, the dainty moods, and pretty expressions of islands. The Isle must be small, too, because since it is yours it becomes a duty to exhaustively comprehend it. Familiarity with its lines of coast and sky, its declivities and hollows, its sunny places, its deepest shades, the sources of its streams, the meagre beginning of its gullies cannot suffice. Superficial intimacy with features betrayable to the senses of any undiscriminating beholder is naught. Casual knowledge of its botany and birds counts for little. All — even the least significant, the least obvious of its charms are there to give conservative delight, and surly the soul that would despise them.

If you would read the months off-hand by the flowering of trees and shrubs and the coming and going of birds; if the inhalation of scents is to convey photographic details of scenes whence they originate; if you would explore miles of sunless jungle by ways unstable as water; if you would have the sites of camps of past generations of blacks reveal the arts and occupations of the race, its dietary scale and the pastimes of its children; if you desire to have exact first-hand knowledge, to revel in the rich delights of new experiences, your scope must be limited.

The sentiments of a true lover of an Isle cannot without sacrilege be shared. The love is an exclusive passion, not of Herodian fierceness, misgiving, and gloom, but of joyful jealousy, for it must be well-nigh impossible to every one else.

Such is this delicious Isle — this unkempt, unrestrained garden where the centuries gaze upon perpetual summer. Small it is, and of varied charms — set in the fountain of time-defying youth. Abundantly sprinkled with tepid rains, vivified by the glorious sun, its verdure tolerates no trace of age. No ill or sour vapours contaminate its breath. Bland and ever fresh breezes preserve its excellencies untarnished . . .

. . . here is the ideal spot, the freest spot, the spot where dreams may harden into realities.

All is lovable — from crescentric sandspit — coaxing and consenting to the virile moods of the sea, harmonious with wind-shaken casuarinas, tinkling with the cries of excitable tern — to the stolid grey walls and blocks of granite which have for unrecorded centuries shouldered off the white surges of the Pacific. The flounces of mangroves, the sparse, grassy epaulettes on the shoulders of the hills, the fragrant forest, the dim jungle, the piled up rocks, the caves where the rare swiftlet hatches out her young in gloom and silence in nests of gluten and moss — all are mine to gloat over . . .

The slowly-heaving sea trailing the narrowest flounce of lace on the beach, the dainty form of Purtaboi, and the varying tones of great Australia beyond combine to complete the scene, and to confirm the thought that here is the ideal spot, the freest spot, the spot where dreams may harden into realities, where unvexed peace may smile.

THE ISLAND

"— fragrant, clean and undefiled . . ."

THE GENIUS OF THE ISLE

Our Island! What was it when we came into possession? From the sea, merely a range display-ing the varied leafage of jungle and forest. A steep headland springing from a ledge of rock on the north . . . an obtruding sandspit to the west, enclose a bay scarcely half a mile from one horn to the other, the sheet of water almost a perfect crescent, with the rocky islet of Purtaboi, plumed with trees, to indicate the circumference of a circle. Trees come to the water's edge from the abutment of the bold eminence . . .

Run the boat on the sand at high-water, and the first step is planted in primitive bush — fragrant, clean and undefiled . . . From the landing-place — rather more up towards the north-east cusp than the exact middle of the crescent bay — extends a flat of black sand on which grows a dense bush of wattles, cockatoo-apple-trees, pandanus palms, Moreton Bay ash and other eucalypts, and the shapely melaleuca. This flat, here about 150 yards in breadth, ends abruptly at a steep bank which gives access to a plateau sixty feet above sea-level . . . The toe of the bank rests upon sand, while the plateau is of chocolate-coloured soil intermixed on the surface with flakes of slate; and from this sure foundation springs the backbone of the island . . .

The plateau is the park of the island, half a mile broad, and a mile and more long. Upon it grows the best of the bloodwoods, the red stringy bark, Moreton Bay ash, various wattles, the gin-gee of the blacks. Pandanus marks the courses and curves of some of the gullies. A creek, hidden in a broad ribbon of jungle and running from a ravine in the range to the sea, divides our park in fairly equal portions . . .

Just above the splash of the Pacific surges on the weather or eastern side, low-growing scrub and restricted areas of forest, with expansive patches of jungle, plentifully intermixed with palms and bananas, creep up the precipitous ascent to the summit of the range — 870 feet above the sea. So steep is the Pacific slope that, standing on the top of the ridge and looking down, you catch mosaic gleams of the sea among the brown and grey tree-trunks . . . The highest peak, which presents a buttressed face to the north, and overlooks our peaceful bay, is crowned with a forest of bloodwoods, upon which the jungle steadily encroaches. The swaying fronds of aspiring palms, adorned in due season with masses of straw-coloured inflorescence, to be succeeded by loose bunches of red, bead-like berries, shoot out from the pall of leafage. In the gloomy gullies are slender-shafted palms and tree-ferns, while ferns and mosses cover the soil with living tapestry, and strange, snake-like epiphytes cling in sinuous curves to the larger trees. The trail of the lawyer vine, with its leaf sheath and long tentacles bristling with incurved hooks, is over it all. Huge cables of vines trail from tree to tree, hanging in loops and knots and festoons . . . Along the edge of the jungle, the climbing fern grows in tangled masses sending its slender wire-like lengths up among the trees — the most attractive of all the ferns, and glorified by some with the title of "the Fern of God" . . .

Birds are numerous, from the scrub fowl which dwells in the dim jungle and constructs of decaying leaves and wood and light loam the most trustworthy of incubators, and wastes no valuable time in the dead-and-alive duty of sitting, to the tiny sunbird of yellow and purple, which flits all day among scarlet hibiscus blooms, sips nectar from the flame-tree, and rifles the dull red studs of the umbrella-tree of their sweetness . . . Cockatoos scream with excitement and gladness; honey-eaters whistle and call; drongos chatter and scold the rest of the banqueters . . . bees and beetles maintain a murmurous soothful sound, a drowsy blending of hum and buzz . . .

— all the freshness of an isle clean and green . . . From the moment the sun illumines our hills and isles with glowing yellow until it drops in fiery splendour suddenly out of sight leaving a band of gleaming red above the purple western range, and a rippling red path across to Australia, the whole realm of nature seems ours to command.

Among such scenes do I commune with the genius of the Isle, and saturate myself with that restful yet exhilarating principle which only the individual who has mastered the art of living the unartificial life perceives. When strained of body and seared of mind, did not the Isle, lovely in lonesomeness, perfumed, sweet in health, irresistible in mood, console and soothe as naught else could? Shall I not, therefore, do homage to its profuse and gracious charms and exercise the rights and privileges of protector?

Among such scenes do I commune with the genius of the Isle . . .

HABITATION

Our castles are built in the air, not because earth has no fit place for their foundations, but for the sufficient reason that the wherewithal for the foundations was lacking . . .

What justification existed for the defacement of the virginal scene by an unlovely dwelling — the imposition of a scar on the unspotted landscape? None, save that the arrogant intruder needed shelter, and that he was neither a Diogenes to be content in a tub nor a Thoreau to find in boards an endurable temporary substitute for blankets.

It was resolved that the shelter should by way of compensation be unobtrusive, hidden in a wilderness of leaves. The sacrifice of those trees unhaply in prior occupation of the site selected would be atoned for by the creation of a modest garden of pleasant-hued shrubs and fruit trees and lines and groves of coconut palms. My conscience at least has been, or rather is being, appeased for the primary violation of the scene, for trees perhaps more beautiful, certainly more useful, stand for those destroyed. The Isle suffers no gross disfigurement . . . no change has been wrought for which the genius of the Isle need demand satisfaction . . .

Prior to departing from civilisation we had arranged for the construction of a hut of cedar, so contrived with nicely adjusting parts and bolts, and all its members numbered, that a mere amateur could put it together. If at the end of six months' trial the life was found to be unendurable, or serious objection not dreamt of in our salad philosophy became apparent, then our dwelling could be packed up again. All would not be lost . . .

Though of scented cedar the hut was ceilingless. Resonant corrugated iron and boards an inch thick intervened between us and the noisy tramplings of the rain and heat of the sun. The only room accommodated some primitive furniture, a bed being the denominating as well as the essential feature. A little shambling structure of rough slabs and iron walls contrived a double debt to pay — kitchen and dining-room.

From the doorsteps of the hut we landed on mother earth, for the verandas were not floored. Everything was as homely and simple and inexpensive as thought and thrift might contrive. Our desire to live in the open air became almost compulsory, for though you fly from civilisation and its thralls you cannot escape the social instincts of life. The hut became the focus of life other than human . . . grey bead-eyed geckoes craftily stalked moths and beetles and other fanatic worshippers of flame as they hastened to sacrifice themselves to the lamp. In the walls wasps built terra-cotta warehouses in which to store the semi-animate carcasses of spiders and grubs; a solitary bee constructed nondescript comb among the books, transforming a favourite copy of *Lorna Doone* into a solid block. Bats, sharp-toothed, and with pin-point eyes, swooped in at one door, quartered the roof with brisk eagerness, and departed by the other.

Finding ample food and safe housing, bats soon became permanent lodgers. For a time it was novel and not unpleasant to be conscious in the night of their waftings, for they were actual checks upon the mosquitoes which came to gorge themselves on our unsalted blood . . .

In the dimness of early morning when errant bats flitted home to cling to the ridge-pole, squeaking and fussy flutterings denoted unwonted disturbance. Daylight revealed a half-concealed, sleeping snake, which seemed to be afflicted with twin tumours. A long stick dislodged the intruder, which scarce had reached the floor ere it died a violent death. Even the snake spectre did not seriously affright the remaining bats, though it confirmed the sentence of their immediate banishment . . .

So we lived, more out of the hut than in it, from October, 1897, until Christmas Day, 1903 . . . The original cedar hut now forms an annexe to a bungalow designed, in so far as means permitted, as a concession to the dominating characteristics of the clime. Around the house is an acre or so given over to an attempt to keep up appearances.

Poultry are comfortably housed; a small flock of goats provides milk and occasionally fresh meat. There are two horses (one a native of the island) to perform casual heavy work; the boat has a shed into which she is reluctantly hauled by means of a windlass to spend the rowdy months; there is a buoy in the bay to which she is greatly attached when she is not sulking in the shed or coyly submitting to the caresses of the waves . . .

A good portion of the house represents the work of my own unaccustomed hands. I have found how laborious an occupation fencing is, and how very exasperating if barbed wire is used; that the keeping in order of even a small plantation in which ill-bred and riotous plants grow with the rapidity of the prophet's gourd, and which if unattended would lapse in a very brief space of time into the primitive condition of tangled jungle, involves incessant labour of the most sweatful kind. A work on structural botany tells me that "the average rate of perspiration in plants has been estimated as equal to that of seventeen times that of man". Only dwellers in the tropics are capable of realising the profundity of those pregnant words.

TROPIC GLORY

Last evening (March 6, 1921) we saw the very gates of heaven. Those who live under sullen skies seldom have a chance of seeing the majestic paintings of the sun; but here, where hills and sea and sky are the mediums in which a tropical sun plays fantastic tricks of bewildering variety, you become accustomed to, though never satiated by, the glories of The Beyond.

All day it had been scorching hot — that kind of hotness that tingles the small of the back and adds two shades of brown to the shoulders during the sun-bath following the noontide wallow in the sea. I had spent an unclad hour clearing away loose coral from one of the favourite runs of the little fishing-net, and had cooled down in the sparkling, noisy streamlet that the wet season stimulates and freshens. That loll in the fragrant water — it comes down the palm- and fern-tree-embowered ravine — created an appetite for lunch, and afterwards influenced a dreamy while of reading.

When I really woke and began to stroll among the mango-trees, the western half of the sky, or rather a big area of it, was sullen — thickly, diabolically blue, as if reeking with fumes from hell. Beneath was a zone of curry-coloured sky, outlining ranges almost black in the intensity of blue.

Away aloft, so high that a backward tilt of the head was necessary, the cloud-bank was edged with light as ineffably variable as the shadows over a wheatfield on a breezy day. Soon

. . . you become accustomed to, but never satiated by, the glories of The Beyond . . .

22

rainbow tints, appearing, disappearing and reappearing magically in detached flakes and patches, and severed by purple rays, hovered and flitted over and along the cloud. Occasionally lightning zig-zagged horizontally across the densest part, and you could just catch the mutterings of thunder.

A great patch of yellow light sprang from the middle of the upper edge of the dusky cloud, like the half of an enormous nimbus, glowing and glittering. Then, with the gentlest of gradations, its yellow gave way to other primary colours, delicately displayed and quivering with fairy-like agitations. A huge ravine opened up, a valley through rainbow-land, leading to a wall as ruddy as imagination may paint, and embossed with a pearl as great as a house.

Twice appeared a strange shape. Picture a bird soaring in a huge, circling flight from north to south, hidden by the cloud-screen save for one fully-extended wing, and that wing displaying bands of blending tints of gold and green and silvery rose, with feather-tips of sepia, fluffy and breathlessly soft. Picture the wing wavering and slowly vanishing, until the final feather seemed the shadow of a golden plume, and as slowly reappearing in all its magnificence — inspiring the hope that the glorious bird of Paradise would emerge and be seen soaring in its proper sphere at the gate of heaven.

All the ships, the ragged remnants, the fragments and frayings of all the rainbows of the most decorative of wet seasons, skirted the cloud or were tossed about in luminous heaps; and then the scene burnt itself out in extravagant redness, leaving the Isle in a lurid gloom, and its inhabitants stiff-necked, but with a rare joy at heart.

. . . the cloud-bank was edged with light . . .

SMILING MORN

A cloudless sky, the long grass wet with the night's gentle shower, a thin veil of mist on the hills, a glassy, steel-blue sea, the air saturated with the essences from myriads of leaves and scented with the last whiffs from the tea-trees and the primal blossoms of the wattles — such are the features of this smiling morn.

A spangled drongo — ardent lover of light and free air — talkatively announced the dawn long before its coming; the noisy pitta — bird of the moist soil and leafy gloom — triumphs in three notes. For an hour the scrub fowl have been violently noisy, but have retired to the recesses of the jungle, whence comes an occasional chuckle of satisfaction or a coarse, triumphant crow. The fasciated honey-eater has loudly called "with a voice that seemed the very sound of happiness"; the leaden flycatcher, often silent but seldom still, has twittered and whispered plaintively; the sun-birds are playing gymnastics among the lemon blossoms, and the centre of activity for butterflies is the red-flowered shrub bordering the wavering path.

Since — sometimes wantonly, often thoughtlessly — man interferes with plants, time out of mind the banqueting-table of the butterflies, is it not a duty to provide substitutes for devastated natural vegetation? When it is discovered that a plant, introduced to give satisfaction to the lust of the eye, provides from year's end to year's end nectar as unfailing as the widow's cruse of oil, is it not becoming to reproduce it plentifully so that excited and virtuous insects may be encouraged to return to former scenes? If not a duty, at least it is a source of happiness, for the particular insects which revel in the nectar of the perpetually flowering shrub are the two most gorgeous butterflies of the land — pleasantly known as Ulysses and Cassandra.

Science changes its titles so frequently that unless the intellect is to be increasingly burdened it is well to refuse to be divorced from the old and often explicit and fulfilling names. Cassandra is the lovely green- and gold-fly which dances in the air so delightfully when he woos his sober, fluttering mate. That of gorgeous royal blue with black edging to the wings and dandyish swallow-tails, which wanders far and wide and flies high and swiftly, is Ulysses . . .

Many other winged creatures flit and glisten in the garden and down along the grass-invaded path between the coconuts. Dragon-flies hover over the moist spots, transparent wings carrying coral-red bodies, and two sand-wasps pilot my steps, following the narrow ribbon of bare ground as a fish the course of a shallow stream, buzzing ominously as if in warning of some possible mischance. They are friends, and will in a moment swerve, and boom back to the shafts they have excavated in sand as depositories for their eggs, and into which they will pack living caterpillars as fresh food for their young. They dig with such deftness and vigour that the sand is expelled in a continuous jet. When the mouth of the shaft, round to exactness, is lumbered with soil, the insect emerges backward and shovels away dog-like with its forelegs. Then it disappears again, until the sand-jet has made another encumbering heap.

These alert and furiously resentful insects are endowed with resourcefulness and "intelligence" in keeping with their physical activities. One had foraged a caterpillar in bulk and weight beyond its flight strength, and was, therefore, compelled to haul it along the toilful earth. On the wing the wasp finds its home unhesitatingly. On the unfamiliar ground it lost its bearings, and, moreover, the lumbering caterpillar had to be tugged through a bewildering forest of grass stems, among which it went astray. During a pause the wasp surveyed the scene, and, locating the shaft, after stupendous exertions deposited its prey conveniently thereto, to find itself confronted with a problem, since the diameter of the caterpillar exceeded that of the shaft. It seemed to reflect for a few moments, and then with feverish haste enlarged the shaft.

Another difficulty had then to be overcome. Was it possible to force such a bulky and unwieldy body head first down — the habitual way? The insect came to a rapid decision in the negative. Backing into the shaft, it seized the caterpillar by the head and drew it down, presently emerging, and how it managed to squeeze past so tight a plug is another of the magics of the morn. Having butted with its highly competent head the caterpillar well home, the wasp selected a neatly fitting stone as a wad, and, filling the shaft with earth, strewed the surface with grass fragments, to the artistic concealment of the site ...

CURIOUS CRINKLED SHADOWS

Before the coming of the obscuring grey of these wet-season days, when the tranquil sea absorbed the lustrous blue of the sky, I discovered myself daydreaming for a blissful moment or two ere the crude anchor of the flattie slipped slowly to the mud twelve feet below. The rough iron and rusty chain cast curious crinkled shadows, and presently, as the iron sank into the slate-coloured mud and the chain tightened, the shadow was single but infirm. Light and the magic of the sea, which, though it takes its ease, is forbidden absolute rest, transformed it until imagination created similitude to a serpent in its natural element. Its half-concealed, formless head was verified by a flake of rust just where a watchful eye might have been, and the sun played upon it.

So here at last was the sea-serpent with alert eye and without end. It was all so realistic and endowed with such benignity and such gentleness of motion that I gazed at it with the gladness of a discoverer. In response to a slight motion of the hand, the sea-serpent wriggled as though in haste; but wriggle as it might, the end never came.

The boat drifted back. The serpent became seriously elongated, but though the beginning was now a grey blotch in the mud, the end was not. I might beat up a little foam with the chain, and see below a giddy dance or at least lively flourishes and swaying. Yet there was something lacking — the end. But for that very commonplace default did there not here exist a very good beginning for another romance of the sea?

The phantom, born of light and limpid salt water and iron into which rust had deeply gnawed, gave zest to the pursuit of shadows. What is commoner under the tropic sun? The boat was now over the sand of the steeply shelving beach, where the water takes the tint of the chrysolite and creatures of fairy lightness come into view. Often on still days small sea-spiders sport under the lee of the boat, each of the eight legs supported by a bubble. With astonishing nimbleness, the spider slips and glides over the surface as a man in laborious snow-shoes over the snow. Having basked in the sun and frolicked with its kind, the spider abandons its pads, takes to its hairy bosom a bubble of air, and dives below. The shadows, not the spiders alone, gave pleasing entertainment. Each vague shadow and the eight bubble-shod feet formed a broochlike ornament on the yellow sand — a grey jewel surrounded by diamonds, for every bubble acted as a lens concentrating the light. When the frail creatures darted hither and thither — the majestic sun does not disdain to lend his brilliance to the most prosaic of happenings — the shadows of the bubbles became jewels or daylight lightnings . . . A wave of the hand dispersed the gay assemblage, but in a few seconds the playful creatures — not too easily to be deprived of their place in the sun — reappeared from nowhere, and the beads and flashes on the floor of old Ocean once more began to glitter.

Small, slim fish took shelter from the intense light. Some hung motionless in the water; others nibbled daintily the green and lazy slime on the batten at the bilge, their gently waving shadows being barely perceptible, for their delicate, semi-transparent bodies absorbed but the merest particle of the brightness of noonday.

The unnoticeable swing of the tide took the responsive boat out from the beach, and again the serpent swayed sleepily. Down in the mud an organised conflict was taking place between a tiny soft-bodied crab and four molluscs which used whip-like tentacles with unceasing energy, while the crab defended itself with every-ready claws. Borne down by numbers, it sank into the mud, the energy of the victors creating a tiny spiral of slush. A huge stingray passed on its way, the edges of extended wings rippling never so gently, its shadow half the size of the boat; and presently, with ghostly glide, a dull-skinned shark came into view with motion so steady and apparently effortless that it might have been a spectre. The pectoral fins swayed listlessly. The swirl of the tail was as tender as a caress. Passing the boat a few yards, it turned with a gracious sweep and nestled in its shade, and, though motionless, it was wide awake. The eyes on each end of the projecting extremities of the head blinked up at the boat. It was comfortable, but suspicious. Was its conscience quite clear? The hammer-head has not the reputation of being an active enemy of man. Why should it be distrustful? This hammer-head would not sleep in the shadow, so let it be made aware of the serpent. I took hold of the chain cautiously, the shark watching, and with a quick turn of the wrist the docile serpent lashed offensively. Then did the shark, frightened of a shadow, flee with mud-stirring haste, like the wicked when no man pursueth.

The hour of day-dreaming was past. I slip over the side of the boat to roll and splash in tepid water limpid almost to invisibility, and to test the wondrous buoyancy of the substantial part of man. Sit down, the lips just awash, so that the accurately ballasted portion cushions on the cleanly sand. Stretch out the legs so that the heels barely rest. Head thrown back and arms extended, fill the lungs to their utmost capacity with the placid, revivifying air, and you will find yourself so uplifted that the heels alone gently touch the sand. At each inspiration almost sufficient air is imbibed to float the whole bulk and machinery of the body. And when the radiant air is all one's own, why be niggardly? Let it be gulped greedily, strongly, wilfully, and let the smiling sea, responding to the embraces of your wide-spread arms, salute your lips with ripples.

The rough iron and rusty chain cast curious crinkled shadows . . .

27

BEACHCOMBING INSTINCTS

Before the rains came thundering on the iron roof of our little hut, the washed-out and enfeebled town-dweller who gave way to bitter reflections on the first evening of his new career, could hardly have been recognised, thanks to the robustious, wholesome effects of the free and vitalising life. Fourteen, frequently sixteen, hours of the twenty-four were spent in the open air, ashore and afloat . . . Is there a human being, taking part in the rough and tumble of the world, who can honestly make confession and say that he has completely suffocated those inherent instincts of savagedom — joy and patience in the chase, the longing for excitement and surprise, the crude selfishness, the delight in getting something for nothing? Society journals have informed me that titled dames have been known to sit out long and wearisome evenings that they may obtain some paltry favour in a cotillion. And when the sea casts up its gifts on these radiant shores, I boldly and with glee give way to my Beachcombing instincts and pick and choose. Never up to the present have I found anything of real value; but am I not buoyed up by pious hopes and sanguine expectations? Is not the game as diverting and as innocent as many others that are played to greater profit? It is a game, too, that cannot be forced, and therefore cannot become demoralising; and having no nice feelings nor fine shades, I rejoice and am glad in it.

And then what strange and varied things one sees! Once a "harness-cask", hostile to every sense, came trundled by waves eager to expel it from the vicinity of these oxless but scented isles. It overcame us as we sailed by, twenty yards off, and the general necessity for temperate diet and restricted dishes came as a sweet and a comforting reflection. No marvel if the ship whence it was ejected was in bad odour among the sailors. Leaving, as it lurched along, a greasy, foul stain on the sea, it may have poisoned multitudes of uncomplaining fishes during its evil course.

Occasionally a case of fruit, washed from the decks of a labouring steamer, drifts ashore. One was the means of introducing a valuable addition to the products of the island. It gave demonstration of how man may unwittingly, and even in opposition to his wit, assist in scattering and multiplying blessings on a smiling land — blessings to last for all time, and perhaps to amend or ameliorate the environment of a budding nation . . .

Again, a German barque, driven out of its course, found unexpectedly a detached portion of the Great Barrier Reef 200 miles away to the south. When the south-easters came, they pounded away so vigorously with the heavy guns of the sea that in a brief space nothing was left of the big ship save some distorted fragments of iron jammed in among the nigger-heads of coral and the crevices of the rocks. A few weeks after, portions of the wreck were deposited on Dunk Island, and the beach of the mainland for miles was strewn with timber. That wreck was the greatest favour bestowed me in my profession of Beachcomber. Long and heavy pieces of angle-iron came bolted to raftlike sections of the deck; various kinds of timber proved useful in a variety of ways. What? was I to leave it all, unclaimed and unregarded — in excess of morality and modesty — on the beach, to be honey-combed by white ants or to rot? or to honestly own up to that sentiment which is the most human of all? Without affectation or apology, I confess that I was overjoyed — that my instincts, pregnant with original sin, received a most delightful fillip. I wallowed for the time being in the luxury of Beachcombing.

Upon sober reflection, I cannot say that I am of one mind with the pastor of the Shetland Isles who never omitted this petition from his long prayer — "Lord, if it be Thy holy will to send shipwrecks, do not forget our island"; nor yet with the Breton fishermen, who to this day are of opinion that wreckage is the gift of God, and who therefore take everything that comes in a reverential spirit, as a Divine favour, whether casks of wine or bales of merchandise. But, after all, who am I that I should claim a finer shade of morality than those, with their sturdy widespread hands and perpetual blessing? . . . And must not I, venturing to regard myself as a truthful historian, frankly admit a sense allied to disappointment when the white blazing beaches are destitute of the most trivial of temptations?

No, the grating of the battered barque, upon which many a wet and weary steersman had stood, now fulfils placid duty as a front gate. No more to be trampled and stamped upon with shifty, sloppy feet — no more to be scrubbed and scored with sand and holystone; painted white, it creaks gratefully every time it swings — the symbol of security, the first outward and visible sign of home, the guardian of the sacred rights of private property, the embodiment of the exclusive. Better so than lying inert under foot on the deck of the barque thrashing through the cold grey seas of the Baltic, or scudding before the unscrupulous billows of Biscay . . .

When there are eight or ten islands and islets within an afternoon's sail, and miles of mainland beach to police, variety lends her charms to the pursuit of the Beachcomber. Landing in one of the unfrequented coves, he knows not what the winds and the tides may have spread out for inspection and acceptance. Perhaps only an odd coconut from the Solomon Islands, its husk zoned with barnacles. The germ of life may yet be there. To plant the nut above high-water mark is an obvious duty. Perhaps there is a paddle, with rude tracery on the handle, from the New Hebrides, part of a Fijian canoe that has been bundled over the Barrier, a wooden spoon such as Kanakas use, or the dusky globe of an incandescent lamp that has glowed out its life in the state-room of some ocean liner, or a broom of Japanese make, a coal-basket, a "fender", a tiger nautilus shell, an oar or a rudder, a tiller, a bottle cast away far out from land to determine the strength and direction of ocean currents, and spinnaker boom of a yacht, the jib-boom of a staunch cutter . . .

That which at the time was the most eloquent message from the sea came close to our door, cast up on the snowy-white coral drift of a little cove, where it immediately attracted notice. Nothing but an untrimmed bamboo staff nearly thirty feet long, carrying an oblong strip of soiled white calico between two such strips of red turkey twill. Tattered and frayed, the flags seemed to tell of the desperate appeal for help of some forlorn castaway; of a human being, marooned on a lonely sandbank on the Barrier, without shelter, food or water, but not altogether bereft of hope . . .

Rarely do we sail about without enjoying the zest of the chance of getting something for nothing. Not yet has the seaman's chest, brass-bound, with its secret compartments full of "fair rose-nobles and bright moidores", been lighted upon; but who can say? Perhaps it has come ashore but now, after leagues of aimless wanderings, and awaits in some cosy cove the next Beachcombing expedition . . .

This is not an apology, but a confession; not a plea of defence, but a justification — a fair and free chronicle, a frank acknowledgment of the tributes of impartial Neptune — Neptune who gives and who takes away — who stealthily filches with tireless fingers, and who, when in the mood, robs so remorselessly, and with such awful, such majestic violence, that it were impious to whimper. Who beachcombed my three rudders, the one toilfully adzed out in one piece from the beautiful heart of a bean-tree log, another cunningly fitted with a sliding fin, and that of red cedar with famous brass mountings? Who owns the pair of ballast tanks once mine? Who the buoy deemed securely moored? Who the paddles and the rowlocks and the signal halyards, lost because of Neptune's whims and violence? Beachcombing is a nicely adjusted, if not quite an exact art. Not once but several times has the libertine Neptune scandalously seduced punts and dinghies from the respectable precincts of Brammo Bay, and having philandered with them for a while, cynically abandoned them with a bump on the mainland beach, and only once has he sent a punt in return — a poor, soiled, tar-besmirched, disorderly waif that was reported to the police and reluctantly claimed.

A mind inclined to casuistry, could it not defend Beachcombing? Does not the law recognise it under the definition of trover? Why bother about the law and the moralities when it is all so pleasing, so engrossing, and so fair?

A BUSH TRACK

It has no beginning. It ends — who shall say where? Every high tide smooths away the footprints of those who use it now, just as it did the erratic tramplings of the host of the past. In those free, unregulated days piccaninnies sprawled and scampered on the hard, glistening beach; young men and girls sported there; men lazed and fought on its convenient spaces; women wandered on the serious business of food-getting. The camps stood a pace or two above high-water mark in the meagre shelter of sighing casuarinas, and were often changed, for there were six miles of gently curving, ripple-embroidered shore on which to rest. To this day most of the traffic is regulated by the tide. High water drives the wayfarer to the loose, impeding sand, over which the great convolvulus sends its tireless tentacles, to be thrown back twisted and burnt by salt surges.

The ebb discovers a broad space, firm and wellnigh unimpressionable. The barefooted traveller may walk for miles and be trackless, so tough and elastic the moist sand. It is not an officious thoroughfare, made formal and precise by coarse hands working to plans correct to a hair, but subject to economic deviations of some soulless contractor. It was not laid with the foundation of the earth, and compacted by heat and stress. It is still in the making, and sand, coral, and shell-grit ground to pollen-like fineness and certain chemicals from the reef outside are among its component parts. One other element invokes perpetual thanksgiving — the flaked mica, which glistens delusively with hues of silver and gold, and gives to the tide-swept track that singular pliancy which resists the stamp of passing generations.

Midway between high and low water is a zone sensible to the airiest tread, being fitted for such temporary effect by a mechanical operation. Millions of the smallest of crabs, sand-tinted, delicate, apprehensive and alert, possess this area, working out their destiny by digging circular shafts. Obedient agents in the execution of the imperative ordinances of Nature, they have the quality of compacting the almost fluid spoil and carrying it to the surface in pellets complementary to the size of the individual, and such pellets retain their rotundity. They are scattered about, not without design, as may be seen if the industrious workers are closely observed, and in such profusion that the feet of the user of a crab-infested zone must press them flat. Then it is that the track becomes visible as far as the eyes reach. But the incoming wavelets, babbling in unison, dissolve the myriads of laboriously lifted pellets, effacing the record of the passing of man. As the tides ebb, the crabs begin their work again, preparing for the next-coming wayfarer. There is something almost incomprehensively great in the tireless activities of the nervous crabs, for not only do they carry compacted sand from their burrows, but they seem to spend odd moments in forming similar globes from material gathered from the surface. Digging, furrowing the surface in stellate patterns, moulding pellets which to the tenderest ripple are but the plaything of a moment, so are the lives of the shy crustaceans spent. What may be the motive for the perpetual labour, as useless, apparently, as the rolling of Sisyphus's stone? For part of the year the beach is the resort of the red-necked sandpiper, which has an enormous appetite for the small, live things of the sea's margin. To bewilder the birds and so reduce the risk to life, Nature imposes the task upon the crabs of forming replicas of themselves not readily distinguishable in size and tint, which represent labour unconsciously expended as life insurance, and serve the subsidiary purpose of detecting the passing of man.

What material has been left by the wayside for the history, not to be altogether despised because of its rusticity, of the unstable ways of one of the ancient peoples of the world, now few in numbers, forgetful of the past, estranged from the customs of their fathers, and dying without mourners and without records? Search the sites of camps the track passes, and there is naught to tell of the manner of those who recently occupied them save a tomahawk or a rare domestic implement of stone, and such stones do not preach thrilling but distinctive sermons. Why hurry along this pleasant way? Is not the one domestic appliance of the long-deserted camps worthy of passing notice? There it rests, half buried in the sand — a worn stone, with two others complementary to it to be had for the searching. It is meet that the most primitive of mills should be examined, and that one of the several and slow processes by which a poisonous, repugnant, and intractable nut was wont to be converted into food should be cited to the credit of the economic forethought of the most thriftless of people.

On adjacent flats and slopes grow survivals from one of the most ancient of all plants — a cycad, that botanical paradox, combining some of the characteristics of the palm and of the pine with the appearance of a tree-fern, while being of distinctive order, which flourished during the age when the iguanodon and the polacanthus and other monstrous and ungainly reptiles roamed the land.

Let us rest awhile reviewing the earlier operations by which its nuts were rendered innocuous, and while the ghosts of the past make and bake their bread.

The fresh nuts of the plant, known as "kim-alo", were roasted, and while hot bruised between two stones, the upper ("oo-kara") a sphere flattened at the poles into which the use of ages wore thumb and finger indentations, the nether ("diban") flat with a saucer-like depression. Fragments of the husks were carefully eliminated. The coarse meal was put into a dilly-bag and placed in running water below a slight fall, from the lip of which fluming, improvised from the leaf of native ginger, conducted a gentle stream. Two days were sufficient to leach the poisonous principle; but if the initial process of roasting the nuts was omitted — as in some districts — the meal was submitted to the purification of water for as long as two months, when it would be tasteless. It was then ground on the nether stone by the "moo-ki" (almost a perfect sphere), used with a rotary action, until reduced to flour-like fineness, when it

What may be the motive for the perpetual labour, as useless, apparently, as the rolling of Sisyphus's stone?

was made into flat or sausage-shaped cakes, wrapped in green leaves and baked. The intractability of the cycad is such that if cattle eat the leaves they die or become permanently afflicted with a disease of the nature of rickets. To the human palate the fresh nuts are inflammatory, and are said to cause intense pain ending with death. That the blacks discovered the means of converting such a substance into desirable food proves that they were often enterprisingly, daringly hungry.

Let us push on, there is far to go. Chance rather than principle, it has been said, turned the paths of old England into roads . . .

Leaving the shore, one branch of the track crosses the high-water fold, follows the bend of a mangrove creek, through which it makes a muddy ford, and is firmly impressed through forest country where every tree is orchid-encumbered, and where the eager soil produces its own varieties. It wriggles up and along a ridge, with the glaucous spathes of grass trees standing like spears on each hand, and where wattle and tough she-oaks grow leanly out of hard soil, thickly strewn with buckshot gravel, rust-coloured.

Soon it descends into a low valley and through a belt of fan-palms and jungle bordering an ever-flowing stream the banks of which are knee-deep in fat, rich loam. Huge tea-trees stand in the water, where the fibrous roots are matted like peat.

Out of the moist coolness the track abruptly ascends to a pleasant forest, and thence drops almost imperceptibly to tea-tree flats intersected by pandanus creeks, which bulge here and there into sedge-margined lagoons. In this "devil-devil" country it is barely the width of the foot, and it wanders sinuously like the trail of a lazy snake. Sometimes it is barely more discernible than such a trail, and again in the soft places it broadens and deepens, for the man with boots has taken the place of the original soft-footed traveller, and horses and cattle are ever fond of the short-cuts which their owners design.

Here a distinct branch is made towards a river, across which Nature, the first of bridge-builders, many a generation ago afforded an easy, dry passage by throwing down a huge tree. It spans from bank to bank, and the wood is worn to slippery smoothness by the passing of shoeless feet. Thence it leads through forest and jungle and mangrove belts to another river, and away south.

The western branch keeps to forest and jungle, following, generally, the ridges, for in the wet season the grass lands are flooded, when the track is but a silvery grey ribbon on a carpet of green. With careless indecision it trends west, with here an angle and there a curve, dipping and twisting, crossing gullies and creeping up slopes. The men whose feet made it in ancient days knew all the landmarks. Mostly it keeps to sound ground, albeit its wanderings perpetuate wayward impulses.

Imagination may follow the blacks of bygone days as they swung past a fallen tree; where sportful youths wandered a few yards to throw grass-tree spears at white-ants' nests on bloodwood-trees; where they turned aside for a drink from the palm creek. Possibly the track deviated to follow the run of a scrub turkey, or because the boys knew of a scrub hen's mound, where the rich pink eggs were raked out by the gins. It was gin's work to overhaul the mounds; the boys did not like to do the digging with their hands, for often little snakes bedded themselves in the warm compost — snakes, though they bite not to the death, make one's hands big and sore. Why incur any risk when there was a well-disciplined woman to take it? There was a turn off (which was officially followed) leading to a huge tree where in the hollow bees had hived; and another straggled up the creek to the pool where eels secrete themselves in the moist, decaying leaves.

Six or seven miles from the beach, where the scarcely discernible crabs, with persistency as eternal as the sea, are strewing the way with millions of tell-tale pellets, the track, skirting swamps, following the bends of a river, passing through forest and jungle, is lost in vagueness and indecision . . .

A Beach Almanac

The most famous of botanists compiled a floral almanac; the months, and in some cases the weeks, being associated with the development and flowering of significant plants. So might it be possible to ascribe to particular months the tokens with which the obliging sea bestrews the beaches ... A few examples of the material on which the delightful work might be undertaken are given, so that the wealth of one brief strip of beach may be taken as typical of a vast stretch of calm waters within the Great Barrier Reef.

The ridges and furrows of the cyclone season, when the clean sand is covered and stained with weed, dead and living molluscs, coral, leaves carried from the hills by flooded streams, all fermenting in the heat, tell that Christmas is past and March not yet over. Many a year passes without such a storm as compels the groaning ocean to ravage its reefs. Then the beaches, during the first three months, are not particularly fertile, nor are the shells to be found special or peculiar. In April many specimens of the mollusc known as tapes, of which there are several species, are cast ashore, empty but fresh. In life the animal buries itself in the mud at the edge of the sand, and some disturbance of natural conditions, possibly due to the fresh water from flooded rivers, causes seasonal mortality ...

April is confirmed, too, but transiently, by the presence of a frail mollusc which is washed ashore attached to seaweed, soon to disappear desiccated by the sun and ground to powder. The shell is semi-transparent with a sandy tint, and in form not unlike that of a common snail. As the weather becomes cooler, a thin, delicate bivalve decorates high-water mark. It is one of the tellinas — semi-transparent, lustrous, and fragile — which occurs in muddy sand, but why the species should be more susceptible to the ills of life during a particular season is not apparent. When the fates do conspire against its welfare dozens of bright specimens may be picked up during a casual stroll, the animal having disappeared. The epidemic the beach thus announced with pink and glittering shells coincides with low night tides, which possibly leave the inefficiently protected animals exposed to the attacks of uncustomary enemies which thrive only when the muddy banks are exposed. The cause of the exhibition of the relics is not of so much concern to the unlearned observer as the relics themselves and the part they play in signifying the progress of the season. If strong winds occur during the cool months, among the wreaths of broken seaweed thrown on the beach may be found unbroken and fresh specimens of a singularly beautiful and fragile univalve known commonly and most appropriately as the "bubble shell", which when alive is a most lovely object, its fine spiral lines being black and faint yellow with faint purple edges, while the mantle is fringed with light blue intermingled with pale yellow ...

When the chill is out of the surface the spring-time of the sea begins. Vegetable life is strenuous, so that one may chance to see a lazy turtle bearing on its back a weedy garden. The water is alive. Miles of space are belted with that plant to which Captain Cook applied a significant name, likening it in its myriads to "sea sawdust" ...

It consists of minute vegetation in bundles, to be individualised under a strong microscope, though when countless billions drift on to the beaches and die and become green and grey with corruption, the fumes are by no means in proportion to the marvellous littleness of the individual plants. Then we know by the organs of scent and sight that August has come. The beaches are foul. The breakers roll in unbroken or with a muddy froth, for the scum acts as oil, calming even troubled water ...

One other season, ephemeral but universal, do the babbling but truth-telling beaches record. No rocky cove, no smooth strand, no rubbish-accumulating creek, no mangrove-fringed islet, no coral esplanade white under the tropic sun, no sand-bank with crest of wind-shaken bush, is free. It is Christmas. Christian and pagan alike tell it to the sea, and the sea tells it to the beaches in — corks.

BABBLING BEACHES

On a breezy day, when the sun scorches the sand and the wind continuously sweeps off the dry surface, and your ears detect the musical sound accompanying the process — vague as the visible part of it is blurred and misty — then it is that you are made aware of the agencies by which time creates geographical differences. Precipitated at the apex of the spit, the sand as it sinks tints the verge of the sea, while the lighter spoil, leaves and wisps of seaweed, trip off on independent voyage. The current from the south pares the spit, preserving its shapeliness. The ebb from the bay maintains the fluent inner curve. The dry wind, the current with its northerly set, and the ebb in conjunction, push the spit to the north, and as the sand advances, vegetation consolidates the work. Then comes the season of northerly winds, when the apex of the spit is forced backwards and outwards into a brief but graceful flourish, in the bight of which small boats may nestle, though the seas roar and show white teeth a few yards away. Since the winds of the north are less in duration and persistency than those from the south and east, the tendency of the spit — in defiance of the yearly setback — is to the north. Driftwood, logs, and huge trees with bare, branchless limbs become stranded, to dry and whiten in the sun and reinforce the sand, and in their decay, with ever contributed seaweed, to make mould for vegetation. The work of encroachment and consolidation is incessant and strangely rapid, for vegetation never lacks pioneers of special character to prepare the way for the less venturesome and less hardy. Often before vegetation appears, coral chips, shells, small stones, and sharp gravel, are concreted into platter-shaped masses which seem to become the base of blocks of rough conglomerate, capable of resisting the attacks of the sea; and a few yards back, where a mangrove-bordered creek once existed, the mud and decayed fragments of wood have been transformed into a black, cheesy substance which might be mistaken for soft coal. So do these beaches lay bare their secrets.

When the mainland streams pour out their floods and the commingled volume hurries north in a mud-tinted, sharply delimited current, and whole trees are cast up on the beaches of far-away isles, vivid examples of the dispersion of animate and inanimate things by purely natural means are afforded. Weighty stones are found locked among roots which, as the wood decays, are deposited on alien sands, thereafter to invite speculation as to origin and means of transport. On one such raft voyaged a living specimen of the white and black banded snake, one of the most singular of the family, for Nature has bestowed on it a placid disposition, and provided it with an unmischievous mouth and fangs so minute that, although classed as venomous, it is not considered injurious to man. Though strange and interesting, on the plea that the family is quite sufficiently represented, the derelict was unwelcome, save as a living proof of the practicability of natural transports. By what grace, indeed, could the creature which earned the Almighty's bitter curse be accepted as "wilsam" — goods of God's mercy driven ashore, no wreck or ship being visible?

This small bay never ceases the laying of tribute at one's feet. There are seasons when the amount is less than at others; but how seldom are its sands trodden without a display of the infinite variety of productions of the ocean? When the mood of the sea is savage and the spoil from the reef is flung in ridges among the vegetation of the shore — coral in blocks and shattered masses, shells, seaweed, sponges, and other dead marine animals and driftwood, heap on heap — days of enthusiastic toil might be spent in sorting out the over-surplus of the secrets of the sea. But for months together the beach maintains its cleanly orderliness, and during these dreamy days the sea will tell of many a pretty treasure which the sands will reveal in the face of the sun.

> *. . . vivid examples of the dispersion of animate and inanimate things by purely natural means are afforded.*

34

A SAILING MISHAP

When I bought a boat to bring hither I knew not the distinguishing term of a single halyard, save the "topping lift", and even that scant knowledge was idle, for I was blankly ignorant of the place and purpose of the oddly-named rope. Necessity drove me to the acquirement of boat sense, and now I manage my home-built "flattie" — mean substitute for the neat yacht which necessity compelled me to part with — very courageously in ordinary weather; and I am content to stay at home when Neptune is frothy at the lips . . .

In the days prior to the fall which my haughty spirit merited, I was vain in the handling of a boat, and my little knowledge proved most dangersome to Paddy (the dog) and others. In holiday humour, with another and two black boys (Willie and Charlie) we drifted out of Brammo Bay on the ebb with idle sails, all serene and bright. Mischance surely was never further away as we conferred, saying that the current and not the breeze was to be depended on this preoccupied morning. Yet a vagrant and wanton puff skipped on the hill-top, snoodled

. . . the intense calm of the morning was giving way before a stiff north-easterly breeze . . .

36

between two steep ridges, whisked coyly out of a bottle-necked gorge, impudently slapped the big jib, and in a trice the skimming dish-boat had made an unbecoming exhibition. Half a mile from land — and not a soul within many miles to send us aid; clinging to the up-turned boat while contemplating the fact that the intense calm of the morning was giving way before a stiff north-easterly breeze — how grim a transformation to the gay little scene of a few moments past! The pursuit of pleasure had led us into dismaying difficulties.

Persuasions, backed by threats of personal violence — for in my hand was the ornamental tiller, hard as iron, to which I had clung while I swam, supporting the passenger who could not swim — started Willie for the shore; and as he swam away there was leisure for a few moments, and we thought of Paddy. Charlie had not seen him.

"That fella drown — finish! Him tie up alonga rigging. No come up one time. My word, poor pfella Paddy; good-bye. Me plenty sorry."

I argued that the dog must have swam for the shore ahead of Willie, but Charlie persisted in his theory.

I could not squat idly on the slippery bottom of the boat with the knowledge that an old and faithful friend was dead as a result of my vanity and carelessness. So I dived among the tangled cordage, but found him not. Then Charlie, forcibly persuaded by the dog-headed tiller, perfunctorily followed my example, also without result. Perhaps the poor dog was floating in the forepart of the boat, where she was decked.

Grasping the chaffing-piece and allowing my body to float away under the boat, I explored with my feet as far as my legs could stretch. By the same plan other parts of the boat were investigated, until my toes touched Paddy's feet, working as though a treadmill. With a shout of joy I dived, seized the dog, drew him down and past the coaming, and in a moment had him safe in the free air.

Fully a quarter of an hour had elapsed since the mishap, and how had Paddy escaped? The sudden and complete capsize had imprisoned a small volume of air against the bottom of the boat. In his game struggles for liberty Paddy had found the gracious bubble, and had kept his shrewd nose in it in the dark all those long minutes.

In the meantime Willie had gained the shore, and in due course paddled out to the scene of the wreck in a frail punt. And the nerves of one individual of the party have thrilled at the thought of a sailing-boat ever since!

In the Making of a Chair

A preponderant part of the furniture of our abode is the work of my own unskilled hands — tables, chairs, bookshelves, cupboards, etc. There is much pleasure and there are also many aches and pains in the designing and fashioning serviceable chairs from odd kinds of bush timber.

In the making of a chair, as in the building of a boat by one who has had no training in any branch of carpentry, there is scope for the personal element. Though the parts have been cut and trimmed with minute care and all possible precision, each, according to requirements, being the duplicate of the other, when they come to be assembled obstructive obstinacy prevails. One of the most fiendish things the art of man contrives is a chair out of the routine design made by a rule-of-thumb carpenter. Grotesque in its deformities, you must needs pity your own mishandling of the obstinate wood. Have you courage to smile at the misshapen handiwork, or do you cowardly discard the deformity you have created? How it grunts and groans as pressure is applied to its stubborn bent limbs! Curvature of the spine is the least of its ills. It limps and creaks when fixed tentatively for trial. Tender-footed, it stands awry, heaving one leg aloft — as crooked and as perverse as Caliban. In good time, botching here, violent constraint there, the chair finds itself or is forced so to do, for he is a weak man who is not stronger than his own chair. So, after many days' intense toil — toil which even troubled the night watches, for have I not lain awake with thoughts automatically concentrated on a seemingly impossible problem, plotting by what illicit and awful torture it might be possible for the tough and stubborn parts to be brought into juxtaposition — there is a chair — a solid, sittable chair, which neither squeaks, nor shuffles, nor shivers. Maybe you are ashamed at the quantity of mind the dull article of furniture has absorbed; but there are other reflections — homely as well as philosophic.

ON WEATHER

" . . . at sundown the weather-god, repenting of his frown, bestowed a glorious benediction."

WORSHIPPER OF THE SUN

Of the graciousness of the sun a special instance has been preserved in my erratic diary. Here it is: November 24, 1908: Spent from 10 a.m. to 1.15 p.m. on the beach and on the Isle of Purtaboi, bare-limbed, bare-bodied, save for scant cotton pants. Above high-water mark the sand was scorchingly hot to the feet. The heat of the glowing coral drift on the Isle forced me promptly to amend my methodic gait to a quick step, though my hardened soles soon became indifferent. Nutmeg pigeons were nesting plentifully on trees and shrubs amongst masses of orchids, and on ledges almost obscured by grass. Brown-winged terns occupied cool nooks and crannies in the rocks, and other species of terns had egg reserves — they cannot be called nests — on the unshaded coral bank. After gazing intently on the white drift, eagerly making mental notes of any remarkable mutations in the colouring of the thickly strewn eggs, and admiring the fortitude or indifference with which the fledglings endured the sizzling heat, I found myself subject to an optical illusion, for when I looked up and abroad the brightly gleaming sea had been changed to inky purple, the hills of the mainland to black. Though absolutely cloudless, the sky seemed oppressed with slaty gloom, and the leaves of the trees near at hand assumed a leaden green. For a few seconds I was convinced that some almost unearthly meteorological phenomenon, before which the most resolute of men might cower, had developed with theatrical suddenness. Then I realised that the intense glare of the coral, of which I had been unconscious, and the quivering heat rays had temporarily deprived my vision of appreciation of ordinary tints. Saturated by vivid white light, my bemused sight swayed under temporary aberration. I was conscious of illusion-creating symptoms, tipsy with excess of sunshine . . .

In civility to his Majesty the Sun do I also proudly testify to his transcendent gifts as a painter in the facile media which here prevail. Look upon his coming and his going — an international, universal property, an ecstatic delight, an awesome marvel, upon which we gaze, of which we cannot speak, lacking roseate phrases. A landscape painter also is he, for have I not seen his boldest brush at work and stood amazed at the magnificence of his art?

Above high-water mark the sand was scorchingly hot . . .

SORCERY OF THE SEA

Do those who live in temperate and cold climates realise the effect of the sun's heat on the sea — how warm, how hot, blessed by his beams, the water may become? The luxuriousness of bathing in an ocean having a temperature of 108°F is not for the multitude who crowd in reeking cities which the sun touches tremulously and slantwise.

On November 21, 1909 (far be it from me to bundle out into an apathetic world whimpering facts lacking the legitimacy of dates), we bathed at Moo-jee in shallow water on the edge of an area of denuded coral reef fully two miles long by a mile broad. For three hours a considerable portion of the reef had been exposed to the glare of the sun, and the incoming tide filched heat, stored by solar rays, from coral and stones and sand. The first wallow provoked an exclamation of amazement, for the water was several degrees hotter than the air, and it was the hottest hour (3 p.m.) of an extremely hot day. No thermometer was at hand to register the actual temperature of the water, but subsequent tests at the same spot under similar conditions proved that on the thermometerless occasion the sea was about 108°F — that is, the surface stratum of about one foot, which averaged from 4° to 6° F hotter than the air. Beneath, the temperature seemed ordinary — corresponding with that of the water a hundred yards out from the shore. This delectable experience revealed that in bathing something more is comprehended than mere physical pleasure. It touched and tingled a refined aesthetic emotion, an enlightened consciousness of the surroundings, remote from gross bodily sensations. For the time being one was immersed, not in heated salt water only but in the purifying essence of the scene — the glowing sky, stainless, pallid, and pure; the gleaming, scarcely visible, fictitious sea and the bold blue isles beyond; the valley whence whiffs of cool, fern-filtered, odorous air issued shyly from the shadowed land of the jungle through the embowered lips of the creek. The blend of these elements reacted on the perceptions, rendering the bathe in two temperatures that of a lifetime and a means also whereby the clarified senses were first stimulated and then soothed . . .

I sat down, steeped chin deep in crystal clearness, warmth, and silence, passively surrendering myself to a cheap yet precious sensation. Around me were revealed infinitely fragile manifestations of life, scarcely less limpid than the sea, sparkling, darting, twisting — strong and vigorous of purpose. Tremulous filaments of silver flashed and were gone. No space but was thickly peopled with what ordinarily passes as the invisible, but which now, plainly to behold, basked and revelled in the blaze — products of the sun. Among the grains of sand and flakes of mica furtive bubblings, burrowings, and upheavals betrayed a benighted folk to whom the water was as a firmament into which they might not venture to ascend.

Sought out by the sun, translucent fish revealed their presence by spectral shadows on the sand, and, traced by the shadows, became discernible, though but little the more substantial.

This peace-lulled, beguiling sea, teeming with myriad forms scintillating on the verge of nothingness — obscure, elusive, yet mighty in their wayward way — soothed with never so gentle, so dulcet a swaying. This smooth-bosomed nurse was pleased to fondle to drowsiness a loving mortal responsive to the blissfulness of enchantment. Warm, comforting, stainless, she swathed me with rose-leaf softness while whispering a lullaby of sighs. Her salty caresses lingered on my lips, as I gazed dreamily intent upon determining the non-existing skyline. Yet, with no demarcation of the allied elements this rimless, flickering moon, to what narrow zone, I pondered, is man restricted! He swims feebly; if he but immerse his lips below the shining surface for a space to be measured by seconds, he becomes carrion. On the mountain-tops he is deadly sick. Thus musing, the sorcery of the sea became invincible. My thoughts drifted, until I dozed, and dozing dreamt — a vague, incomprehensible dream of floating in some purer ether, some diviner air than ever belonged to wormy earth, and woke to realities and a skate

— a little friendly skate which had snoodled beside me, its transparent shovel-snout half buried in the sand. Immune from the opiate of the sea, though motionless, with wide, watery-yellow eyes, it gazed upon me as a fascinated child might upon a strange shape monstrous though benign, and as I raised my hand in salutation wriggled off, less afraid than curious . . .

. . . the incoming tide filched heat . . . from coral and stones and sand.

A "Temperate" Climate

As to climate, will general credence be given to the statement that Dunk Island is more "temperate" than Melbourne? We experience neither the extreme heat nor the extreme cold of the metropolis of Victoria — nearly 2,000 miles to the south; we have four or five times the volume of rain, yet a greater number of fine days — days without rain. The general principle that where the rainy days are fewest the amount of rain is greatest, is apt to be forgotten . . . Here in the tropics we have the finer weather — no excess of either heat or cold, no sudden, constitution-shattering changes . . . Dunk Island has a mean temperature of about 69 deg.; January is the hottest month, with a mean of 87 deg., and July the coolest, mean 57 deg. Taking the official readings of Cardwell (twenty miles to the south), I find the greatest extremes on record occurred in one year, when the highest temperature was 103.3 deg. and the lowest 36.2 deg. At Geraldton (Innisfail — twenty-five miles to the north) the extremes were 96 deg. and 43.4 deg.

Rainfall and temperature, the proportion of clear to cloudy skies, calms, the direction, strength and the duration of winds, do not wholly comprehend distinctive climatic features. There are other conditions of more or less character and note, some hard to define, yet ever present. Here the air is warm and soothing, seldom is it crisp and never really bracing. Hot dry winds are unknown, but in the height of the wet season — which coincides with the dry season of the Southern States — the moisture-laden air may be likened to the vapour of a steam bath. While the rain thunders on the roof at the rate of an inch per hour, inside the house it may be perspiringly hot. After a fortnight's rain the damp saturates everything. Neglected boots and shoes grow a rich crop of mould, guns demand constant attention to prevent rust, and clothes packed tight in chests of drawers smell and feel damp. But the atmosphere is so wholesome that ordinary precautions for the prevention of sickness are generally neglected without any fear of ill consequence.

However sharply defined by reason of the personal discomfort it inflicts, this steamy feature of the wet season is no more a general characteristic than the hot winds are of Victoria. Warm as the rains are, they bring to the air coolness and refreshment. Clear, calm, bright days, days of even and not high temperature, and of pure delight, dovetail with the hot and steamy ones. The prolificacy of vegetation is a perpetual marvel; the loveliness of the land, the ineffable purity of the sky, the glorious tints of the sea — green and gold at sunrise, silvery blue at noon, purple, pink and lilac during the all too brief twilight, a perpetual feast.

For six months it may be said the prevailing wind is the south-east, followed by gentle breezes from the east and north-east. North-easters begin in September and are intermittent until the beginning of the wet season. The south-east monsoons are regular and consistent; the north-east, which precede the rainy monsoon, fitful and wayward, never continuing long in one stay, and lasting but four out of the twelve months. Rare is the wind from the west, rarer from the south-west. North-easters are a pronounced feature. They work up by diurnal and easy grades from gentleness to strength, thunder coming as a climax. After a succession of calm days of gentle breezes from the east-south-east and east, the north-easter begins softly, and daily gathers courage and assumption, to find in the course of a week or two its haughty spirit subdued by thunder and rain showers. Calms prevail for a few days. Easterly breezes come, to give way to the north-east again, and so the programme is repeated with variations which none may foresee, and which set at naught the lengthiest experience. At last, at Christmas or the New Year, the rains come with a boisterous beginning. A north-easter accompanied by thunder lasted a whole July afternoon. It was as strange as a crop of mangoes would have been at that time of year.

> . . . dew which releases the prisoned odour of flowers
> irresponsive to the heat of the sun . . .

During the cool season — a generous half of the year — dews are common — not the trivial barely perceptible moisture called dew in some parts, but most ungentle dew, which saturates everything and drips from the under sides of verandas as the sun warms the air; dew which bows the grass with its weight, soaks through your dungarees to the hips, and soddens your thick bluchers, until you feel and appear as though you had waded through a swamp; dew which releases the prisoned odour of flowers irresponsive to the heat of the sun, which keeps the night cool and sweet, which with the first gleam of the sun makes the air soft and spicy and buoyant, and inspires thankfulness for the joy of life.

Are we not all apt of fall into the error of estimating the character of a country by its extravagances rather than its average and general qualities? . . .

Even in the matter of cyclones — often quoted as one of its detriments — North Queensland has nothing to hide. At intervals Nature does indulge in a reckless and violent outburst, but not more frequently here than in other parts of the world. Year after year the seasons are passive and pleasant, and in every respect considerate of humanity and encouraging to humanity's undertakings. Then, abandoning for a few hours her orderly and kindly ways, Nature runs amok, raving and shrieking. Her transient irresponsibleness and mischievousness are then cited as everyday, persistent vices. Not so. Nature is rational even in her most passionate moments. Vegetation, rank and gross as in an unweeded garden, requires vigorous lopping and pruning. These twenty-year-interval storms comb out superfluous leaves and branches, cut out dead wood, send to the ground decayed and weakly shoots, and scrub and cleanse trunks and branches of parasitic growths. All is done boldly, yet with such skill that in a few weeks losses are hidden under masses of clean, insectless, healthy, bright foliage. Trees and plants respond to the stimulus with magical vigour, for lazy, slumbering forces have been roused into efforts so splendid that the realism of tropical vegetation is to be appreciated only after Nature has swept and sweetened her garden . . .

. . . the ineffable purity of the sky, the glorious tints of the sea . . . purple, pink and lilac during the all too brief twilight . . .

THE SCENE-SHIFTER

In a few hours came "the season's difference". The scene-shifter worked with almost magical haste, with silence, and with supreme effect. The gloomy days and nights of misty hill-tops and damp hollows, where the grass was sodden and the air dull and irresponsive to sound, gave way to bright sunshine, cloudless skies, calm seas, echoing hills, and the tinge of that which for lack of the ideal word we call "spring". Spring does not visit the tropical coast, where vegetation does not tolerate any period of rest. When plants are not actually romping with excess of vital force, as during the height of the wet season, they grow with the haste of summer. And yet immediately on the dispersal of the mists of July the least observance could not fail to recognise that a certain and elaborate change had taken place. The mango-trees had been flowering for several weeks in a trivial, half-hearted way, but when the sun sent its thrills down into the moist soil the lemons and pomeloes began to sweeten the air; the sunflower-tree displayed its golden crowns among huge soft leaves, and the last blooms of belated wattles fell, showing that it is possible for tributes representative of May and September to be paid on one and the same date.

The scene-shifter came softly "as the small rain upon the tender herb" but with an orchestra of his own. Years of observation have shown that the weather does control the habits of some birds — birds of distinct and regular methods of life. Two such are common — the nutmeg pigeon and the metallic starling. Both species leave this part of the North during the third week of March, flying in flocks to regions nearer the equator. For several weeks the starlings train themselves for the long Northern flight and its perils, dashing with impetuous speed through the forest and wheeling up into the sky until they disappear, to become visible again as black dots hurtling through space when the sunlight plays on their glossy feathers as the course of the flock is changed. With the rush of a wind of small measure but immense velocity, the flock descends earthwards, manoeuvring among and over the trees, perfecting itself by trials of endurance and intricate alertness. The birds return during the first week in August, in small and silent companies, to reoccupy favourite resorts in common. The nutmeg pigeons are also of exact habit, the time for their return generally coinciding with that of the starlings. This year (1916) both birds were noticed just after the scene-shifter had swept the hills of mists, and now other birds seem to have awakened to the conditions which the starlings and the nutmegs brought with them from hotter lands. The swamp pheasants are whooping and gurgling, and that semi-migratory fellow, the spangled drongo — a flattering name, for he jangles but does not spangle — sits on the slim branch of the Moreton Bay ash which held last year's nest and chatters discordances in the very ears of his responsive mate. They will start building a loose nest on the brittlest branch forthwith, and while the lady sits on her three eggs he will screech defiances to the high heavens and perform aerial gymnastics with delirious delight.

The sun-birds are searching the lemon blooms. The breast of the gay, assertive little bird is far richer in tint than the brightest of the lemons. A minute ago one perched on a ripe fruit as if to shame it by contrast, and the fruit has since seemed a trifle dull of tint, and with light-hearted inconsequence the pair are now probing narrow throats of papaw flowers. The ground has been too much overgrown with grass and weeds for the comfort of the little green pigeons which come strutting down the paths for seeds and crumbs. Dry soil, which may be easily scanned and scratched, is more to their liking, so they keep to the forest, where in some places the undergrowth of wattles is so dense that the sun may not visit the ground, and the bare places glitter with seed.

When rain was seriously deficient, proof was given that some proportion of the wattle seeds eaten by pigeons are not digested. In the crevices of logs supporting the water-trough, which proved to be a popular refreshment spot of many species of birds, clamorous with thirst, seeds were deposited, and when the rains came the trough was fringed and decorated with pinnate leaves of sprouting wattles, some of which grew so strongly, notwithstanding the absence of soil, save that which occurs from the slow decay of seasoned bloodwood, that if summary measures had not been taken the trough might have been embowered. The season seems to have been too damp for the night-jars, though quite to the taste of all species of pigeons. In the course of a few minutes the voice of the timid, tremulous, barred-shouldered dove came from among the yellow-flowered hibiscus of the beach, while the pheasant-tailed pigeon sounded its rich, dual note, the red-crowned fruit pigeon tolled its mournful chime, and the guttural of the magnificent fruit pigeon — often heard, but seldom seen — came from the jungle close at hand. Not one of these birds was visible, nor was the fluty-voiced shrike thrush, which answers every strange call and mimics crude attempts to reproduce its varied notes. The blue kingfisher is investigating the tumour made by white ants in the bloodwood wherein the nest is annually excavated, and soon the chattering notes of the pair will be heard. A week ago few signs of the approach of the scene-shifter were discernible. He has come, and plants and birds respond to his genial and becoming presence — plants with richer growth and more abundant flowers, birds with the unreflecting gaiety of nuptial days.

The gloomy days and nights of misty hill-tops and damp hollows . . .

Wet Season Days

Just as in the spring a young man's fancies lightly turn to thoughts of love, so at the beginning of each new year in tropical Queensland the minds of the weather sages become sensitive and impressionable. All the tarnish is rubbed off the recollection of former ill manners on the part of the weather, when about the middle of January the wind begins to bluster and to abuse good-natured trees, shaking off twigs and whirling branches like a tipsy bully striving to dislocate a weak man's arm at the shoulder. We remember dubious events all too vividly when the recitation of them does not make for mutual consolation.

In January, 1909, for two days the sea burst on the black rocks of the islet in the bay in clouds of foam. It was all bombast, froth and bubble, or rather a gentle back-hander, for the cyclone was playing all sorts of naughty pranks elsewhere. But why were we apprehensive? In disobedience to the scriptural injunction, we had observed the clouds and the birds. Twice a flock of lesser frigate-birds — those dark, fish-tailed high-fliers which are for ever cutting animated "W's" in the air with long lithe wings — had appeared. Seldom do they come unless as harbingers of boisterous weather. On each recent occasion they had been absolutely trust-

This . . . luminous cloud had bewitched the commonplace, converting familiar surroundings into fairyland . . .

worthy messengers. Watching them soaring and swooping, we said one to another: "Behold the cyclone cometh!" But it did not. With a passing flick of its tail it passed elsewhere.

Altogether, however, we had very queer weather and two or three "rum" sorts of nights. On the 19th the morning was calm, the sky brilliantly clear. A north-east breeze sprang up at noon. Deep violet thunder-clouds gathered in the west, and, muttering and grumbling, rolled across the narrow strait slowly and sullenly. Australia scowled at our penitent Island, threatening direful inflictions — lightning, thunder, and an overwhelming cataclysm. Behind that frowning Providence there was a smiling face. The good storm, albeit black and angry, behaved benignly. Gentle rain came, and a picturesque little electrical display to a humming accompaniment of far distant thunder, followed by a soothingly cool south-westerly breeze. Just at sundown the weather-god, repenting of his frown, bestowed a glorious benediction.

All afternoon a damp pall had overhung the Island, mopping up feeble sounds and strangely muffling the stronger. Now it was translated. Lifting so that the summits only of the hills were capped, the haze (for it became nothing more) assumed a luminous yellow saffron suffused with sage green. Against this singularly lovely, ample "cloth" branches and leaves of steadfast trees stood out in high relief. All the lower levels became transparently clear, the definition of distant objects magically sharpened, spaces translucent. In a sea which shone like polished silver the islet was a gem — green enamel, amethyst rocks, golden sand. The bold white trunks of giant tea-trees glowed; the creamy blooms of bloodwoods were as flecks of snow; the tips of the fronds of coconut palms flickered vividly as burnished steel; the white-painted house assumed speckless purity. All light colours were heightened; ruddy browns and sombre greens seemed to have been smartened up by touches of fresh paint and varnish. An idealistic artist had revealed for once living tints and uncomprehended hues.

Was it not a landscape fresh from Nature's brush, divinely transmogrified by one bold smudge of yellow-green haze? Or was the effect partly due to the dust raised by the golden fringe of the blue mantle which the sun trailed over the glowing hills? I know naught of the chemistry of colours, nor why this yellow-green medium should so clarify and etherealise the atmosphere. But was ever clear sunset half so affecting? This tinted, luminous cloud had bewitched the commonplace, converting familiar surroundings into fairyland itself. If all the world's a stage, this truly was one of the rarest transformation scenes.

What was about to happen? Surely this mysterious colouring portended some astounding phenomena? Again, nothing did happen, save a stilly night and grey.

A Cyclone

Heaving, as with deep-drawn breaths, out from the beach the sea seemed to be both restless and angry, as glistening rollers heaved themselves on to the strand, to be shattered into spray. They rifled the Barrier Reef, threw on the sand lumps of coral to which brown seaweed hung, like the scalps of mermaids, and swept them to and fro with savage persistency. They brought driftwood from afar, and claimed all sorts of sun-dried relics from previous depositary moods.

After a time the sea became silent again, with a sparkling, wavering ripple, while the noise of its assault on the mainland beach had the tone of distant, unceasing thunder.

Ten days before the second storm, while the sky was cloudless and the air serene, a change in the quality of the heat was felt. During the first three months of the year — the period of heavy rainfall — the temperature is generally humid. Suddenly it became dry and burning, with a tingling intensity, as rare as uncomfortable. For the time the moist vapours of a mild steam-bath were dispersed by scorching breath as from a furnace, to the discomfort of animal life and the injury of vegetation.

Early on the morning of Sunday, 10th March (1918), the sky became overcast. A fresh southerly breeze had sprung up during the night. A short, confused sea tumbled in the channel, and the usually placid bay mimicked its sport. With fearsome steadiness of purpose, the wind developed as it veered to the east. At 5 p.m. it was travelling at furious speed, twisting branches from trees and thickening the now gloomy skies with leaves. Consistently with the strength of the wind the barometer fell until between 9 and 10 p.m., when, with a conglomeration of terrifying sounds varying from falsetto shrieks to thunderous roars, the centre of the cyclone seemed to bore down on the very vitals of the island.

The devastating assault lasted about half an hour; it was followed by a lull, succeeded by another attack of violence from the north and north-west; . . . the demons of the air were crazy with fury . . . Only while the core of the storm was passing was lightning seen or thunder heard. Then the whole mass of tumultuously-racing clouds and vapour was luminous at frequent intervals, and the rumble of the thunder almost continuous — but the glow was weak and tremulous, and the thunder timorous, as if the electricity was a cowed captive at the chariot-wheels of triumphing Wind.

Throughout the night rain was incessant; but its torrential tramplings on the resonant, ceilingless roof were not to be detached from the discordancies of wind and wave, save only while breath was held in expectation of whatsoever might happen after the terrifying lull. The gauge overflowed at 10.50 in., so that the exact quantity for the twenty-four hours during which all ordinary concerns and interests were wafted aside cannot be stated; but, by comparison with results of previously recorded deluges, the fall must have exceeded 14 in., the greater volume of which should be ascribed to about five hours.

Being in perfect sympathy with each other's fury, wind, rain and sea, in a common tongue, spoke threats of ruin and devastation, and fulfilled them all in more or less degree. And it has to be confessed that the crash and confusion of the awe-inspiring night, after three years of healing, still ring in the ears.

While the rage lasted, a slight degree of comfort was attained from considering the suddenness of the storm and its very violence. At its lowest the barometer indicated nothing out of the normal; but its marvellous activity as the wind gathered in force, the sensational drop immediately prior to the crisis, the recovery as the depression passed over, and the subsequently revealed fact that the course of the storm was brief — little over a hundred miles — show that it was home-brewed. Subsequent information proved that the dangerous phase was not experienced for more than twenty miles to the south and twenty-four miles to the south-west . . .

At sunrise on Sunday a leafy wilderness; at sunrise on Monday a leafless wilderness, wanting only grey skies, snow on the hills, and ice on the pools to suggest an English winter scene. Along the beach, on the flat, on the spurs of the range, astonishing transfiguration. The shrub-embroidered strand is now forlorn, its vegetation, up-rooted and down-beaten, naked roots exposed to critical view. Not a shrub has escaped, and broken and shattered limbs of tough trees appeal for sympathy. The country is foul with wreckage.

Rain ceased two days after the storm, giving way to dry air under a cloudless sky, and the effects of the visitation were revealed in harsh crudeness and nakedness. Not a single tree escaped more or less serious injury. Those not uprooted or broken at the trunk, are almost limbless and entirely leafless. Instead of a compact mantle in various shades of green, hills and spurs — and even valleys and the rims of ravines — have assumed a tattered and frayed raiment of brown, as if a mighty flame had singed the verdure.

All the minor secrets of the land are bare; the "verdurous glooms" of yesterday are open to the inquisitive sun; the streams, fair-running but foul-tasting now, are blocked with decaying vegetation, and the flat lands are strewn with fallen timber.

Ravished by the profligate wind, once tender and lovable scenes flaunt their wretchedness and woe, and seem to appeal for consolation. The islet in the bay — hitherto a garden to the water's edge, offering to the admiration of the sun and sea masses of golden-brown orchids and red clumps of umbrella-trees, of incomparable luxuriance and beauty — is but a bare rock with a forlorn crest of seared shrubs . . .

Huge coconut palms, that a few hours ago might have vaunted their stately straightness, lie uprooted or broken at the base, or lean at pitiable angles . . .

The veering of the wind to the north-west, since it took place about the hour of high water, occasioned a tidal wave, evidences of which strew the green places of yesterday a hundred yards beyond the strand. Shrubs four feet high are buried in white coral sand . . . Here, too, every exposed rootlet, every twig and fragment of drift-wood, is the crest of a sand-ridge in miniature, telling the direction whence came the wind's final onrush . . .

Thousands of maritime birds were killed, and those of the land suffered in like degree. Here the only species which seems to be in pre-storm numbers is the swiftlet, the home of which, in secret places among huge granite rocks, was safe against the shake of anything less than an earthquake . . .

Forlorn birds, made tamer by one irresistible touch of Nature, flit mournfully among the battered branches. They are silent. None of the cheerful jeers and chuckles of the scrub-fowl comes from the trampled jungle; the great flight of terns, which settled on the sand-spit on Sunday and sat in a dense crowd, head to sea, has been dispersed. A solitary, wind-wearied gannet sleeps, head under wing, in the sun.

Shrubs four feet high are buried in white coral sand . . .

RESTORATION

The loveliness of the Isle is of the past; but do I love it the less while it bears the stripes of its chastisement? Shall I not rather attempt to comfort and soothe it and heal its scars? Behold, how it blossoms in its distress! ... Even a great, bullying, maniacal wind has its compensations ... How soon did Nature begin her soothing duties!

In the shattered forest the sun searched out spots sheltered from its rays for many a generation, and germinated seeds of jungle plants which had been dropped by careless birds or carried by idle winds. A thick undergrowth is springing up, which from present appearances may permanently transform the country. Instead of forest, there will be forest in the process of conversion into jungle, and in years to come there will be specific jungle vegetation ...

... the big wind will have to its credit denser and more beautiful growth; instead of grassy glades, an almost impenetrable entanglement; palms will sprawl over lofty trees; huge vines, with stems as thick as a man's thigh and bearing pods a yard long, will spread a network over all; and instead of the forest's comparatively dry surface will be maintained a moist, sweet-smelling soil, and steamy conditions and half-lights. In time, too, the gradual accumulation of vegetable mould must tend inevitably to the enrichment of the land ...

After such a visitation, probably the most conspicuous trees of the coast are the tea-trees, for the lustful wind tore off their weather-stained layers of bark, revealing naked limbs and branches of a pale-red tint. The tea-tree's bark is composed of an infinite number of layers, thin as tissue paper; within a few weeks of its ravishment, the exterior became white, and, contrasted with the seared and stricken forest, each looked like an emblem of purity and an example of strength. How few of these magnificent trees were overthrown whose roots had obtained secure hold! Few were snapped below the spring of the branches, or otherwise mutilated. Most were stripped of foliage, but slender branches and twigs stand out as an elaborate fretwork against the sombre hue of the battered and slowly recovering background. Over a fair extent of country not a single instance of an uprooted tea-tree is to be seen, save where the tidal surges had attacked its base; and hundreds exultingly display clean trunks and limbs and all the elaborate and beautiful complexity of branches and twigs, now glistening with silvery leaf-buds ...

Different, but scarcely less sturdy, stand the bloodwoods. Few are uprooted, fewer broken at the trunk; but how horribly are most maimed and disfigured! ...

Less at ease under extraordinary conditions, the Moreton Bay ash-trees suffered greatly. In the thick of the sheltered forest they lie, scores uprooted, scores severed at the trunk, and most of them more or less seriously mutilated by loss of limb. This tree is more susceptible to decay than bloodwood, and offers more inviting food to white ants, though when seasoned it becomes almost imperishable ...

Forest mahogany, or messmate, another eucalypt plentifully represented, shows contemptible subservience to the will of the wind in all phases of disastrous ruin; ...

Of the wattles, that which is known locally as the black — the toughest and the densest — behaved with the greatest staunchness, though many were destroyed by the uprooting and severing force of the wind. It would seem that the weak spot of many a specimen was about ten or twelve feet from the ground; ...

Figs, soft-wooded, but willing to bend before the wind, do not show very serious effects, though many in exposed parts were cast down. Slim shrubs of upright habit and pithy texture escaped almost scot-free, being pliable and submissive, and pandanus palms stood the test bravely in comparison with many trees which vaunt a tougher nature ...

A SPINNER OF SAND

When the smoke of the belated steamer was a mere smudge in still air far to the south-west, and there was naught to do but to wait for tidings, good or bad, from the sick and discomforted world — the din of which actually reaches these placid scenes — was it not meet to study the sand, a field of intense though noiseless industry, of edifying determination, of competitive forces working undesignedly to a common purpose, of exemplary utility? . . .

If you believe that Nature's restorative operations are performed unceasingly, with never-failing design and often with the exhibition of wonderful power, you may not be altogether astounded at the antics of seemingly inanimate things. On this flat a year ago was a thick sward of grass, perpetually mulched by millions of needles from the beach oaks. The cyclone buried both the grass and the mulching, so that the new surface was unprotected from shifting winds. To encourage the growth of plant-life retentive of sand, Nature employs certain advance agents, the successive office of each of which is to create ever so meagre an amelioration of the harsh conditions. Behold how one of these agents works.

Ordinarily the fallen needle — or branchlet — of a beach oak is absolutely passive. Like the tree of the Bible, "In the place that it falleth there shall it be". But here is one with its terminal spike of withered flowers that *moves*, though lacking apparent impulse, with a succession of jerks. It may be ten inches long, light of course, yet unaccountably mysterious in its actions. The terminal plume lifts and sways, as if some unfortunate creature were semaphoring signals of distress. May these dry things live and brave the light of day with frolicsome waverings?

Look at the other end, and for a moment the mystery deepens. It is slowly settling upright in the sand. Was ever conjurer's trick more entertaining! Take hold of the plume; you will find a weak resistance to the strain you exert, and then the needle may be withdrawn. Let it lie for a moment, and again it apparently becomes invested with life. The plume lifts from the sand, wavers, and begins to heave itself upright, the frequent pauses in the operation proving that the task is a mighty one, demanding rests. Carry investigations a trifle further, and you will discover a sand-coloured grub, a trifle more robust of figure than the needle, holding the end with mandibles backed by definite purpose. Not one-tenth the length of the needle, the insect exerts almost magical strength, and is, moreover, endowed with determination to obey the dictates of Nature. Though apparently disliking exposure to the sunlight, yet, should the needle be withdrawn from its grip, the insect after an interval slowly and cautiously emerges, hastens to it, drags it once more to the entrance of its shaft, and withdraws, the waving plume registering each tug.

It is as if a six-foot man were to take hold of a flagstaff about a third the circumference of his own body and ten times his length, and retreat into the sand, dragging the staff with him. There is a circumstance, however, in favour of the herculean grub. Its shaft has been dug beforehand, though the entrance closes automatically and is not discoverable on the surface; further, it has a casing of web, reinforced with minute grains of sand. The shaft may be traced down six and eight inches. When you look about, you will find similar operations in progress by the dozen over every square yard of the sandy area. Indeed, in some places the casings of the shafts are so close together that there may be three or four in the space of a square inch. Some occupants are working on needles, or portions thereof, three and four inches long. The higher-minded grubs, those that tend to improve the conditions of the multitude, try to get ten-inch needles down eight-inch shafts, and not only try but succeed; for do they not nibble away the superfluous length, and as they nibble does not the plume tell of gigantic concentration of effort, crowned with the flourish of success? Thus do these sober-tinted, scarcely discernible grubs check the mobility of sand and make loam upon which plants may feed and be vigorous!

REFUSE OF AGES

If one wanted proof of the significance of Kipling's saying that last year's nuts are this year's black earth, it lies at hand. Just before the cyclone a diminutive garden, solely for utilitarian purposes, was made in sand fronting the beach, and with a short, narrow, spongy depression, tributary to a little creek, as a background. Tall tea-trees and many pandanus palms flourished there in the peaty soil which was never dry, and where the frontal ridge rose from swampy levels the sand was black with the mouldering vegetation of centuries.

Adjacent to the crude fence once stood a huge coral-tree which had had its day and ceased to be, and the soft wood as it decayed formed heaps of tindery stuff that mingled with the sand, helped to this end by the industry of scrub-fowls.

For generations before the coming of white men the great coral-tree was the centre of activities of the Aboriginal proprietors of the Isle. Some of their dead were buried beneath its shade. The living feasted there, for have not their stone ovens been unearthed? Birds lodged in the big tree. Being deciduous and of succulent foliage, it contributed largely to the enrichment of the absorbent sand which its roots explored far and near . . .

Taking a hint from Nature, it was decided to form a vegetable garden where water and sandy humus, enriched by the deposition of the refuse of ages, were available. Tons of vegetable mould were transferred a few yards; tons of decayed manure from the milking shed were added as a special stimulant, and to give it body; and the work was wellnigh completed when the storm and its attendant tidal wave desolated the scene. The buoyant elements of the soil were carried off like froth, and deposited in the peaty hollow where the pandanus palms stood, ever refreshed; little but salt sand, raw from the beach, remained on the scene which had absorbed so much enthusiastic labour. The fencing had to be restored, the beds reformed, and some of the disarray of the spiteful breeze smoothed with hasty hands, for the season was advancing . . .

How speedily, notwithstanding the ruffianly check, did the site justify itself! It might have been thought that the very heart had been taken out of the soil, but elements inappreciable to the eye remained in the seemingly intractable sand, and soon gave positive evidence of their existence. Seeds germinated with almost magical spontaneity, and plants of varied character made extraordinary growth . . .

It was seen that vagrant tomato plants grew among the beach rubbish . . . Cabbages, beans, green peas, carrots, parsnips and radishes, with neglected sunflowers, are giving good returns, though for several weeks the weather has been by no means propitious for succulent greens, and oft-times serious affairs have interfered with regularity in watering the beds.

Let it be remembered that most of the crops in the primitive garden belong to cool, if not cold, climates, and that here — well within the tropics — in almost pure sand, in some spots hot enough at noon to blister the feet, no check has been sustained by plants usually associated with cloudy skies and dripping mists. On the untended sand-ridge beyond the highest limit of the tidal wave pumpkins and vegetable marrows have gone on doing more than justice to themselves, some plants having lived through two seasons productively . . .

SOUNDS, SILENCES AND SCENTS

". . . the silken rustle of the butterflies becomes audible . . ."

WOOER OF THE MUSES

Such is the silence of the bush that the silken rustle of the butterflies becomes audible and the distinctive flight of birds is recognised — not alone such exaggerated differences as the whirr of quail, the bustle of scrub fowl, and the whistle and clacking of nutmeg pigeons, but the delicate and tender characteristics of the wing notes of the meeker kinds of doves and the honey-eaters, and also the calculated flutterings of the fly-catchers. In the whistling swoop of the grey goshawk there is a note of ominous blood-thirstiness, silent though the destroyer has sat awaiting the moment for swift and decisive action . . .

Apart from the tricks which memory plays upon the solitary individual, inviting him by scents and sounds to scenes of the past, I find that the moist unadulterated atmosphere is a most compliant medium for the transmission of certain sorts of sound waves. The actual surface of the sea — differing from its resonant bulk — seems to sop up rather than convey sounds, though on given planes above its level sounds travel unimpeded for remarkable distances. The resonance of the atmosphere appears at times to be dependent on the tone and quality rather than on the abruptness and loudness of the sound. I have listened with strange delight to the rustle of the sea on the mainland beach — two and a half miles distant — when the air has been so idle that the sensitive casuarinas — ever haunted by some secret woe upon which to moan and sob — have been mute and unable to find excuse for the faintest sigh . . .

However listless the air, the coral-reef, though its crowded life is inarticulate and mute, is ever brisk with minor but strenuous noises. Splashes and gurgles, sighs and gasps, coughs and sneezes, sharp clicks and snaps and snarls — telling of alarms, tragic escapes, and violent death-dealings — blend with the continuous murmur of the sea, and are occasionally punctuated by sudden slaps and thuds as a blundering hammer-head shark pursues a high-leaping eagle-ray, or the red-backed sea eagle dashes down upon a preoccupied bream, the impact of its firm breast embossing a white rosette on the blue water.

In the absence of vibratory media the noises of the reef are isolated, furtive, echoless — staccato accidentals and dull dissonances out of tune with the soothing theme of the sea. Hence, when, as I wandered absorbed in an inspection of minor details, and a mellow whistle, constant but varying in volume, broke in upon my musings, it was vain to repress the thrill of excitement. A sound so foreign and incongruous also had a certain element of mystery. In a flash unsensational ponderings were displaced by a picture of a steamer in distress far away. Had I not on a similar occasion of a secret-disclosing tide heard through seven miles of insulted and sullen air the flop of an inch or so of dynamite exploded by a heartless barbarian for the illicit destruction of vivacious fish? Had I not listened with amazement to the buzz of a steamer's propeller and the throb of her engines six miles away when unaccustomed "nigger-heads" of coral showed yellow in the sun? The calm, shallow sea conveyed the sounds with marvellous fidelity and surety. Yet this unaccountable call came from a quarter whence steamers may not venture, and was I not the only whistler within a range of many miles? No steamer ever gloated or warned or appealed in so fluty a note — plaintive, slightly tremulous, nervously imploring.

Alert, I tracked the strange sound along an eccentric course to its haunt, finding nothing more than the empty shell of a huge sea urchin, which in accord with a whim of the sea had floated and was now held aloft slantwise to the lips of the wind, firm in the branching tines of stag's-horn coral. A rustic pipe — giving forth a sonorous moan, now cooing and crooning, now bold and confident, and again irresolute and unschooled. Not too sure of instrumentalism, oft the note was hesitating, soliciting a compliant ear as became a modest wooer of the muses, polishing his unceremonious serenade to some shy mermaid, or hooting at shyer silence.

A TROPIC NIGHT

For a week the wet monsoon had frolicked insolently along the coast, the intermittent north-east breeze, pert of promise but flabby of performance, giving way to evening calms. Then came slashing south-easters which, having discourteously bundled the cloud banks over the mountains, retired with a spasm upon the reserves of the Pacific.

All day long the sea had been pale blue with changeful silvery lights, and now the moon, half-way down on her westward course, shines over a scene solemn in its stillness — the peace and repose more impressive than all the recent riot and haste.

Here on the verge of the ocean, at the extreme limit of the spit of soft, shell-enamelled sand, where the breakers had roared in angry monotone, the ears thrill with tender sounds. Though all the winds are dead, the undertones of the sea linger in lulling harmonies. The tepid tide on the warm sand crisply rustles and hisses as when satin is crumpled and smartly rent. Weird, resonant tappings, moans, and gurgles come from a hollow log drifting with infinite slowness. Broken sighs and gasps tell where the ripples advancing in echelon wander and lose their way among blocks of sandstone. As the tide rose it prattled and gurgled, toying with tinkling shells and clinking coral, each tone separate and distinct, however thin and faint. My solitary watch gives the rare delight of analysing the night thoughts of the ocean, profound in its slumber though dreamily conscious of recent conflict with the winds. All the frail undertones suppressed during the bullying day now have audience. Sounds which crush and crowd have wearied and retired. The timid and shy venture forth to join the quiet revelry of the night.

On its northern aspect the sand spit is the steeper. There the folds of the sea fall in velvety thuds ever so gentle, ever so regular. On the southern slope, where the gradient is easy, the wavelets glide up with heedless hiss and slide back with shuffling whisper, scarce moving the garlands of brown seaweed which a few hours before had been torn from the borders of the coral garden with mischievous recklessness.

The sounds of this most stilly night are almost wholly of the faintly pulsing sea — sibilant and soft. Twice have the big-eyed stone plovers piped demoniacally. Once there were flutterings among the nutmeg pigeons in the star-proof jungle of the crowded islet to the south. A cockatoo has shrieked out in dismay at some grim nightmare of a snake. Two swamp pheasants have assured each other in bell-like cadences that the night is far spent, and all is well.

As the moon sinks a ghostly silence prevails. Even the subdued tones of the sea are hushed. Though I listen with aching intentness no sense of sound comes to my relief. Thus must it be to be bereft of hearing. This death-like pause, this awful blank, this tense, anxious lapse, this pulseless, stifling silence is brief. A frail moan, just audible, comes from the direction of the vanishing moon. There is a scarcely perceptible stir in the warm air — a sensation of coming coolness rather than of motion, and a faint odour of brine. A mile out across the channel a black band has settled on the shining water . . .

While I loll and peer and listen I am alert and still, for the primitive passions of the universe are shyly exercised. To be sensitive to them all the faculties must be acutely strained. With this lisping, coaxing, companionable sea the serene and sparkling sky, the glow beyond the worlds, the listening isles — demure and dim — the air moist, pacific and fragrant — what concern of mine if the smoky messenger from the stuffy town never comes? This is the quintessence of life. I am alive at last. Such keen tingling, thrilling perceptions were never mine before. Now do I realise the magnificent, the prodigious fact of being. Mine not only a part in the homely world, but a fellowship with the glorious firmament.

It is night — the thoughtful, watchful, wakeful, guardian night, with no cloud to sully its tremulous radiance. How pretty a fable, I reflect, would the ancients have associated with the

Southern Cross, shimmering there in the serene sky! Dare I, at this inspiring moment, attempt what they missed, merely because they lacked direct inspiration? Those who once lived in Egypt saw the sumptuous southern jewel, and it may again glitter vainly for the bewilderment of the Sphinx if the lazy world lurches through space long enough. Yes, let me invent a myth — and not tell it, but rather think of the origin of the Milky Way and so convince myself of the futility of modern inventions . . .

As I gaze into those serene and capricious spaces separating the friendly stars I am relieved of all consciousness of sense of duration. Time was not made for such ecstasies, which are of eternity. The warm sand nurses my body. My other self seeks consolation among the planets.

> *"This huge stage presenteth naught but show*
> *Whereon the stars in secret influence comment."*

A grey mist masks the winding of a mainland river. Isolated blotches indicate lonely lagoons and swamps where slim palms and lank tea-trees stand in crowded, whispering ranks knee-deep in dull brown water. The mist spreads. Black hilltops are as islands jutting out from a grey supermundane sea . . .

As if by magic the mainland is blotted out. The sea is dark and death-like, the air clammy, turgid, and steamy. Heavy vapour settles upon the hills of the Island, descending slowly and with the passivity of fate, until there is but a thin stratum of clear air between the gloomy levels and the portentous pall.

Lesser islands to the south are merely cloud-capped. This lower level with blurred and misty edges may not be further compressed, but the air is warm, thick, sticky, and so saturated with vegetable odours that even the salt of the sea has lost its savour.

. . . now the moon . . . shines over a scene solemn in its stillness . . .

A low, quavering whistle heralds the approach of a nervous curlew, running and pausing, and stamping its script — an erratic scrawl of fleurs-de-lis — on the easy sand. Halting on the verge of the water, it furtively picks up crabs as if it were a trespasser, conscious of a shameful or wicked deed and fearful of detection. It is not night nor yet quite day, but this keen-eyed, suspicious bird knows all the permanent features of the sand-spit. The crouching, unaccustomed shape bewilders it; it pipes inquiringly, stops, starts with quick, agitated steps, snatches a crab — a desperate deed — and flies off with a penetrating cry of warning.

A long-billed shore plover takes up the alarm, and blunderingly races towards instead of from me, whimpering "plin, plin" as it passes and, still curious though alert, stops and bobs and ducks — all its movements and flight impulsive and staccato.

The grey mist whitens. A luminous patch indicates the east. The light increases. The cumbersome vapour is sopped up by the sun, and the coo-hooing of many pigeons makes proclamation of the day. Detached and erratic patches of ripples appear — tiptoe touches of sportful elves tripping from the isles to the continent, whisking merrily, the faintest flicks of dainty toes making the glad sea to smile. Parcelled into shadows, bold, yet retreating, the dimness of the night, purple on the glistening sea, stretches from the isles towards the long, orange-tinted beach.

Let there be no loitering of the shadows. The gloomy isles have changed from black to purple and from purple to blue, and as the imperious sun flashes on the mainland a smudge of brown, blurred and shifting, in the far distance — the only evidence of the existence of human schemes and agitations — the only stain on the celestial purity of the morning — betokens the belated steamer for the coming of which the joy-giving watches of the tropic night have been kept.

Now do I realise the magnificent, the prodigious fact of being . . . a fellowship with the glorious firmament.

READING TO MUSIC

As I lounged at mine ease on the veranda, serenely content with the pages of a favourite author, I became conscious of an unusual sound — vague, continuous, rhythmic. Disinclined to permit my thoughts to wander from the text, at the back of my mind a dim sensation of uneasiness, almost of resentment, because of the slight audible intrusion betrayed itself. Close, as firmly as I could, my mental ear the sound persisted externally, softly but undeniably . . . In a few minutes the annoyance — if the trivial distraction deserved so harsh an epithet — changed, giving place to a sense of refined pleasure almost as fatal to my complacency, for it compelled me to think apart. What was this new pleasure? Ah! I was reading to an accompaniment — a faint, far-off improvisation just on the verge of silence, too scant and elusive for half-hearted critical analysis . . .

Still fain to read, but with the niceties of the art embarrassed, I began to question myself. Whence this pleasant yet provoking refrain? Not of the sea, for a glassy calm had prevailed all day; not of the rain which pattered faintly on the roof. This sound phantom that determinedly beckoned me from my book — whence, and what was it?

Listening attentively and alert, the mystery of it vanished. It was the commotion, subdued by the distance of three-quarters of a mile, of thousands of nutmeg pigeons — a blending of thousands of simultaneous "coo-hoos" with the rustling and beating of wings upon the thin, slack strings of casuarinas. The swaying and switching of the slender-branched and ever-sighing trees with the courageous notes of homing birds had created the curious melody with which my reading had fallen into tune.

And the sound was audible at one spot only. The acoustic properties of the veranda condensed and concentrated it within a narrow area, beyond which was silence. Chance had selected this aerial whirlpool for my reading.

Again taking my ease, the mellow "roaring" of the multitude of gentle doves commingling with the aeolian blandness of trees swinging under the weight of the restless birds, became once more an idealistic accompaniment to the book. I read, or rather declaimed inarticulately, to the singularly pleasing strain until light and sound failed — the one as softly and insensibly as the other. I had enjoyed a new sensation.

Relieved of the agreeable pressure of the text, my thoughts turned to the consideration of bird voices — more to the notes of pigeons, their variety and range. There are sounds, little in volume and rather flat than sharp, rather moist than dry, which seem to carry farther under favouring atmospheric conditions than louder and more acute noises. The easy contours of soothing sounds created in the air seem to resemble the lazy swell of the sea; while fleeter though less sustained noises may be compared to jumpy waves caused by a smart breeze. Pitched in a minor key sounds roll along with little friction and waste, whereas a louder, shriller stinging note may find in the still air a less pliant medium. The cooing of pigeons — a sound of low velocity — has a longer range than the shrieking of parrots. My pet echo responds to an undertone. A loud and prolonged yell jars on its sensitiveness — for it is a shy echo, little used to abrupt and boisterous disturbances . . . On this stilly, damp evening the air in the corner of the veranda happened to be resilient to the mellow notes of far-away pigeons.

SWEET AIRS

It came after unexampled drought. Far-off thunder had heralded it the day before; but heavy clouds had so often gathered and had dispersed without affording the parched soil any refreshment, that signs which under ordinary conditions would have betokened the break of the season were frankly discredited.

Filmy, heated vapour tinged the hills. The still, hot air, saturated with the essence of smoke from many "burnings off" on the mainland, quivered in response to the swiftly approaching disturbance. Clouds gathered suddenly. A startling clap of thunder sounded near by, and big, widely-dispersed drops began to splutter on the dust and to stutter on the roof. Other sounds were deadened.

Rain was so eagerly desired that, merely to enhance the pleasure of anticipation, we preferred to assert that it would not come. Most of the tall, bladyy grass had become as yellow as hay, and there were actually bare patches, revealing bluish-grey soil whereon the little blue doves squatted and pecked, almost invisible until sheer nervousness made them rise. Of other grasses and of herbs many had become crisp underfoot, and brown; but with the first gentle sprinkling dry soil and faded leafage sent up an incense as from flowers blossoming in the dust.

Another loud peal from a fast-gathering, ominous cloud — the base of which rested on the nearest hill, and began to descend, fixed and determined of purpose — and the welcome din began. All surroundings were blotted out by a grey mantle of warm but invigorating rain, while lightning played and thunder rattled and our spirits began to jubilate. The time of doubt was over.

In half an hour the smaller watercourses, where they were not banked up with leaves, ran headlong races to the flat, spread out into pools, and gave the soil more than it could gulp. Like a man rescued at the last moment in a dry and thirsty land, it could not absorb liberal helpings, but had to be content with trivial doles until it became accustomed to the effects of long-denied moisture. Soon the storm travelled across the sea, vapour gathered on the hills against an inky background, and all the birds began to call — the swamp pheasant the loudest and most mellow, the scrub-fowl the merriest, with its coarse hilarity and contented chuckles.

To the south the blue-black bank of thunderous cloud rested on the sea, with never so slight a blur where rain beat on the lustreless surface. Most of the Isles were hidden; some were mere misty blots, while those near at hand stood out preternaturally green and bold, with the slaty sea enveloping their fringe of mangroves. All this dull shade and breathless calm seemed to exist for a single purpose — to intensify the vividness of the nutmeg pigeons, that trailed in irregular procession from the mainland to the restful Isles. Snow-white and swift, they flew low over the sea in companies of ever-changing formation, and the islet near at hand suddenly seemed transformed — its almost leafless trees and shrubs burst in white bloom, and the blending of wing-beats and coos came as one of the pleasant sounds of early evening . . .

. . . the freshly-fallen and decaying leaves underfoot give forth an odour rich and varied; one must stop occasionally to fill the lungs with so potent and pleasant a balsam, and to give thanks for enjoying it on such a generous scale. All the air is saturated with its invigorating principles. Gums and wattles, the huge-leaved "gin-gee", tea-trees, the ripe, orange-tinted fruit of the pandanus along the gullies, the big spreading figs on the edge of the jungle, the pungent native ginger, the full-fruited nutmeg, the few last flowers of the milkwood, the resiniferous gum of the "tangebah", the patchouli-like ixora, and the sodden grass — all contribute to the medley of perfumes, and create a longing for some magic art by which the combination could be fixed, materialised, and sent to those who may still believe that Australia is a scentless land . . .

The Season of Scents

It is the season of scents, and the native, untended, unpampered plants are easily and gracefully first in an uncatalogued competition . . . Just now, in some situations, the old gold orchid rivals the mango in showiness and fragrance; the pencil orchid dangles white aigrettes from the trunks and branches of hundreds of trees, saturating the air with a subtle essence as of almonds and honey; and the hoya hangs festoons from rocks and trees in such lavish disregard of space and the breathings of less virile vegetation, that the sensual scent borders on the excessive. On the hill-tops, among rocks gigantic of mould and fantastic of shape, a less known orchid with inconspicuous flowers yields a perfume reminiscent of the violet; the shady places on the flats are showy with giant crinum lilies . . .

The most elemental of all incenses — that which arises from warm, dry soil sprinkled by a sudden shower — is undoubtedly invigorating. The spirituous scent of melaleuca-trees burdens the air, not as an exhalation but as an arrogant physical part of the Isle, while a wattle shyly proclaims its flowering by a scent as intangible and fleeting as a phantom . . .

An early or late arrival among flowers and fruit cannot be hailed or chidden where there is but trifling seasonable variation. Without beginning and without end, the perpetual motion of tropical vegetation is but slightly influenced by the weather. Who is to say that this plant is early or that late, when early or late, like Kipling's east and west, are one? It is not that all flowering trees and plants are of continuous growth. Many do have their appointed seasons, producing flowers and fruit according to date and in orderly progress, leaving to other species

It is the season of scents . . .

. . . the sensual scent borders on the excessive.

the duty of maintaining a consecutive, unbroken series which defies the mechanism of cold countries with their cast-iron calendars.

Here but three or four trees deign to recognise the cool season by the shedding of their leaves. The fig discards — by no means consistently — its foliage in obedience to some spasmodic impulse, when the many thin branches, thick-strewn with pink fruit, stand out against the sky as aerial coral, fantastically dyed. But in two or three days burnished brown leaves burst from the embraces of elongated buds which, rejected, fall — pink phylacteries — to decorate the sand, while in a week the tree wears a new and glistening garment of green. The flame-tree slowly abandons its foliage; but before the last yellow-green leaf is cast aside the fringe of the blood-red robe soon to overspread has appeared. The white cedar permits its leaves to become yellow and to fall lingeringly, but its bareness is merely for a week or so. So also does the foliage of the moo-jee turn to deepest red and is discarded, but so orderly is the disrobing and the never varying fashion of foliage that the tree averts the scorn of the most respectable of neighbours.

Month after month of warm days and plenteous rain during the early part of 1909 produced an effect in the acacias which cannot be too thankfully recorded. The blooming season extended from March 29th to July 17th, beginning with *Acacia cunninghami* and ending with the third flush of *A. aulacocarpa*. During a third of the year whiffs of the delicious perfume of the wattle were never absent, for two flushes of *A. flavescens* filled in the brief intervals between those of *aulacocarpa*. This latter, the commonest of the species on the island, produces its flowers in long spikes in the axils of the leaves on the minor branches, weighting such branches with semi-pendulous plumes laden with haunting perfume. The fragrance of the bounteous, sacrificial blooms saturates miles of air, while their refuse tricks out the webs of spiders great and small with fictitious favours, and carpets the earth with inconstant gold.

NEIGHBOURING ISLES AND "AUSTRALIA"

"Five islets, wildernesses of leafage, trip out to the east."

Isles Rediscovered

Dunk Island has four satellites and seven near relations ... The official chart has been revised, the original and comely titles of the blacks being substituted for the exotic names of the map-makers ...

Many of the geographical titles of the blacks are without meaning, being used merely to indicate a locality. Others were bestowed because of the presence of a particular tree or plant or a remarkable rock. Some few commemorate incidents. Two places on Dunk Island perpetuate the names of females. The coastline is so varied that specific names for localities a few hundred yards apart hardly seem necessary; but the original inhabitants, frugal of their speech, found it less trouble to strew names thickly than to enter into explanations one to another when relating the direction and extent which the adventures and the sport of the day led them. Few names for any part of the island away from the beach seem to have existed, although the sites of camps along the edge of the jungle, and even in gullies as remote as may be from the sea, are even now apparent. Camps were not honoured by titles, but all the creeks and watercourses and other places where water was obtainable were so invariably, and camps were generally, though not always, made near water ...

Not to many men is permitted the privilege of choosing for his day's excursion from among so many beautiful spots, certain in the knowledge that to whichsoever he may elect to flutter his handkerchief is reserved for his delight; certain that the sands will be free from the traces of any other human being; certain that no sound save those of nature will break in upon his musings and meditations.

Purtaboi, the first and the nearest of the satellites, lies three-quarters of a mile from the middle of the sweep of Brammo Bay — always in view through the tracery of the melaleuca trees. Mungumgnackum and Kumboola, to the south-west, are linked at low water spring tides to Dunk Island and to each other; and Woolngarin, to the south-east, is separated from the rocky cliffs and ledges of the island by 300 yards of deep and swiftly-flowing water.

Purtaboi — dainty and unique — its hill crowned with low-growing trees and shrubs, a ruddy precipice, groups of pandanus palms, beach lined with casuarinas, banks of snow-white coral debris, ridge of sharp-edged rocks jutting out to the north-western cove and outlying reef of coral, tangle of orchids and scrub all in miniature — save the orchids — gigantic and gross and profuse of old-gold bloom. In October and November hosts of sea-birds come hither to nest, and so also do nutmeg or Torres Strait pigeons, blue doves, peaceful doves, honey-eaters, wood-swallows, the blue reef heron, and occasionally the little black cormorant. The large-billed shore plover deposits her single egg on the sand, merely carelessly whisking aside the casuarina needles for its reception. Hundreds of terns (six species) lay their eggs among the tinkling coral chips, and discarding all attempts at concealment, practise artistic deception. So perfect is the artifice that the eggs are frequently the least conspicuous of the elements of the banks of drift, broken coral and bleached shells ...

Low-lying Mungumgnackum — the abode of the varied honey-eater, the tranquil dove, and the brooding-place of the nightjar — and lovely Kumboola, lie to the south-west, a bare half-mile away. Kumboola's sheltered aspect is thickly clad with jungle; a steep grassy ridge springs from the blue-grey rocks to the south-east; and on the precipitous weather side grow low and open scrub and dwarf casuarina. Here is a natural aviary ... Sundown at Kumboola towards the end of September, when the sea laps and murmurs among the rocks, and great white pigeons gather in thousands on the dark foliage, or "coo-hooing" and flapping, disappear beneath the thick leafy canopy, and all the other birds are saying their goodnights, or

Kumboola's sheltered aspect is thickly clad with jungle ...
On Timana are gigantic milkwood trees ...

asserting their rights, or protesting against crowding or intrusion, is an ever-to-be-remembered experience . . .

Of entirely different character is the last of the satellites to be mentioned, Woolngarin . . . it is naught but a confused mass of weather-beaten rocks, the loftiest not being more than fifty feet above high water. A few pandanus palms, hardy shrubs and trailers, and mangroves, spring from sheltered crevices, but for the most part the rocks are bare. The incessant assaults of the sea have cut deep but narrow clefts in the granite, worn out sounding hollows, and smoothed away angularities. Here a few terns rear their young, and succeeding generations of the sooty oyster-catcher lay their eggs just out of the reach of high tide. A never-ending procession of fish passes up and down the channel, according as the tide flows and ebbs . . .

The neighbouring islands include Timana, two and a half miles from the sandspit of Dunk Island and one and a half miles from Kumboola. Bedarra lies a little to the southward; Toolghar three-quarters of a mile from Bedarra; Coomboo half a mile from Toolghar; and the group of three — Budjoo, Kurrumbah and Coolah — still further to the south-east . . .

On Timana are gigantic milkwood trees which need great flying buttresses to support their immense height, their roots being mainly superficial. For many generations two ospreys have had their eyrie in one of these giant trees, fit nursery for imperial birds! . . . A heavy, slovenly-patched mantle of leafage, impervious to sunlight, covers the Isle of Timana, creating a region of perpetual dimness from western beach to eastern precipice, where orchids cling and palms peer on rocks below. All the vegetation is matted and interwoven, only the topmost branches of the milkwood escaping from the clinging aspiring vines . . . cockatoos and metallic starlings are plentiful. Although there is no permanent fresh water, the pencil-tailed rat leaves numerous tracks on the sand, and scrub fowls keep the whole surface perpetually raked . . .

A mile beyond Timana is Bedarra, with its lovely little bays and coves and fantastically weathered rocks, its forest and jungle and scrub, and its rocky satellite Peerahmah. Several of the most conspicuous landmarks are associated in the minds of the blacks with legends, generally of the simplest and most prosaic nature. About this rough rock Peerahmah is a story . . . In the far away past two nice young gins, they say, were left by themselves on Dunk Island, while the others of the tribe went away in canoes to Hinchinbrook. Tiring of their lonesomeness, they made up their minds to regain the company of their relatives by swimming from island to island. Kumboola was easily reached; to Timana it is but a mile and a half, and a mile thence to Bedarra. Leaving the most easterly point of Bedarra, they were quickly caught in the swirl of a strong current and spun about until both became dazed and exhausted. As they disappeared beneath the water they were changed to stone, and the stone rose in fantastic shape, and from that day Peerahmah has weathered all the storms of the Pacific and formed a feature in the loveliest scene these isles reveal.

The largest of the neighbouring isles, Bedarra, has less than a square mile of superficial area; the smallest but four or five acres. The smaller are made up of confused masses of granite, for the most part so overgrown with fig trees, plumy palms, milkwoods, umbrella trees, quandongs, eugenias, hibiscus bushes, bananas and lawyer vines, as to be unexplorable without a scrub-knife; for the soil among the rocks is soft and spongy, the purest of vegetable mould, and encourages luxurious growth. The jungle droops over the grey rocks on the sheltered side. Twisted Moreton Bay ash and wind-crippled scrub spring up among the clefts and crevices on the weather frontage — the south-east — while a narrow strip of sand, the only landing-place, is a general characteristic of the north-west aspect . . .

The islands immediately to the south-east form the (rest of) the Family group — triplets, twins and two singles. I like to think approving things of them; to note individual excellences; to familiarise myself with their distinguishing traits; to listen to them in their petulance and anger, and in that sobbing subsidence to even temper; to their complacent gurglings and sleepy murmurs.

A Little Cove

Among the islets of the Family group, sprinkled between Hinchinbrook and Dunk islands, not one is denied distinction. All are, for the most part, rugged on the Pacific slope, though some decorate even that exposed aspect with vegetation of a sumptuousness that conceals the crude, confused masses of granite. Each has a truncated sand-spit jutting out to the north-west, while two have masses of snow-white coral spoil, which clinks and chinks underfoot, and upon which shrill-voiced terns scatter, with careless profusion, daubed and spotted eggs. The waves that break on it with measured stride, scarcely whiter than the coral, wallow among its finger-shaped fragments, combing and rustling them, until all point obediently to the reef whence old Ocean tore them . . .

When one wanders among such scenes, where there is no sign of traffic save that of his own footprints, no sound save the confidential whispering of the sea, the thin screams of terns and the whimsical cackling of scrub-fowl in the jungle, he becomes a part of the realm of Nature, a trivial and insignificant item soon to disappear, but for a brief space supreme — the only part of teeming Nature capable of disinterested joy in all the other parts. The sea will quickly smooth away the last trace of his trespassing feet, and will moan and gurgle in cool crevices whither bottle green crabs scurry when the red-backed sea-eagle soars vigilantly overhead. Yet for a time he has been absorbed into the scene. He possesses it and is possessed by it, and will bring away with him a loving remembrance of it which entices beyond power of abstinence.

There is, of course, one scene which combines more of excellences than the others, however admirable individually. A little bay lies open to the turbulent south-easters, yet lacks not a sheltering cove wherein a small boat may nestle. The cove is formed by a bold and rounded mass of granite, on which pandanus palms and straggling shrubs find foothold. The boat glides round the sturdy rock, revealing a white beach, the sand of which has been ground to such singular fineness that it feels as silk underfoot. Where the anchor rests, it is rippled in correspondence with the gentle heaving of the sea, while patches of golden-brown weed sway to the same poetic motion. Coarse grass marks time at high-water limit.

From a low pinnacle of rock, on which an osprey is fond of perching, the virtues of the wider scene are best revealed. Five islets, wildernesses of leafage, trip out to the east. A mass of fantastic rocks, round which confusing currents swill, intercepts the fairway, and beyond the islets are the Brooke group, with Goold Island and Hinchinbrook to the right to complete the picture. The bay beneath is shallow close inshore, for coral is industriously building substantial domes and fragile lacework in limestone. The reef gleams dull-red through the blue water, and white and pale green patches show where sand has occupation of the unallotted places.

On a very still and clear day you may see turtles browsing on the weed below, and at any time they may burst upwards through the surface with splash and bubble for gulps of scented air.

On the rocks, piled high, is a long pencil-cedar log, weathered almost to the tone of the granite. It has reposed there, with but slight changes of position, for fifteen years and more, and the salt spray and the tepid rains have done it but small harm; but the rocks have fretted its sides as it has rolled uneasily when the seas have sought to claim it again. The old log is the one relic of the coarse effects of the hands of man. Few visit the spot. All its charms are held in reserve.

HEIGHTS OF HINCHINBROOK

Porpoises, snow-white terns sitting on drifting wood, sea-eagles, ospreys, sea-snakes, sails, the smudge of steamer-smoke and its ten-mile plume, sunlit isles and speckless sky, with no sound save the purring of the engine and the prattle of the water against the bows ... Here was, indeed, the freedom of the sea — the sea in its happiest and most alluring and loveliest of moods. No restrictions existed. The little boat sought out ways of her own, nosing shoal-showing buoys and beacons, and hugging the land whensoever and wheresoever she chose ...

Seen from such a low level, the heights of Hinchinbrook and all the shoulders and spurs and ridges of the mountain demand uninterrupted attention, for are they not transformed? Bold and clean-cut, the skyline with its abrupt declivities, its peaks and contours — here the profile of a giant with beetling brows, long, slim nose and babyish lips, there a succession of irregular notches and knolls — are projected against a perfectly limpid atmosphere, while in vale and gorge

"Just a faint cloud of rose shall appear,
   As if in pure water you dropped and let die
   A bruised, black-blooded mulberry."

And this tinted haze seems to magnify trees and obtruding rocks, revealing hitherto well-guarded secrets. The sources of torrents which in the wet season seam the brown rocks with silver, now cushioned with moss and islanded with yellowing sedges, are shown by an occasional flash and glitter as the sun plays upon them at a reflective angle ...

A few miles back Leafe Peak was a perfect cone of delicate blue. More than once it has seemed to change its position, and now it might stand for a model of Castle Hill, Townsville, as that was wont to be ere nakedness shamed its base. There is legend extant that the name is derived from the ribbon of leaves which almost invariably stretches from the mangroves and jungle at the foot to the mangroves of the flats of the mainland; and it is further said that hereabouts the northern and the southern current meet, creating the watery ridge defined by leafy flotsam ...

In popular imagination the mountains of Hinchinbrook, however picturesque and grand, are too severe, rugged and precipitous to tempt any but the boldest and toughest of athletes; but a resident of the Herbert district undertook many years ago to demonstrate that from a mountaineering point of view the difficulties of ascent were not so great as appearances suggested. For the love of the thing he rowed across the channel from Lucinda Point, fought his way through the jungle, scaled the shoulders of Mount Diamantina, and signalled his presence at the great rock on the summit by smoke in such a short space of time that the Mount might well have felt humbled. A singular feature of the boulder surmounting the rugged height is that it seems to be a pivot round which other elevations swing — at least, such is the illusion as the boat runs down the channel and out to sea to the south-east, and from whatsoever aspect the stern boulders of the mount are viewed, they seem to express aloofness and disdain. Not so the nooks and coves in the sheltered parts of the channel, which coax little boats to spend quiet hours within rocky arms, and promise gurgling lullabies the livelong night.

Within such a cove the boat lay in silence and serenity. In the deep shadow of the morning a fast steamer, blurred with mist, came rushing down the channel — a white blotch with a backward-curling smudge of smoke, calling to mind one of Turner's masterpieces; but that famous picture lacks the foreground of bold declivities and the distances of hills aglow with the beams of the rising sun. Thence the course was to the northern extremity of Pelorus Island, avoiding the shallow shoals opposite Lucinda, and, when a clearance was made, direct to Pioneer Bay in Orpheus Island . . .

. . . the course lay almost due south, miles to the westward of the steamer track, close past Dido Rock, with its outlying sandbank, snow-white in the distance — not much larger than, and somewhat of the shape of, an upturned boat. Most of these islands, rocks and shoals bear the names of men-of-war, derived in the first instance from the classics. Is it not possible, then, that the steep-faced, weather-scored rock which bears the name of Dido caught the fancy of surveyors who had in mind the citadel that valiant woman built on the African coast, when a storm drove her fleet there, and she bought of the inhabitants as much land as could be encompassed by a bull's hide cut into thongs?

Swarms of welcome swallows issued from the crevices of the red rock, circled round the boat, twittering greetings, and flew back to their nests when their invitations to stay were disregarded. At Herald Island, where anchor was dropped at four o'clock in the afternoon close inshore, flocks of swallows again paid the boat respect, perching on the rigging and spars, and making themselves easy and familiar. Two or three spent the night on board, and the rest of the colony seemed to have homes among the low granite boulders and blocks that fringed the shore just above high-water mark. Here, as elsewhere, the sea was sparklingly clear, so that isolated rocks crowned with brown, wavy seaweed, rounded masses of coral and dead shells, gleaming white, were revealed, and the merging tints, pale-green to deep-blue as the water deepened off-shore where the sand was soft and pure white, made the heart glad. It was invigorating, too, to wallow in such stainless water before sunrise, the air being crisp and the only sound that of the cheeping of the welcome swallows.

Suddenly clouds gathered in the south-west, and before a moaning wind the serenity of the sea fled, chased by white horses. The boat lay snug under the spit until the early snack of coffee and biscuit was disposed of — then, rejoicing as a strong man to run a race, she swept disdainfully round its apex and with frolic and saucy capers flew homewards.

. . . the heights of Hinchinbrook and all the shoulders and spurs and ridges of the mountain demand uninterrupted attention . . .

Isle of the Papaw

About fourteen miles north from Dunk Island, and three miles off the coast of North Queensland, lie the Barnard Islands, so named in 1819 by Captain (afterwards Admiral) Phillip P. King, in honour of his friend Edward Barnard.

Though condemned to spend most of the time as two isolated, jungle-covered knolls, the southernmost portion of the group (generally known as the South Barnards), is a single formation. A shallow sea separates the detached parts, but low-water spring tides expose a broad bond of union, an irrefragable proof of their oneness and indivisibility. The alliance may be secret, but is very secure. It frets the intemperate sea, and makes it froth and roar with rage. Outlasting all the blustering fury, it is stolidly irresponsive, too, when the coiling coquette gently slaps its face with the softest of white flounces. This rustic bond, defiant to all the moods of the unstable sea, confirms the legitimacy of the union of the Isle, and forms an interesting feature in a pretty scene.

Another reef, or ridge, or causeway, true as a surveyor's line, juts out from the western point, almost parallel with the main and complete connecting-link. This smaller spur acts as a breakwater, and the terminus is furnished with a rough T, which, though rather jumbled and broken seems to indicate that Nature designed, in her off-hand way, a plan worthy the imitation of man.

The smaller of the ridges is basaltic, and in its ruggedness resembles the jaw of "some pre-Adamite beast setting its teeth against the sky"; yet the larger portion of the Isle is coarse sandstone, or rather conglomerate, with basaltic blocks and boulders. A miniature bluff, sixty or eighty feet high, accentuates the south-western aspect, and at the base of it are strewn huge blocks which the vortices of the sea have torn down . . .

The better half of the Isle may be best described as a mass of conglomerate and basalt resting upon a platform of basalt of extreme density. At a rough estimate it is less than twenty acres in area.

Originally, save for two or three of the steeper individual slopes, the whole surface was covered with jungle. A great part still remains, the luxuriousness of which seems extraordinary when one regards the thinness of the soil and apparent sterility of the rough conglomerate . . . Very many years ago the islet was the headquarters of a bêche-de-mer fisherman. He began the clearing of the western aspect, where the soil is red and very fertile. Then another took up his abode, extended the clearing, planted coconut palms, several kinds of fruit trees, sugar-cane, sweet potatoes, taro, etc., etc., and went his way. The last-comer revels in the fruits of former industry . . .

The chief vegetable feature of the islet nowadays is the marvellous robustness of its papaws. Upon this ideal spot the plant has set its foot, and is at home. No one who admires the papaw could, without breach of courtesy, attribute to it the vulgar habit of crowding upon and elbowing away other vegetation possessing equal rights to a common plot. But if the papaw is not in this particular republic of vegetation becoming tyrannically rude, it is at least very boldly asserting its rights. On the slopes, on the edges of the jungle, among basalt boulders, on the highest elevation, on rocky terraces, where there is no soil save in cracks and crevices, deep in the heart of the jungle are self-centred groves of papaws. At the base of a romantic cliff of basalt reposes a forest of papaws — not spindly weaklings, but sturdy plants, thirty feet high, fruitful and odorous. Up and over the verge of this little basaltic precipice the facile wind blows from a befittingly narrow ravine, heavily freighted with perfume of a whole grove, down upon the lusty heads of which we admiringly gaze.

It is the very paradise of papaws. They flourish in places, and situations, and under conditions hitherto considered impossible or unseemly in such a discreet and orderly plant.

They have abandoned all reserve, submitting to the touch and strong embraces of the aboriginal plants of the isle, and even stamping them underfoot or shoving them away from accustomed places.

In genial air, and soil to its liking, the natural habit of the papaw finds true expression. With its tap-root squeezed and flattened in the crevice of a rock, it sends its feeders over the surface, gripping like a parasite, and gathering sustenance from uncompromising conglomerate. The gale may uproot a seemingly ambitious plant, but it will not die. It grows as it lies recumbent, with a kink in its neck, gamely contending for its share of sunlight, and offering abundant and easily gathered tribute — fruit large and without spot or blemish. Tons of papaws might be gathered where, according to accepted tradition, the plant could hardly be expected to grow. Is there a satisfactory reason for the wonderful vigour of the desirable plant among basalt and conglomerate?

Yes, plainly so.

Possibly for thousands of years this islet has been one of the "rookeries" of the white nutmeg pigeon. Millions have mated and reared families here, and thousands do so to this day (1910). On the 11th August we saw the first flight of the season of nesting birds. So vast are the flocks that the very rocks must have become saturated with manure; for the birds breed during the first part of the wet season, and the average annual rainfall is about 140 inches.

A gardener will tell you that, if you place a quarry at his disposal and provide him with manure and water, he will convert it into a garden. Nature on this spot provides an apt illustration, and this sumptuous display of fruitfulness reacts on the birds ...

Silent Green River

A few minutes past the deck glistened in the sun as each rollicking billow sent its herald over the bows, and here the surface of the river is almost rippleless. Shallows and uncertainties perplex its union with the ocean. Sombre green mangroves screen its muddy banks at full tide and trail leathery leaves and the tips of spindly fruit on its placid surface. Pendant roots and immersed branches create on each hand a continuous scroll of wavering ridges and eddies bordered with the living tints of the steadfast wall of leafage. The sun so burnishes the midstream ribbon that the boat seems to float on an invisible element. Though the topmost leaves of the mangroves fail to disclose any movement in their air, an unceasing and inharmonious hum tells of the sea idly shouldering the orange-hued sands outside.

The original inhabitants of the country knew the stream as Marang. None call it so; but half stranded on the bank at the mouth lies a raft typical of the past, and of the ease and resource with which those of the day were wont to avail themselves of Nature's suggestions in the art of crossing flooded waters. The name of the river has gone, but not that of the three buoyant logs lashed together with strips of cane which with sullen lurch, take the wash of the boat. The boys jerk their heads in the direction and murmur "wur-gun", and speculate on the last user. The day is young. For the time being the best the ancient river has to show — the quintessence of the season, superb October — shall be ours. The cloudless sky is richly blue, lighter in shade than the shapely mountain which seems to block the way miles ahead. The sun gives a taste of its quality, not to fret or discomfort, but merely to add a slightly richer tint to skin glowing with previous marks of his fervour and favour.

All the sounds of the little engine are maliciously exaggerated as the boat forges ahead. The silent green river has become vociferous with echoes, which snap and grunt, groan and hiss, in mockery of inevitable and earnest doings . . . Surely the uncouth imps of the dimly-lit jungles need not proclaim their spite with such exaggerated fuss.

With but little effort of imagination the boat becomes stationary on a shining ribbon with strips of dark green on each side, and the banks glide past with never so gentle undulations. The tide screens most of the mud on which the many-rooted trees stand. Some are in full bloom, the hawthorn-like flowers breathing perfume as from an orangery soliciting the raids of millions of bees. Scents cling to the placid surface. It is as a stream of scent, bounded and confined by changeful tints as the sun toys with the shadows, and curve after curve, reach after reach, slip by. Sometimes the chattering boat heads due east. South she knows too, and then she bows her duty to the west, along reaches which run straight and clean as a canal; and round hairpin bends she sweeps with disdainful air, as if conscious of besoiling banks.

Gradually the monopolistic mangroves become more tolerant of the rights of other vegetation. Tea-trees with white papery bark and pale yellow flowers dripping with spirity nectar, the sunflower-tree with its masses of gold, an occasional wattle, and slim palms mirror themselves, and here and there compact jungle, with its entanglement of ponderous vines and smothering creepers, shoulders away the salt-loving plants. Scents may vary as the river's fringe; but only a delicate blend is recognised — the breathings of honey-secreting flowers and of sapful plants free from all uncleanliness. Many trees endure sadly the decoration of orchids in full flower, some lovely to look on and deliciously scented. The snowy plumes of one species sway gently, as if offering friendly greeting. A worthy similitude to the lily of the valley clings to a decaying limb, and a passing smudge of lustrous brown is but the reflection from a mass of the commonest of the dendrobiums which encumbers a long-suffering host. Where forest trees and wattles guard the bank the water is of a different hue, as if the face of the river had

. . . slim palms mirror themselves . . . All is wonderfully still.

76

absorbed less of the actualities of the sun. The screen of vegetation is not only higher, but it is varied and impresses its individuality. Only during the pelting rains of the wet season may this delightful stream be monotonous, for at intervals brief and narrow vistas open out on patches of yellowing grass, and beyond lie forest-clad hills.

All save the boat is wonderfully still. The birds are silent, for this is the first hot day of the season, and they have retired to the patches of jungle where shade and dimness afford relief from the sunlight spaces. For many a mile a cormorant, lacking valour to double on its tracks, has fled before the boat, settling out of sight ever and anon, only to be scared further from its nest. A mangrove bittern sitting humpbacked on a root and roused from its night thoughts has flown ahead, following the bends of the stream until it crossed a familiar loop and so evaded incessant harrying.

No murmur of the sea is audible, though the water is as briny as at the mouth. Mangroves still reinforce the muddy banks at intervals, and big barramundi swirl aside to give the boat precedence in the narrow way ... crocodiles basking on their sides, as many as seven on a sunny morning in the cool season, "miscreated gigantic vermin" ... Crocodiles have their moods. Sometimes they are lazy and indifferent and will not be disturbed though the boat may clink and chatter as it passes ... More often the faculties of the crocodile are disappointingly acute. He is visible for such a fragment of time that the authoritative man who has promised sport looks foolish and tries to relieve the strain by the relation of anecdotes in which circumstances have not been all in favour of the illusive creature ...

Here is a tall hibiscus with coarse leaves, diversely lobed, and great pink, fragile flowers, each with a blotch of maroon at the base and each containing a fat and lumbering bee spangled with maroon-tinted pollen. A trailing eugenia bears dark red flowers shaped like a mop, and a tiny white lily with petals and strangely protuberant anthers scents the air as with honey and almonds.

The tide ebbs fast. All the country teems with entertainment, and the river, cool in the dusk, and black, reflects the dead mangroves, white and spectral, on its brink ...

THE PLANTS WHICH
CROWD EACH OTHER

"Such communicable trees should stand together, commenting on passing events, booming in unison with the cyclone, and mimicking the tenderest tones of the idlest wind ..."

BEACH PLANTS

Strolling on the curving footway of broken shells and coral chips marking the limit of the morning's tide, a vague attempt was made to catalogue the plants which crowd each other on the verge of salt water, and so to make comparison with that part of Australia the features of which provoked Adam Lindsay Gordon to frame an adhesive phrase concerning bright scentless blossoms and songless, bright birds. Excluding the acacias and eucalypts, said to have given sameness to the scenes among which the exotic poet ranged, a long list might be compiled; nor will the pleasant sounds of the afternoon be set down in formal order to the vexing of his memory, for possibly he never heard the whoop and gurgle of the swamp pheasant or the blended voices of hundreds of nutmeg pigeons mellowed by half a mile of still, warm air.

Nor may such unassuming vegetation as the grasses — at least a dozen varieties — find place in an enumeration which appeals primarily on the grounds of prominence, though it would not do to despise the soft and pleasant carpet beneath the orderly row of casuarinas which the tide planted during the last big cyclone with gardener's art. The common name for the trees — "she" (or "shea" oaks, as the late F. Manson Bailey preferred) — mimics the sound of the wind among the branches, which the slightest zephyr stirs and the storm lashes into sea-like roar. The bright green of the grasses sets off the dull green and bronze of the steadfast harps of the beach. At certain seasons and in some lights, when the sun is in the west, the minute scales at the joints of the slender, pendulous branchlets shine like old gold, producing a theatrical effect which, if not experienced before, startles and almost persuades to the belief that the complaining trees have been decorated by one who "has sought out many inventions". But the slant of the sun alters, the light fades, leaving them sombre in hue and whispering more and more discreetly as the night calm settles over the scene. Such communicable trees should stand together, commenting on passing events, booming in unison with the cyclone, and mimicking the tenderest tones of the idlest wind. During a storm, when the big waves crash on the beach and the casuarinas are tormented, the tumult is bewildering; but however loud their plaint, very few suffer, though growing in loose sand; for the roots are widespread and, like the trunk and main branches, tough, while the branchlets stream before the wind.

Close behind the screen of casuarinas is a magnificent specimen of a wide-spreading shrub, in form a squat dome, which commemorates the name of a French naturalist — *Tournefortia argenta*. The leaves, crowded at the ends of thick branchlets, are covered with soft, silky hairs of a silvery cast, which reflect the sun's rays . . .

At high-water mark stands one of the terminalias with big terminal light green leaves, musty flowers, and purple fruit — gold, silver, and purple in close array — while over the sand the goat-footed convolvulus sends long, succulent shoots bearing huge pink flowers complementary to the purple of the beach-pea.

Under the she-oaks young coral trees have sprung up, but the red flowers are of the past, and so also have the gold and white of the calophyllums disappeared. But in the evening the breeze brings whiffs of a singular savour, pleasant yet not sweet, which comes from the acre or two of native hops a few yards back. The bruised leaves thereof give off anything but an attractive odour, yet the faint natural exhalations from the plant are sniffed eagerly and to the revivification of pleasant recollections.

Among a crowd of massive shrubs sprawls a plant of loose habit known as *Caesalpina bonduc*, the long clinging branches and the pods of which are armed with hooked prickles. It is a plant of wide range, for the bluish-grey seeds are said to be used in Arabia for necklets. In the idle days of the past the blacks were wont to enclose a single seed in a miniature basket woven of strips of cane for the amusement of infants — probably the first of rattles. It has seized for support some of the branches of a rare tree (*Cerbera manghas*) which bears long, glossy, lanceolate leaves, large, pink-centred, white flowers, delicately fragrant, and compressed oval fruit, brilliantly scarlet. The tempting appearance of the fruit is all that may be said in its favour, for it is hard and bitter, and said to be vicious in its effects on the human system; hence the generic title, after the three-headed dog, guardian of the portals of the infernal regions . . .

Another small tree, suggesting in its regular and well-balanced shape the use of the pruning-knife, is *Guettardia speciosa*, the flowers of which are white with a tinge of pink in the centre and highly fragrant. The fruit is a hard, woody drupe, containing small seeds . . .

To unaccustomed eyes the pandanus palm is chief among the noticeable features of the flora of the coast of tropical Queensland. Two species are represented on these accommodating sands, each suffering no ill from imbibing salt water, each exhibiting the peculiarity whence the genus derives its common name — the screw palm the arrangement of the long, narrow, prickle-edged leaves displaying in the most regular and demonstrative style the perfect spiral . . . The huge, bright orange-tinted fruit of the species known as *tectorius* is highly attractive in appearance, and to the uninitiated offers pleasing hopes and delicious expectations. It is, however, delusive, being constituted of woody drupes in close clusters collected into a globular head, with meagre yellow pulp at the base of each group, the pulp having an aromatic and unsatisfactory flavour . . .

The cockatoo apple, which has several useful qualities, flourishes exceedingly. The ripe fruit, green and insipid, was wont to be eaten by the blacks, bark from the branches was twisted into fishing-lines, that of the roots used for poisoning fish, while the leaves, heated over the fire until the oil exuded, were applied to bruised and aching parts of the body. Extraordinary tenacity of life distinguished the tree, the axe, fire, and poison failing under some circumstances to vanquish it.

Another and closely related member of the same family is *Barringtonia asiatica*, which, so far

Magnificent representatives of the umbrella-tree . . . are massed in groups . . .

as local experience is to be trusted, is restricted to the beaches, growing lustily in pure sand at the very verge of high-water mark. The glossy leaves of this many-branched tree often exceed a foot in length; the flowers, too, are large and singular in style, the petals being comparatively insignificant, while the numerous stamens attain a length of four inches and are of a lovely shade of red. Like its relative, the cockatoo apple, the flowers of the barringtonia have a meaty smell, which seems to attract many species of insects . . .

One of the loveliest and most remarkable plants of the beach is the seacoast laburnum, with its pinnate leaves of sage green, hoary with silvery fur as soft as seal-skin, and bearing terminal spikes of golden flowers with scent invoking slight comparison with mignonette. The thick, silky leaves, the yellow flowers, and the strange pods, are distinctive qualities . . . The pods begin as slender, silvery, dangling threads, which speedily lengthen and become constricted. When the breeze flusters the shrubs, revealing the undersides of the leaves at a reflective angle and shaking the tasselled pods, and the splashes of gold sway hither and thither . . . it might be likened to the tree of the sun described by Marco Polo — green on one side, but white when perceived on the other . . .

Almost within reach from high water are representatives of a tall, shining-leaved shrub known as *Morinda citrifolia*, the flower-heads of which merge into a berry which has a most disagreeable odour and a still more objectionable flavour. It is related that when La Perouse was cast away on one of the islands of the South Pacific, a native undertook to ward off the pangs of hunger by converting the fruit into an edible dish. But his manipulation seemed but tö intensify original nauseousness, and the brave Frenchman and his companions found semi-starvation more endurable than the repugnant mess.

Magnificent representatives of the umbrella-tree, unique among the many novelties of the tropical coast, are massed in groups or stand in solitary grace close to the sea. Queensland has a monopoly over this handsome and remarkable tree, the genus to which it belongs being limited to a single species occurring nowhere else in a native state. Discovered by Banks and Solander at Cooktown in 1770, the second record of its existence, it is believed, was made from specimens obtained on this island by Macgillivray and Huxley in 1848. Possibly the very trees which attracted their attention still crown their rayed and glossy leaflets with long, radiating rods thickly set with red, stud-like flowers . . .

Few of the ornaments of the beach are more noticeable than that known commonly as the sunflower-tree and by the natives as gin-gee, with its big leaves, soft of surface when young, but harsh and coarse at maturity. The golden flowers, grouped in huge heads, are rich in nectar, attracting birds and butterflies by day and flying foxes at night. The fruit, enclosed in a crisp capsule, is tough and leathery, in shape a flattened oval, and is entirely covered with silken seeds lying close and dense as the feathers of the grebe. When numbers of the capsules open simultaneously, the seeds float earthwards like a silvery mantle or stream before the wind like a veil. Rarely the capsule falls to the ground complete, and then the parting of the valves reveals the fruit, in form not unlike a small fish covered with glistening scales. The soft white wood is generally condemned, but duly seasoned it becomes tough, and is durable when not exposed to the weather. Like other quick-growing trees, the gin-gee takes no long time in arriving at maturity, and its life is comparatively brief. Often big trees die from no apparent cause, and the wood becoming dry and tindery, the limbs crash to the ground suddenly, and in a few months the whole substance disappears in dust and mould.

Though the flowering season of the calophyllum is of the past, the tree which bestows on the beaches the deepest shade and is handsome in all its parts must not be disregarded, for does it not, ever and anon, strive after a higher purpose than the production of goodly leaves, white flowers, and nuts "harsh and crude"? On rare occasions the external covering of the nut turns yellow on the tree, and is then found to enclose a thin envelope of pulp of aromatic and rather gratifying flavour. Such a phenomenon seems to manifest inherent excellencies, a laudable effort towards self-improvement, a plea for assistance on the part of some approving and patient man, an indication of the lines on which he might cooperate. The tree does not need gloss for its perfect leaves or fragrance for its flowers, nor need the qualities of its pink wood of wavering figure be extolled. With the exception of the stamens, all parts of the inflorescence, inclusive of the long pedicles, are milk-white, and the perfume is as sweet and refreshing as an English spring posy. Chemists tell us that the oil from the kernels contains a green pigment which changes to yellow on saponification, and that the resin is emetic and purgative, and healing when applied as plaster. If botanical science can develop the meritorious tendencies the fruit occasionally exhibits, the calophyllum would certainly rank as one of the most wonderful of all tropical fruits . . .

Two eucalypts — bloodwood and Moreton Bay ash — and two acacias are represented, the former developing into great trees of economic value, the latter being comparatively short-lived and ornamental. The young shoots of *Acacia flavescens* are covered as with golden fleece, and its globular flowers are pale yellow. The wood resembles in tint and texture its ally, the raspberry-jam wood of Western Australia, though lacking its significant and remarkable aroma. *Acacia aulacocarpa* displays in pendant masses golden tassels rich in fragrance.

The yellow-flowered hibiscus (cotton-tree) overhangs the tide, and the small-leaved shrub the blacks name tee-bee, the pink, semi-transparent fruit of which is eaten in times of stress, springs from pure sand . . .

The length of the beach thus casually examined is not more than a quarter of a mile long, and no plant mentioned is more than a few yards from high-water mark, the soil being almost pure sand. Imagine some three square miles of country varied by hills and flats of rich soil, with creeks and ravines, precipices and bluffs, dense jungle and thick forest, hollows wherein water lodges in the wet season, and granite ridges, and then endeavour to comprehend the botany of one small island of the tropical coast! . . .

The golden flowers, grouped in huge heads, are rich in nectar . . .

83

A Jungle Flower

During September, the flowery month, and the early part of October many parts of the coast of North Queensland are decorated with a plant of remarkable beauty, which seems to have escaped general notice, though well deserving the admiration of all who take pleasure in purity, in simplicity of form, and in rich perfume.

It is the fate of most flowers that grow in deserts, where no man abides, to die uncommended; but this delightful shrub, sometimes developing into a small tree, is a denizen of country which is desert only in the poetic sense, for the soil is fertile, the rains frequent and abundant, and (as a consequence of stimulating natural conditions) given over to glorious vegetation, varied in character, refreshing to behold in the mass, and teeming with novelties which make appeal to all lovers of plants; and not without rarities to those who make even casual study of the science of botany. Though conspicuous by reason both of flowers and fruit, this desirable plant has no common or pet name. Botanists have termed it *Randia fitzalanii*. It belongs to the same family as the gardenias, and in common with several of its relatives is endowed with strong and pleasant perfume ...

Just now on this Isle are scores of specimens of the glossy-foliaged shrub on the very margin of the sea, flowering profusely. Many of the leaves are about six inches long, smooth and shining, the flowers of the purest white, and the scent that of the family in its quality of pervasiveness.

Randia fitzalanii seldom flourishes when fully exposed to the sun. Its place is rather under the shade of taller and sturdier vegetation, and it finds ideal conditions alike at the mouths of shrub-obstructed creeks and among boulders overhung with trees and screening vines, where the struggle for existence always seems tense and unnecessary. Is it a sort of conscious vanity which impels the graceful plant to occupy deeply-shadowed, if not gloomy, spots? There, at least, are its intensely-white starry flowers set off to the best advantage, and there they last longer and breathe out becoming odours which for the time being monopolise the attention of the passer-by. Simple in form, the flowers are produced in loose, irregular groups, and are proportionately thick and leathery, with less tendency than others of the family to become brown when fading. Posies of the white flowers appear scattered among the glossy leaves, looking like patches of enamel, precisely cut; since there are few winds to disturb such sheltered, well-embowered scenes, the effect is that of formality and primness contrasted with the unkempt, disorderly luxuriance of the jungle.

Large, rotund fruit follows the flowers as a rule, but this season has been so gracious that some plants are displaying flowers and fruit simultaneously. The latter, however, may not ripen for months, and when it does so, though attractive by reason of its size — that of an average orange — and yellowish colour, it is inedible, being hot, insipid and astringent. Blacks confess that at times hunger has driven them to it, but many other vegetable products of repugnant appearance are preferred to this seductive-looking fruit. One cannot with easy mind complain against the laws of nature when a plant which gives pleasure to the eye with its big leaves and white flowers, and ravishes the sense of smell, yet fails in respect of edible fruit; but it may be quite within reason, and in no spirit of fault-finding, easy to imagine that in time to come some ingenious and patient horticulturist will set to work to improve the fruit — and so, peradventure, bestow on the world a novelty which, like the orange, will produce fine foliage, deliciously perfumed flowers and a something excellent to eat.

THE CONQUERING TREE

On the deltas and banks of all the rivers and creeks of North Queensland and on many of the more sheltered beaches, the mangrove flourishes, that ambitious tree which performs an important function in the scheme of Nature. Its botanical title reveals its special character — *Rhizaphora*. Very diverse indeed are the means by which plants are distributed. While some are borne, some fly and others float. The mangrove is maritime. While still pendant from the pear-shaped fruit of the parent tree, the seed, a spindle-shaped radicle, varying in length from a foot to four feet, germinates — ready to form a plant immediately upon arrival at a suitable locality. A sharp spike at the apex represents the embryo leaves ready to unfold, while the roots spring from the opposite and slightly heavier end. The weight is so nicely adjusted that the spindle floats perpendicularly or nearly so, when owning a separate existence from the parent tree, it drops into the water, and begins its remarkable career.

It has been suggested that the viviparity of the mangrove is a survival of a very remote period in the development of the earth — that a mangrove swamp represents an age when the earth was enveloped in clouds and mist; and that with the gradual decrease in tepid aqueous vapour the viviparous habit, then almost universal, was lost, except in the case of this plant . . .

Whole battalions of living mangrove radicles fall into the rivers during February and March. Out at sea miles from the land you may cross the sinuous ranks of the marine invaders — a disorderly, planless venture at the mercy of the wind and waves. Myriads perish, hopeless, water-logged derelicts, never finding foothold nor resting-place. But thousands of these scouts of vegetation live to fulfil the glorious purpose of winning new lands, of increasing the area of continents. This arrogant plant not only says to the ocean, "Hitherto shalt thou come, but no further; and here shall thy proud waves be stayed", but unostentatiously wrests from it unwilling territory.

Plants like animals require "food convenient for them", certain constituents of the soil, certain characteristics of environment, that they may flourish and fulfil their purpose. This delights in conditions that few tolerate — saline mud, ooze and frequent flooding by the salt sea. Drifting into shallow water the sharp end of the spindly radicle bores into the mud. At once slender but tough roots emerge in radiating grapples, leaves unfold at the other extremity, and the plan of conquest has begun. During the early period of its life there is nothing singular in the growth of the plant. In a few months, however, it sends out arching adventitious roots, which on reaching the mud grasp it with strong finger-like rootlets. These arching roots, too, send out from their arches other roots that arch, and the arches of these similarly repeat themselves, and so on, until the tree is underpinned and supported and stayed by an elaborate and complicated system, which while offering no resistance to the sweep of the seas, upholds the tree as no solid trunk or stem could. Then from the plan of arches spring offshoots, in time to become trees as great as the parent. Aerial roots start a downward career from the overhanging branches, anchoring themselves in the mud. Some young seedling drops and the pointed end sticks deep in the mud, and grows forthwith, to possess arching and aerial roots of its own, and to make confusion worse confounded. The identity of the original founder of the grove is lost in the bewildering labyrinth of its own arches, offshoots, and aerial roots, and of independent trees to which it has given the mystery of life. One floating radicle with its pent-up energy, having after weeks of drifting and swaying this way and that to the slightest current and ripple, grapples Mother Earth and makes a law to the ocean. Among the interlacing roots seaweed, sodden driftwood and leaves lodge, sand collects, and as the level of the floor of the ocean is raised the sea retires, contributing by the flotsam and jetsam of each spring-tide to its own inevitable conquest.

Not to one plant alone is the victory to be ascribed. As in the army there are various and distinct branches of service, so in this ancient and incessant strife between land and water, the vegetable invaders are classified and have their appointed place and duties. Neither are all the constituents of a mangrove swamp mangroves. In the first rank will be found the hardiest and most highly specialised. The roots of the red mangrove spread over the surface and have vertical kinks. The roots and the accessories act as natural groynes, causing the waves to swirl and to precipitate mud and sand . . .

No less remarkable is the help that the white mangrove affords in the conquest with its system of strainers . . . erect, obtrusive, respiratory shoots from the roots, slender in comparison, resembling asparagus shoots or rake tines (called by some cobbler's pegs) and which strain the sea, retaining light rubbish and assisting to hold and consolidate it all. Each of the plants mentioned is equipped in a more or less efficient manner for the special purpose of taking part in the reclamation of land. In some the roots descend from the branches to the mud where roots ought to grow; in others, roots ascend from the mud to the upper air, where, ordinarily, roots have no sort of business. Each possesses varying and distinct features well designed to aid and abet the general purpose.

Other species of marine plants have their duty too. That which is known as the river mangrove — which does not confine itself to rivers — comes to sweeten the noisome exhalation of the mud, and with its profuse white, orange-scented flowers, to invite the cheerful presence of bees and butterflies. The looking-glass tree, with its large, oval, glossy, silver-backed leaves and boat-shaped fruit, stands with the river mangrove along the margin farthest from the sea, not as a rearguard, but to perform the function of making the locality the more acceptable to the presence of plants which luxuriate in sweetness and solid earth. Another denizen of the partially reclaimed area of the mangrove swamp is the "milky mangrove", or river poison tree, alias "blind-your-eyes". In India the sap of this tree is called tiger's milk. It issues from the slightest incision of the bark, and is so volatile that no one, however careful, can obtain even a small quantity without being affected by it. There is an acrid, burning sensation in the throat, inflamed eyes and headache, while a single drop falling into the eyes will, it is believed, cause loss of sight. Yet a good caoutchouc may be prepared from it, and it is applied with good effect to ulcerate sores, and by the blacks of Queensland and New South Wales for the relief of certain ulcerous and chronic diseases; while in Fiji the patient is fumigated with the smoke of the burning wood. Several of the plants produce more or less valuable woods . . .

A weird and stealthy process is this invasion of the ocean, which leads to the alteration and amendment of the surface of the globe. Here, may be watched the very growth of land — land creeping silently, irresistibly upon the sea, yet with a movement which may be calculated and registered with exactitude. Having fulfilled its purpose, the mangrove suffers the fate of the primitive and aboriginal. Tyrannous trees of over-topping growth, which at first hesitatingly accepted its hospitality, crowd and shove, compelling the hardy and courageous plant to further efforts to win dominion from the ocean. So the pioneer advances, ever reclaiming extended areas as the usurping jungle presses on its rear . . .

Drifting into shallow water the sharp end of the spindly radicle bores into the mud.

SILENT STRANGLER

The fig-tree . . . begins life as a parasite. A thin slender shoot, tremulously weak, leans lightly on the base of some tall tree, and finding agreeable conditions, clings and grows. A harmless, tender, thong-like shoot it is — a helpless plant, that could not stand alone or exist but for the hospitality of another of strength and substance. Soon a second shoot, slight and frail, emerges near the root, but at a different angle from its aspiring brother, and others as delicate as the first follow, until the trunk of the host is sprawled over by naked running shoots, grey-green in colour, crafty and insidious. As they increase in age the shoots flatten on the under surface and cross and recross. Wheresoever they touch they coalesce. The trunk becomes enveloped in living lace — in a network, rather, living, ever growing and irregular — the meshes of which gradually decrease in dimension. All the while squeezing and causing decay, the meshes close up. The trunk of the host is completely enclosed; it is the dying core of a living cylinder, for the first shoots have long since crept up among the branches, have expanded their leaves, and are busy sapping the life-blood of the tree at all points. A greedy intractable, implacable foe, it gives no quarter, but flourishes upon its dead or dying friend, upon which in its youth it leaned delicately for support. Finally it weaves its slender shoots among the topmost leaves of its victim, and having outgrown its growth, flourishes on its decay.

This vegetable usurper produces immense crops of small purple figs, the favourite food of many birds. So bountiful are its crops, and so much are they appreciated, that one perceives, almost without reflection, its due and proper place in the harmony of nature. To complete the cycle, birds frequently, after eating the fruit, "strop" their beaks on the bark of a neighbouring tree. Now and again a seed thus finds favourable conditions for its germination, and then the parasite sends exploring roots to the ground, forming as they descend intricate lace-work, while shoots repeat a similar process as they climb further up the trunk and among the branches. Then the fate of the host seems less cruel, for the end is speedier.

Delicious fruit is produced by a somewhat similar fig growing in the locality and displaying, though not in such a cruel manner, parasitical tendencies. Passing from green to orange with deep red spots to rich purple, the fruit — about the size of an average grape — indicates arrival at maturity by the exudation of a drop of nectar. Clear as crystal, the nectar partially solidifies. Fragrant and luscious, pendant from the polished fruit, this exuberant insignia of perfection, this glittering drop of vital essence, attracts birds of all degree. It is a liqueur that none can resist, and which seems, so noisy and demonstrative do they all become, to have a highly exhilarating effect on their nerves. Birds ordinarily mute are vociferous, and the rowdy ones — the varied honey-eater as an example — losing all control of their tongues, call and whistle in ecstasy. The best of the fig-tree's life is given for the intoxication of unreflecting birds.

The trunk becomes enveloped in living lace . . .

THE HOST

Standing with its feet awash at high tide, the huge fig-tree began life as a parasite, the seed planted by a beak-cleaning bird in a crevice of the bark of its fore-runner. In time the host disappeared, embraced and absorbed. Now the tree is a sturdy host. Another fig envelops some of its branches, two umbrella-trees cling stubbornly to its sides, a pandanus palm grows comfortably at the base of a limb, tons of staghorn, bird's-nest, polypodium, and other epiphytal ferns, have licence to flourish, orchids hang decoratively, and several shrubs spring aspiringly among its roots. But the big tree still asserts its individuality. It is the host, the others merely dependants or tenants. Most of the functions of the tree are associated with the sea. Twice a year it studs its branches with pink fruit, food for many weeks for a carnival of birds, the relics of the feast dully carpeting the sand. Before the first fruiting the old leaves fall, and for a brief interval the shadows of branches and twigs, intricate, involved, erratic, might be likened to unschooled scribblings, with here a flourish and there a blot and many a boisterous smudge. Soon — it is merely a question of days — the swelling buds displace millions of leaf-sheaves, pale green and fragile, which fall and, curling in on themselves, redden, and again the yellow sand is littered, while overhead fresh foliage, changing rapidly from golden, glistening brown to rich dark green, makes one compact blotch. And when the wind torments sea and forest, and branches bend and sway, and creepers drift before it, the white blooms of the orchids, so light and delicate that a sigh agitates them, might be "foam-flakes torn from the fringe of spray" and tossed aloft . . .

In time the host disappeared, embraced and absorbed.

Mauve, Green and Grey

About 600 feet above sea-level, looking across the Family group to the great bulk of Hinchinbrook, there is an irregular precipice, half concealed by the trees and plants that decorate its seams and crevices and spring up about its cool and ever gloomy base.

During the greater part of the year water trickles down the grey face of the rock in narrow gleaming bands, and wheresoever are the faintest footholds there is a flower — mauve in its modesty. It is not common enough to possess a familiar name, but botanists have called it *Boea hygroscopica*, for it is always found near water, invariably pure, cool, fern-filtered mountain water. From the damp rock the roots of the plant, matted and interwoven, may be peeled off in a thin layer, for the plant is epiphytical, depending as much upon heat, moisture and light as on any constituents of the soil for sustenance. When the season is exceptionally dry, the thick, soft wrinkled leaves become parched and shrivelled; but a shower restores their vigour and lovely, tender green, and fresh flowers slightly resembling the violet, but borne on scapes six or eight inches long, bloom within a few hours of the revivification of the plant. In moist seasons the plant, true to its hygrometic character, continuously blooms, and while it braves the hottest sun on the bare places of the burning rock as long as its roots find moist spots, it will also be found in the shade below, where the flowers are richer in colour, more of purple than mauve, and, rarely, pure white. Generally the plant depends upon others or cracks or crevices in rock for foothold. It shares the grasp the spongy moss may take on the slippery surface, or when the root, thin as whipcord, of a certain fig-tree has crept across the face of the grey rock forming a ridge or barricade against which decayed vegetation accumulates, there the *Boea* flourishes, displaying in indeterminate line of mauve flowers above oval, crimpled leaves. Mauve, green and grey — the mauve of the Victorian age, the green of the cowslip, the grey of glistering, weathering granite.

. . . and wheresoever are the faintest footholds there is a flower . . .

91

Tissue Paper and Spiced Honey

Few of the forest trees are more picturesque than the paper-bark or tea-tree (*Melaleuca leucadendron*), the "tee-doo" of the blacks. It is of free and stately growth, the bark white, compacted of numerous sheets as thin as tissue paper. When a great wind stripped the superficial layers, exposing the reddish-brown epidermis, the whole foreground was transfigured. All during the night alone in the house, I heard the great trees complaining against the molestation of the wind, groaning in strife and fright; but little had I thought that the violation they had endured had been so coarse and lawless. The chaste trees had been incontinently stripped of their decent white vesture, leaving their limbs naked and bare. In the daylight they still moaned, throwing their almost leafless branches about despairingly, their flesh-tints — dingy red — giving to the scene a strangely unfamiliar glow. This outrage was one of the most uncivil of the wrong-doings of the storm wind "Leonta". But within a week or so the trees assumed whiter than ever robes; pure and stainless, the breeze had merely removed soiled linen. The picture had been restored by the most ideal of all artists.

The blossoms of the melaleuca come in superabundance, pale yellow spikes odorous to excess. When the trees thus adorn themselves — and they do so twice in the year in changeless fashion, in the fulness of the wet season — the air is saturated with the odour as of treacle slightly burnt. The island reeks of a vast sugar factory or distillery. Sips of the balsamic syrup are free to all, and birds and insects rejoice and are glad. A perpetual murmur and hum of satisfaction and industry haunt the neighbourhood of the trees as accompaniment to the varied notes of excitable birds. Chemists say that insects imprisoned in an atmosphere of melaleuca oil become intoxicated. Insects and birds certainly are boldly familiar and hilarious during the time that the trees offer their feast of spiced honey.

Every tree is a fair, and all behave accordingly, chirping and whistling, humming and buzzing, flitting and fluttering, in the unrestrained gaiety of holiday and feast-day humour. Always an impertinent, interfering rascal, the spangled drongo, under the exhilarating influence of melaleuca nectar, degenerates into a blusterer. He could not under any circumstances be a larrikin; but the grateful stimulant affects his naturally high spirits, and he is more frolicsome and boisterous than ever. The path between the coconuts to the beach passes close to two of the biggest trees, and from each as I strolled along, one sublime morning when the whole world was drenched with whiffs, strong, sweet and spirity, a drongo, flushed with excitement, flew down, bidding me begone in language that I am fully persuaded was meant to provoke a breach of the peace. The saucy bullies, the half-tipsy roysterers, tired of domineering over every participator of the feast, dared to publicly flout me, defiantly sweeping with their tails the air, as an Irishman, "blue mouldy for want of a bateing", sweeps the floor with his coat, and chattered and scolded in every tone of elated bravado. The bibacious drongo can be as demure as any. When he comes to dart among the eddying insects, glorying in the first cool gleams of the sunshine, he will take his ease on a mango branch, make jerky bows and flick the fine feathers of his tail, and "cheep" in timorous accents. He is sober then, quite parsonified in demeanour; his speech "all in the set phrase of peace", and would be scandalised by the mere mention of melaleuca nectar ...

When the melaleuca blossoms, bees seem to work with quite feverish haste; but the honey gained is dark in colour and has a certain pungent, almost acid, flavour. Holding a frame of comb to the light, you see the clear gold of the bloodwood and the tawny tints of the melaleuca as erratically defined as geographical distinctions in a tinted map ...

A Prickly Climbing Palm

Perhaps the most impressive feature of the jungle — that which takes fast hold, clings most tenaciously, and leaves the most irritating remembrances — is what is known as the lawyer cane or vine. It is a vegetable of tortuous ambitions, that defies you, that embarrasses with attention, arrests your progress, occasionally envelops you in a network of bewildering, slender, and cruelly-armed tentacles, that everywhere bristles with points, that curves back on itself, and makes loops and wriggles; that springs from a thin, sprawling and helpless beginning, and develops into almost miraculous lengths, and ramifies and twists and turns in "verdurous glooms", ascends and descends, grovels in the moist earth and among mouldy leaves, clasps with aerial rootlets every possible support, and eventually clambers and climbs above the tallest tree, twirling its armed tentacles round airy nothings. It blossoms inconspicuously, and its fruit is as hard, tough and dry as an argument on torts. Ordinary mortals call it a vine. Botanists describe it as a prickly climbing palm, and no jungle is complete without it. There are several varieties of this interesting plant, all more or less of a grasping, clinging character, and each of vital importance in the republic of vegetation.

Sometimes when it is severed with a sharp knife there flows from the cane a fluid bright and limpid as a judge's summing up; occasionally it is all as dry as dust and as sneezy, and its

. . . a network of cruelly-armed tentacles, that everywhere bristles with points . . .

prickly leaf sheathes the abode of that vexing insect which causes the scrub itch.

This plant produces lengths of cane similar in every respect to the schoolmaster's weapon — familiar but immortal — varying in diameter from a quarter of an inch to an inch and a half, and in length, as some assert, to no less than 500 and 600 feet. Certainly 300 feet is not uncommon, and one can readily concede an additional 100 feet, knowing the extravagance of the remarkable palm under ordinary circumstances. And the cane weaves and entangles the jungle, binds and links mighty trees together, and with the cooperation of other clinging, and creeping, and trailing plants — some massive as ship's cables, and some thin and fine as fishing-lines — forms compact masses of vegetation to penetrate which tracks must be cut yard by yard ... gloriously rampant jungle. In all this the lawyer cane is the most aggressive and hostile. Not only are there prickles on the ten-feet thongs, but the leaves and leaf-sheaths are thickly beset. In one species the six-feet-long leaves bear upon the margins and upper surface long, thin, needle-like points, black and glossy, and attaining a length of three inches; the main rib bears stout re-curved prickles, while the sheaths which envelop the cane are densely covered with dark brown or black points one inch and more long.

One cannot cut jungle and escape bloodshed, for the long tentacles of the lawyer catch you unawares sooner or later, and then, for all are set with double rows of re-curved points, do not endeavour to escape by strife and resistance — it is no use pulling against those pricks — but by subtlety and diplomacy. The more you pull, the worse for your skin and clothes; but with tact you may become free, with naught but neat scratches and regular rows of splinters. The points of the hooks to which you have been attached anchor themselves deep in the skin, and tear their way out and rip and rend your clothes, and your condition of mind, body and estate, is all for the worse.

But the uses of the lawyer cane are many and various. Blacks employ it as ropes, as stays for canoes, and, split into narrow threads and woven, for baskets and fish-traps; and white men find it handy for all sorts of purposes, from boat-painters and fenders to stock-whip and maul-handles. Suppose a tree that a black wishes to climb presents difficulties low down, he will procure a length of lawyer cane, partly biting and partly breaking it off, if he lacks a cutting implement. Then he will make a loop, so bruising and chewing the end that it becomes flexible and ties almost as readily and quite as securely as rope. Ascending a neighbouring tree, he will manoeuvre one end over a limb of that which he wishes to climb, and slip it through the loop, and run it up until it is fast. A cane fifty feet long, no thicker than one's little finger, fastened to the upper branch of a tree, has on trial borne the weight of three fairly-sized men. Thus tested, the black has no hesitation or difficulty in rapidly ascending, and in lowering down young birds, or eggs (wrapped in leaves), or whatsoever his quest.

Another cane-producing plant (*Flagellaria*), though innocent of the means of grappling, succeeds in overtopping tall trees and smothering them with a mass of interwoven leafage. Each of its narrow leaves ends in a spiral tendril, sensitive but tough, which entwines itself about other leaves and twigs. Feeling their respective ways, the tender tips of leaves of the one family touch and twist, and the grasp is for life. Though not of such extravagant character as the lawyer vine, the *Flagellaria* seems to be endowed with perceptive faculty almost amounting to instinct in selecting the shortest way toward the support necessary for its plan of existence, which is to climb, not to grovel. It spurns the ground. New shoots spring from old rhizomes in the clearings, and turn towards the nearest tree as though aware of its presence, as the tendrils of a grape vine instinctively grope for the artificial support provided for it. Progress along the ground is slow, but once within reach, the shoot rears its head, stretches out a delicate finger-tip, and clings with the grasp of desperation. A vigorous impulse thrills the whole plant. It has found its purpose in life. With the concentration of its energies, its development is rapid and merciless. Its host is rapidly enveloped in entangling embraces, smothered with innumerable clinging kisses.

A Lost Chord

Powerful as nutmeg pigeons are on the wing, some suffer lingering deaths in consequence of a singular characteristic of one of the trees of the jungle. Tall and graceful, with luxuriant glossy leaves, there is nothing uncanny about the tree. In style and appearance it is the very antithesis of the "upas-tree", upon which legendary lore cast unmerited responsibility . . . It is no myth. There is no exaggeration in the statement that the character of the Queensland tree is actually murderous, and that it counts its victims by the thousand every season. Of the great host it destroys, all save a few may be very small and very feeble . . . Neither spike nor poison is used nor any sensational means of destruction, but nevertheless the tree is sure and implacable in its methods.

The seed-vessels of the Queensland upas-tree, "ahm-moo" of the blacks (*Pisonia* species), which are produced on spreading leafless panicles, exude a remarkably viscid substance, approaching bird-lime in consistency and evil effect. Sad is the fate of any bird which, blundering in its flight, happens to strike against any of the many traps which the tree in unconscious malignity hangs out on every side. In such event the seed clings to the feathers, the wings become fixed to the sides, the hapless bird falls to the ground, and as it struggles heedlessly gathers more of the seeds, to which leaves and twigs adhere, until by aggregation it is enclosed in a mass of vegetable debris as firmly as a mummy in its cloths. Small birds as well as lusty pigeons, spiders and all manner of insects; flies, bees, beetles, moths and mosquitoes, as well as the seeds of other trees are ensnared. Spiders are frequently seen sharing the fate of

The seed-vessels . . . which are produced on spreading, leafless panicles, exude a remarkably viscid substance . . .

the flies, fast to seeds in the humiliating posture in which Br'er Fox found Br'er Rabbit on the occasion of the interview with the Tar Baby ...

On some of the islands where the tree is plentiful numbers of pigeons meet a dreary fate every season. The maturity of the seeds coincides with the hatching out of the young, and inexperienced birds pay dearly for their inexperience. The natural glutin is produced while the slim, fluted, inch-long seeds are green, but its virtue remains even after the whole panicle has withered and has fallen. So tenacious is it and prompt, that should a panicle as it whirls downward touch the leaves of lower branches of the parent, or of any neighbouring tree, it sticks and becomes a pendant swaying trap in a new position. At first glance it is not easy to identify the tree to which the obnoxious feature belongs.

The seeds occasion even dogs considerable distress, and might easily be the cause of death to them. As the dog endeavours to remove them from his feet and sides with his teeth, his muzzle is fouled, and he very soon exhibits confusion and alarm, and rolling about in frenzied attempts to free himself, gathers more and more of the seeds and accumulated rubbish.

One is led to ponder upon the purpose of this provision — to endeavour, if possible, to find its justification. Insects lured by the sweetness of the exudation are callously entrapped, and why so? Do the seeds require the presence of animal matter to ensure germination? In that case the tree is indirectly carnivorous, and therefore decidedly entitled to recognition among the curiosities of the island. Is the glutin secreted to secure the wide dispersal of the seeds? If so, the object is largely self-defeated, for seeds by the hundred cling as they fall to the branches of the parent tree, and to those of its lowly neighbours. Certainly some proportion of the seeds which reach the ground must be borne hither and thither by the agency of that eternal scratcher, the scrub fowl. But even a bird of such immensely proportionate strength may be seriously troubled by them ... If the glutin is provided to prevent birds consuming the kernels, then the object is perfectly served; otherwise no very satisfactory reason is apparent why the tree should be invested with the means of destroying even humble forms of life. Is this one of the "lost chords" in the harmony of nature?

FRUITS

". . . the mango in its infinite variety possesses charms as engaging as those of Cleopatra . . ."

DEPENDENT UPON MAN

No one need starve or pine for lack of wholesome appetising and nutritious food while the banana grows as it does in North Queensland, and common as it is, the banana is one of the curiosities of the vegetable world. One writer says: "It is not a tree, a palm, a bush, a vegetable, nor a herb; it is simply a herbaceous plant with the stature of tree, and is perennial." He adds that the fruit contains no seed, though he qualifies the latter statement by remarking that he has heard of fully developed seeds occasionally appearing in the cultivated fruit "when left to ripen on the tree", and further that wild varieties of the banana which propagate themselves by seed are reported to be found in some parts of Eastern Asia. A high botanical authority includes in his description of the species indigenous to Queensland, "Fruit oblong, succulent, indehiscent; seed numerous; tree-like herbs. Herbs with perennial rhizome."

There are three if not more species of bananas native to Queensland, and they form a conspicuous feature of the jungle. With remarkable rapidity one of the species shoots up a ruddy symmetrical, slightly tapering stem — smooth and polished where the old leaf-sheaths have been shed — to a height of twenty and thirty feet, producing leaves fifteen feet long and two feet broad, small and crude flowers, and bunches of dwarf fruit containing little but shot-like seeds. The energy of these plants seems to be concentrated in the production of an elegant and proud form, the fruit being a mere afterthought . . .

In the most popular of the cultivated varieties, the far-famed *Musa cavendishii*, there is little of graceful form, save the broad leaves mottled with brown. All the vitality of the plant is expended in astonishing results. A comparatively lowly plant, its productions in suitable soil are prodigious. In nine or ten months after the planting of the rhizome, it bears under favourable conditions a bunch weighing as much as 120 lb. to 160 lb. and comprising as many as forty-eight dozen individual bananas. So great is the weight that to prevent the downfall of the plant a stake sharpened at each end — one to stick in the ground and the other into the soft stem — is needed to buttress it. Before the fruit has fully developed, other shoots have appeared; but each plant bears but one bunch, and when that is removed the plant is decapitated and slowly decays, and the second and third and fourth shoots from the rhizome successively arrive at the bearing stage and are permitted to mature each its bunch and then fated to suffer immediate decapitation. And so the process goes on for five or seven years, by which time the vigour of the soil has been exhausted, and moreover the rhizomes, originally planted about a foot deep, have grown up to the surface, and are no longer capable of supporting a plant upright. Then a fresh planting of rhizomes elsewhere takes place. It must not be thought that the banana defertilises the soil. Phenomenal crops of sugar-cane are produced on a "banana-sick" land.

A traveller relating his tropical experiences glorifies the banana, stating that he has eaten it "ripe and luscious from the tree". In North Queensland bananas ripening on the plant frequently split, and seldom attain perfect flavour. The ripening process takes place after the fully-developed bunch is removed and hung up in a cool, shady, well-aired locality. Then the fruit acquires its true lusciousness and aroma. Other climes, other results, perhaps; but a banana, "ripe and luscious from the tree", is not generally expected in North Queensland. The fruit may mature until it falls to the ground, yellow and soft, yet lack that delicate finish, that benign essential, the craft of man bestows. It would seem that the plant has been cultivated for so long a period that it has become dependent upon man not only for its existence but for the excellence of its crowning effort. An abandoned banana grove soon disappears, for although seeds are undoubtedly produced, the occasions are so rare that the reproduction of the cultivated varieties depends solely upon the rhizome, and these very speedily deteriorate if neglected . . .

The ripening process takes place after the fully-developed
bunch is removed . . .

MANGOES AND MANGOES

Now, the mango in its infinite variety possesses charms as engaging as those of Cleopatra . . .
A mango might be designated the unspeakable eatable, for who is qualified to determine the
evanescent savours and flavours which a prime specimen of the superb fruit so generously
yields? Take of a pear all that is mellow, of a peach all that is luscious, of a strawberry all that is
fragrant, of a plum all that is kindly, of an apricot all its aroma, of cream all its smoothness.
Commingle with musk and honey, coriander and aniseed, smother with the scent of musk
roses, blend with cider, and the mixture may convey a dim sense of some of the delectable
qualities of one kind of mango. To do justice to the produce of the very next tree another list
of triumphant excellences might be necessary. A first-class mango is compact of so many
sensations to the palate, its theme embraces such rare and delicate surprises, that the true
artist in fruit-flavours is fain to indulge in paraphrase and paradox when he attempts to record
its virtues and — yes, its vanities.

There are mangoes and mangoes. The very worst is not to be wholly despised. For the best
there are due moods and correct environments. For some, the lofty banquet-hall, splendid
with reflected lights and the flash of crystal and silver and the triumphal strains of a full band
hidden by a screen of palms and tree-ferns. There are others best to be eaten to slow, soft
music in a flower-bedizened glade of fairy-land.

September is the season of scents. Partly as a result of the dryness of the month, the mango-
trees continue to bloom as though each had determined (for the time being) to abandon all
notion of utility and to devote itself solely to the keeping up of appearances. Appearances are
well worth maintaining, for however trivial from a florist's point of view the flower of the
mango in detail, yet when for six weeks on end the trees present uniform masses of buff and
pink, varied with shades of grey and pale green, and with the glister of wine-tinted, ribbon-like
leaves, and the air is alert with rich and spicy odour, there is ample apology ever ready for the
season and the direct results thereof. The trees are manifestly over-exerting themselves, in a
witless competition with others which may never boast of painted, scented fruit. There is not a
sufficient audience of aesthetics to tolerate the change of which the mango seems ambitious.

A Perfect Diet

That which makes women beautiful for ever; which renews the strength of man; which is a sweet and excellent food, and which provides medicine for various ills, cannot be said to lack many of the attributes of the elixir of life, and is surely entitled to a special paean . . . How few there are who recognise in the everyday papaw one of the most estimable gifts of kindly Nature?

Some who dwell in temperate climes claim for the apple and the onion superlative qualities. In the papaw the excellences of both are blended and combined. The onion may induce to slumber, but the sleep it produces is it not a trifle too balmy? The moral life and high standard of statesmanship of an American Senator are cited as examples of the refining influences of apples. For every day for thirty years he has, to the exclusion of all other food, lunched on that fruit. Possibly the papaw may be decadent in respect to morals and politics. The grape, lemon, orange, pomelo, and the strawberry, each in the estimation of special enthusiasts, is proclaimed the panacea for many of the ills of life. One writer cites cases in which maniacs have been restored to reason by the exclusive use of cherries. The apple, they say, too, gives to the face of the fair ruddiness, but the tint is it not too bold, compared with maiden blush which bepaints the cheek of the beauty who rightly understands the use of the vital principle of the papaw? Those who have complexions to retain or restore let them understand and be fair.

In North Queensland the plant grows everywhere. In the dry, buoyant climate west of the coast range, and in the steamy coastal tract, on cliff-like hill-sides, on sandy beaches a few feet above high-water mark, among rocks with but a few inches of soil, and where the decayed vegetation of generations has made fat mould many feet deep, the papaw flourishes. It asks foothold, heat, light and moisture, and given these conditions a plant within a few months of its first start in life will begin to provide food — entertaining, refreshing, salubrious — and will continue so to do for years. Its precociousness is so great and its productiveness so lavish, that by the time other trees flaunt their first blossoms, the papaw has worn itself out, and is dying of senile decay, leaving, however, numerous posterity. The fruit is delicate, too, and soon resolves itself into its original elements. Pears and peaches are said by the artistic to enjoy but a brief half hour of absolute perfection. The artist alone knows the interval between immaturity and deterioration. The refined and delicate perception of the exquisite and transient aroma and flavour of fruits deserves to be classed among the fine arts. Some people are endowed with nice discrimination. They are of the order of the genius. The higher the poetic instinct, generally the better qualified the individual to detect and enjoy the fugitive excellences which fruits possess. Can a gourmand ever properly appreciate rare and fragile flavours? Though he may be a great artist in edible discords — things rank and gross and startling — can he in the quantity of inconvenient food he consumes, be expected to pose as a critic of the most etherealised branch of epicureanism? The true eater of fruit is of a school apart, not to be classed with the individual who, because of the rites and observances of the table, accepts, in no exalted spirit, a portion of fruit at the nether end of a feast. He is one who has attained, or to whom has been vouchsafed, a poignant sense of all that does the least violence to the sense of taste and smell; but, moreover, who is capable of discovering edification in things as diverse as the loud jackfruit and the subtle mangosteen — who can appreciate each according to its special characteristics, just as a lover of music finds gratification of a varied nature in the grand harmonies of a Gregorian Chant and in the tender cadences of a song of Sullivan's. Are those who have sensitive and correct palates for fruit not to be credited with art and exactitude, as well as critics of music and painting and statuary, and connoisseurs of wine?

. . . Only those who grow it themselves, who learn of the relative merits of the produce of different trees, and who can time their acceptance of it from the tree, so that it shall possess all its fleeting elements in the happy blending of full maturity, can know how good and great a papaw really is ... But the papaw, delicate and graceful, is more than a mere fruit. If we give credence to all that scientific research has made known of it, we shall have to concede that the papaw possesses social influences more potent than many of the political devices of this socialistic age.

But there may be some who do not know that the humble papaw belongs to the passion-fruit family, a title bestowed on account of a fancied resemblance in the parts of the flower to the instruments of Christ's sufferings and death. And it is said to have received its generic name on account of its foliage somewhat resembling that of the common fig. A great authority on the botany of India suggested that it was originally introduced from the district of Papaya, in Peru, and that "papaw" is merely a corruption of that name. The tree is, as a rule, unbranched, and somewhat palm-like in form. Its great leaves, often a foot and a half long, borne on smooth, cylindrical stalks, are curiously cut into seven lobes, and the stem is hollow and transversely partitioned with thin membranes.

One of the most remarkable characteristics of the papaw is that it is polygamous — that is to say, there may be male and female and even hermaphrodite flowers on the same plant. Commonly the plants are classed as male and female. The males largely predominate. Many horticulturists have sought by the selection of seeds and by artificial fertilisation to control the sex of the plant so that the fruit-bearing females shall be the more numerous but in vain. Some, on the theory that the female generally obtains a more vigorous initial start in life, and in very infancy presents a more robust appearance, heroically weed out weak and spindly seedlings with occasionally happy results. The mild Hindoo, however, who has cultivated the papaw (or papai to adopt the Anglo-Indian title) for centuries, and likewise wishes to avoid the cultivation of unprofitable male plants, seeks by ceremonies to counteract the bias of the plant in favour of masculine attributes. Without the instigation or knowledge of man or boy, a maiden, pure and undefiled, takes a ripe fruit from a tree at a certain phase of the moon, and plants the seed in accordance with more or less elaborate ritual. The belief prevails that these observances procure an overwhelming majority of the female element. The problem of sex, which bewilders the faithless European, is solved satisfactorily to the Hindoo by a virgin prayerful and pure.

On plants which have hitherto displayed only masculine characteristics, small, pale yellow, sweetly-scented flowers on long, loosely-branched axillary panicles, may appear partially or fully developed female organs which result in fructification, and such fruit is ostentatiously displayed. The male produces its fruit not as does the female, clinging closely and compact to the stem, but dangling dangerously from the end of the panicles — an example of witless paternal pride. This fruit of monstrous birth does not as a rule develop to average dimensions, and it is generally woodeny of texture and bitter as to flavour, but fully developed as to seeds.

The true fruit is round, or oval, or elongated, sometimes pear-shaped, and with flattened sides, due to mutual lateral pressure. As many as 250 individual fruits have been counted on a single tree at one and the same time. The heaviest fruit within the ken of the writer weighed 8 lb. 11 oz. They hug the stem closely in compact single rows in progressive stages, the lower tier ripe, the next uppermost nearly so, the development decreasing consistently to the rudiments of flower-buds in the crown of the tree. The leaves fall as the fruit grows, but there is always a crown or umbrella to ward off the rays of the sun. When ripe, the most approved variety is yellow. In the case of the female plant growing out of the way of a male, the fruit is smaller in size, and seedless or nearly so.

Another curious, if not unique point about this estimable plant is that sometimes within the cavity of a perfect specimen will be found one or two infant naked fruits, likewise apparently perfect. Occasionally these abnormal productions are crude, unfashioned and deformed.

Ripened in ample light, with abundance of water, and in high temperature, the fruit must not be torn from the tree "with forced fingers rude", lest the abbreviated stalk pulls out a jagged plug, leaving a hole for the untimely air to enter. The stalk must be carefully cut, and the spice-exhaling fruit borne reverently and immediately to the table. The rite is to be performed in the cool of the morning, for the papaw is essentially a breakfast fruit, and then when the knife slides into the buff-coloured flesh of a cheesy consistency, minute colourless globules exude from the facets of the slices. These glistening beads are emblems of perfection. Plentiful dark seeds adhere to the anterior surface. Some take their papaw with the merest sensation of salt, some with sugar and a drop or two of lime or lemon juice; some with a few of the seeds, which have the flavour of nasturtium. The wise eat it with silent praise. In certain obvious respects it has no equal. It is so clean; it conveys a delicate perception of musk — sweet, not florid; soft, soothing and singularly persuasive. It does not cloy the palate, but rather seductively stimulates the appetite. Its effect is immediately comforting, for to the stomach it is pleasant, wholesome, and helpful. When you have eaten of a papaw in its prime, one that has grown without check or hindrance, and has been removed from the tree without bruise or blemish, you have within you pure, good and chaste food, and you should be thankful and of a gladsome mind. Moreover, no untoward effects arise from excess of appetite. If you be of the fair sex your eyes may brighten on such diet, and your complexion become more radiant. If a mere man you will be the manlier ...

The papaw and the banana in conjunction form an absolutely perfect diet. What the one lacks in nutritive or assimilative qualities the other supplies. No other food, it is asserted, is essential to maintain a man in perfect health and vigour. Our fictitious appetites may pine for wheaten bread, oatmeal, flesh, fish, eggs, and all manner of vegetables but given the papaw and

The peculiar properties of the milky juice which exudes from every part of the plant ...

the banana, the rest are superfluous. Where the banana grows the papaw flourishes. Each is singular from the fact that it represents wholesome food long before arrival at maturity.

Then as a medicine plant the papaw is of great renown. The peculiar properties of the milky juice which exudes from every part of the plant were noticed two hundred years ago. The active principle of the juice known as papain, said to be capable of digesting two hundred times its weight of fibrine, is used for many disorders and ailments, from dyspepsia to ringworm and ichthyosis or fish-skin disease.

By common repute the papaw tree has the power of rendering tough meat tender. Some say that it is but necessary to hang an old hen among the broad leaves to restore to it the youth and freshness of a chicken. In some parts of South America papaw juice is rubbed over meat, and is said to change "apparent leather to tender and juicy steak" ... A common-place experiment was tried. A small piece of beef wrapped up in a papaw leaf during twenty-four hours, after a short boiling became perfectly tender; a similar piece wrapped in paper submitted to exactly similar conditions and processes remained hard ... By its power of dissolving stains the papaw has acquired the name of the melon bleach; the leaves, and a portion of the fruit are steeped in water, and the treated water is used in washing coloured clothing, especially black, the colours being cleaned and held fast.

In the country in which it is supposed to be endemic it is believed that if male animals graze under the papaw tree they become *blasé*; but science alleges that the roots and extracted juice possess aphrodisiac properties, and who among us would not rather place credence upon this particular fairy tale of science than the fairy tales of swarthy and illiterate and possibly biassed gentlemen.

And as to its beauty-bestowing attributes, an admirer's word might be quoted as a final note of praise —

"The strange and beautiful races of the Antilles astonish the eyes of the traveller who sees them for the first time. It has been said that they have taken their black, brown, and olive and yellow skin-tints from the satiny and bright-hued rinds of the fruit which surround them. If they are to be believed, the mystery of their clean, clear complexion and exquisite pulp-like flesh arises from the use of the papaw fruit as a cosmetic. A slice of ripe fruit is rubbed over the skin, and is said to dissolve spare flesh and remove every blemish. It is a toilet requisite in use by the young and old, producing the most beautiful specimens of the human race."

BIRDS AND THEIR RIGHTS

"Sired by a sunbeam, born of a flower, gaiety its badge, might be said in fable of the sun-bird . . ."

DAYBREAK FUGUE

Before there is any visible sign of the break of day, some keener and finer perception than man possesses reveals it to the noisy pitta, or dragoon bird, which in duty bound makes prompt proclamation. Man trusts to mechanism to check off the watches of the night; birds to a self-contained grace more sensitive if not so viciously exact. The noisy pitta bustles along the edge of the jungle rousing all the sleepy heads with sharp interrogative whistles before there is the least paling of the eastern sky. He scents the sun as the ghost of Hamlet's father the morning air. His version of "Sleepers, wake", echoes in the silence in sharp, staccato notes. Seldom heard during the heat of day, they are oft repeated at dusk and late in the evening. Of all the birds of the day his voice is the last as well as the first, and from that the natives derive his name, "wungobah".

As the dawn hastens a subdued fugue of chirps and whistles, soft, continuous and quite distinct from the cheerful individual notes and calls with which the glare is greeted, completes a circle of sounds ... the listener is in the centre of ripples of melody which blend with the silence almost as speedily as the half lights flee before the pompous rays of the imperial sun ... a general exclamation of pleasure on the recovery of the day from the apprehension of the night, a mutual recognition, an interchange of matutinal compliments. Those who take part in it may be jealous rivals in a few minutes, but the first impulse of each new day is a universal paean, not loud and vaunting, but mellow, sweet and unselfish.

Of all the birds of the day his voice is the last as well as the first ...

An Earthly Psalmist

Australian, truly; but, unlike the emu, the black swan, the lyre-bird, the kookaburra, and others, the swamp pheasant is not exclusively so. Familiarly known as a pheasant, and having one feature at least in common with the family, it makes no claim to direct relationship. Science seems somewhat bewildered by its contrarieties; it is placed among the cuckoos, its formal title being *Centropus phasianinus*—pheasant-like spur-foot — while the approved vernacular name is a combination, pheasant-coucal.

In common with most birds, the swamp pheasant has its exclamatory season. During the cool months it seldom breaks the silence; when the leaves of the purple-fruited terminalias begin to redden and fall, when the native nutmegs are soft, furry and brown, and before the calophyllums blossom, the pheasants, responding to the universal thrill, assume their status as the loudest (save the harsh-voiced channel-billed cuckoos) and most persistent singers of the forest. Perhaps the term "singer", applied to sweet-voiced birds generally, should not be associated with one of such original and powerful style . . .

Has any poet attempted to rhyme its moods and music, any artist shown it save as a staid creature incapable of frolic and destitute of fun? Ideally at home on the peaty margins of pandanus swamps, revelling in seclusion, rejoicing triumphantly in otherwise silent places, a lover of sunshine as well as of cool shades, the long, dusky bird, when accustomed to the presence and the ways of man, surely reveals its gift of humour; else why those pranks, swinging its tail, ducking its head, ruffling itself to twice its natural bulk while chortling impertinences? . . .

This earthly psalmist of rare felicity in the expression of its emotions seems proud of its gifts and fond of exercising them. Harken now to the succession of full-sounding, slow, booming notes, accentuated by balanced rests, as if the vocalist were conscious of a flawless performance and studied it with the air of a libant, pausing between sips of the exquisite. Listen again to the quick, crisp, trippingly airy outbursts of merriment. Are they improvisations of a thoughtless moment, tossed into space? And how delicately do a pair in concord harmonise as, perched on a dead limb, they make muscial a square mile of attentive forest!

What is richer, more inspiring to serene and lofty thought, more soothing, less worldly than the bubbling chant heard on a September midnight, when the winds are still? Wakened from innocent and happy dreams, the bird seems to assure its fellows that all is well — not boisterously or in loud and authoritative terms, but in tones bespeaking sympathy and love. It might be repeating that chiming phrase —

"*He, watching over Israel,*
 Slumbers not nor sleeps."

A few seconds of thrilling silence, and another organ-voiced dreamer of all that is consoling takes up the theme, in the same subdued, hushing, almost apprehensive cadence. It is the warranty of mutual confidence and hope, blended with supplication for preservation from the perils of the night. A distant sleeper responds cautiously, each note distinct and mellow; and so the sound is borne away until lost in musical throbs, and the whole Isle has heard the pheasants reassuring each other against the powers of darkness.

Swift as Light — Silent as Dawn

Though showing no fear of human beings, even when the home cave is visited, swiftlets cannot be considered among the familiars of man. A bird that rarely rests during daylight, except when brooding, and is as free as the air, neither fears nor favours its admirers; but when the wings of ants and termites glitter in the light of the newly-risen sun they disdain the presence of onlookers.

Shall we stand for a while to watch the varied behaviour of banqueting birds this steamy morning, when the passing of the wet season is denoted by the mingling of the fragrance of the last blossoms of the tea-trees with the sweetness of the first of the wattles? . . .

The rhythmic evolutions of the bolder of the feasters — a bewildering succession of curves and undulations — might be an unstudied ballet; or they might represent a throng of fairies weaving, with gossamer imperceptible to mortals, a complicated design on the blueness of the sky and the greenness of the foliage. For all the fervency and haste, no jostlings or conflict of claims to the best share of a profuse gift disturbs the harmony of the pattern.

On foot a hopeless cripple, on wing the picture of ease and grace, the swiftlet wheels in circles of varying radii, interrupted by turns of excelling certainty. Audaciously fearless, it often passes silently within arm's reach; when on the instant it swerves within a few inches of your head, then and only then a wisp of sound may be heard.

Splendid are the gifts bestowed upon the little bird in compensation for degenerate legs, which, to vary Shakespeare's phrase, nothing can but cling — eager, defiant, persistent flight, as swift almost as light, as silent as dawn, and sight marvellous in acuteness and adaptability. At one moment it flies as effortless as the drift of wind-blown thistledown, the next as unwaveringly as an arrow. Does it not often race the fast-fleeting light? In company with semi-blind bats it scours the dusk, taking toll of insects that sport boldly in the dark, and in an instant shoots over the hill and down through the gloomy jungle to its quarters, there to thread its way along crevices a hand's breadth wide, and to alight without hesitation at the edge of its nest among hundreds of others on the roof of an obscure dormitory.

Swiftlets' nests are unique among those of Australian birds. Restricted by reason of aerial life in the choice of material, the bird makes a framework of vegetable substances consolidated with saliva. In one cave all the birds had used as a base a grey-green moss, which hangs from trees in specially damp situations and can be seized during flight. Another and considerably larger colony favoured what appeared to be the stems of a thin, wiry grass, and on the only occasion on which they were caught in the act of nest-building all were filching dried "needles" from beach oaks, picking and choosing without slackening speed, each carrying off a single strand.

On a dull day the single white egg seems to glow as if it were slightly phosphorescent; perhaps that effect is produced by a slight reflection from the grey gelatine which forms a considerable part of the nest.

Delicately formed, sober in tint, with a fluff of grey at the base of the tail, short of beak and woefully lacking in leg, the swiftlet is well proportioned and planned for its part in the scheme of Nature; this is to keep in check certain winged insects of destructive character, that otherwise might make the life of man miserable and defeat his efforts to become a habitant of lonely places. What quantity does a single colony dispose of between dawn and dusk? When the local supply runs short, the daily range for forage must be considerable; but what is distance to a creature whose speed may be safely estimated at over a mile a minute? The rivers of the mainland, the mangrove swamps, the lily lagoons are pleasant and profitable resorts, and the open spaces miles further inland are available at the cost of a trifle of time. It is safe to assume, too, that a bird of such high power must exhaust its vital force rapidly, and that there must be constant renewal. Two or three colonies represent, therefore, free agencies operating for the benefit of man to an extent and worth beyond estimation.

When the homing birds appear at dusk there is no slackening of wing. They have flown and feasted, probably without cessation, all the hours of light, and now for rest. Daylight abroad is not for chatter either; but do they ever shuffle each into a tiny nest or cling beside a brooding mate, without greeting associates with a gritty sort of twitter? — just the sort of sound appropriate to a home in the hollow heart of a granite boulder, bewilderingly dim on the brightest noon.

Deprived as it is of the impulse of legs, how does a frail, light bird, submissive to all the functions of life on the wing, rest and incubation excepted, rise from a flat surface on the rare occasions when it alights? Fly-like, it clings to the slanting roof of its home, thence drops, and is away. That is easy enough. But it has been seen to rise from unlittered, level sand, and the feat is performed so quickly that the effect is as if it were tossed upward by a force foreign to itself. No doubt the instantaneous impact of both wings against the sand gives the initial impetus. Scores brooding breast deep, and one after another popping into the air, present a sight that few have had the privilege of witnessing . . .

THE SUN-BIRD

Sired by a sunbeam, born of a flower, gaiety its badge, might be said in fable of the sun-bird, as in temperament and tint it parades its right to such parentage ... One of the most self-assertive of birds of the Island is also one of the least ... Garbed in rich olive green, royal blue, and bright yellow, and of a quick and lively disposition, small as he is, he is always before his public, never forgetful of his appearance, or regardless of his rights. Feeding on honey and on insects which frequent honey-supplying flowers, the sun-bird is generally seen amid surroundings quite in keeping with the splendour of his plumage. The best part of his life is passed among blossoms, and he seems to partake of their beauty and frailness. The gold of the gin-gee, the reds of the flame-tree, the umbrella-tree, and of the single and double hibiscus are reflected from his shining feathers, as he flutters and darts among the blooms, often sipping on the wing after the habit of the humming-bird — which he resembles even to the characteristic expansion of the tail feathers. When in September the flame-tree is a dome of red, sun-birds gather by the score — the gayest of all the revellers. Uncommon length of bill enables them to probe recesses of flowers forbidden others, and they seem proud of the superiority ...

There is a spell in the nectar of the flame-tree as irresistibly attractive to taste of birds as the colour is to the sight of man. Although the tree bursts into bloom with truly tropical ardour, they await the coming banquet with unaffected impatience. Then one of the prettiest frolics of the sun-bird is revealed. Time cannot lag with such gay, saucy creatures, so while they wait half a dozen or more congregate in a circle and with uplifted heads directed towards a common centre sing their song in unison. Whether the theme of the song is of protest against the tardiness of the tree, or of thanks in anticipation, or of exultation in race, or of rivalry, matters not; but one is inclined to the last theory, for none but males take part in it. The sun glints on their burnished breasts, their throats throb, their long bills quaver with enthusiastic effort, and the song still matters not, for it is but a thin twittering, so feeble and faint as to be inaudible a few yards off. Patience and stillness are the price of it. And with a squeak in chorus the choir disperses, to meet and sing again in a few minutes in another part of the reddening tree.

Sired by a sunbeam, born of a flower, gaiety its badge ...

Flight Soft as a Falling Leaf

To work out its destiny the night-jar depends on secret doings and on flight soft as a falling leaf. It is a bird of the twilight and night. Startled from brooding over its eggs or yet dependent chicks, it is ghost-like in its flittings and disappearances. In broad daylight it moves from its resting-place as a leaf blown by an erratic and sudden puff, and vanishes as it touches the sheltering bosom of Mother Earth. Mark the spot of its vanishment and approach never so cautiously, and you see naught. Peer about and from your very feet that which had been deemed to be a shred of bark rises and is wafted away again by a phantom zephyr.

The chick which the parent bird has hidden remains a puzzle. It moves not, it may not blink. Its crafty parent has so nibbled and frayed the edges of the decaying brown leaves among which it nestles that it has become absorbed in the scene. There is nothing to distinguish between the leaf-like feathers and the feather-like leaves. The instinct of the bird has blotted itself out. It is there, but invisible, and to be discovered only by the critical inspection of every inch of its environment. You have found it; but not for minutes after its instinct has warned it to possess its soul calmly and not to be afraid. So firm is its purpose that if inadvertently you put your foot on its tender body it would not move or utter cry. All its faculties are concentrated on impassiveness, and thus does Nature guard its weakest and most helpless offspring.

While you ponder on the wonderful faith of the tiny creature which suffers handling without resistance, the shred of bark, driven by the imperceptible zephyr, falls a few yards away, and in an agony of anxiety utters an imploring purr, or was it an imprecation? That half purr, half hiss has been the only sound of the episode. It is a warning to be gone and leave Nature to her secrets and silences.

THREE FISHERS

Chief among the birds of prey are the osprey, the white-headed sea-eagle, and the white-bellied sea-eagle. The great wedge-tailed eagle is a rare visitor, and is not a fisher. The others are resident and are industrious practisers of the art which, according to their interpretation, is anything but gentle. As they indulge in it, the sport is so rough and boisterous and clumsy that one wonders that so many fish should be caught. Each soars over the sea in circles at a height of about sixty feet or eighty feet, and when fish are seen flies down and, plunging into the water, seizes its prey with its talons. Unless the bird is watched closely its attitudes while preparing for the downward cast and during the descent are misunderstood. "And like a thunderbolt he falls" is quite, according to local observations, an erroneous description of the feat performed by the fishing eagle. Take as an example of the others the actions of the noble bird the white-headed sea-eagle. As it circles over the blue water its gaze is fixed and intent. Flight seems automatic — steady, fairly swift, rippleless. Immediately a fish is sighted, attitudes and poses become comparatively strained and awkward. Flight is checked by the enormous brake-power of outspread tail, and backward beating wing. The eagle poises over the spot, stretches out its legs, and extends its talons to the utmost; flies down in a series of zig-zags, and with the facial expression of the dirty boy undergoing the torture of face-washing, plunges breast first with outstretched wings with a mighty splash into the water. Disappearing for four or five seconds, it finds it no easy task to rise with a two-pound mullet ...

The circumstance that baffles is that fish are so unobservant or so slow that they do not always, in place of sometimes, escape. For the excuse of the fish it must be acknowledged that very few members of the tribe are fitted with eyes for star-gazing. The eagle captures a dinner, not by the exercise of any very remarkable fleetness or adaptiveness or passion for fishing, but because of certain physical limitations on the part of the fish.

"As is the osprey to the fish, who takes it
  By sovereignty of nature."

The subserviency of fish to the osprey was noted by the ancients, who attributed a fabulous power of fascination to the bird so that as it flew over the ponds the fish "turned their glistering bellies up" that it might take liberal choice. Certainly some limitation on the part of the fish seems to operate in favour of the osprey, otherwise the clumsy fisher would oft go hungry.

It goes against the grain to speak slightingly of the knightly, white-headed sea-eagle — a friend and almost a companion; but as any one may see that it fishes not for the sport but for the pot, and that the plunge into the water is a shock that is dreaded, no injustice is done ... The white-headed sea-eagle, which seems, and with good reason, to be proud of its ruddy back, appears to have no enemy of its kind. While the osprey and the white-bellied sea-eagle fall out and chide and fight, it looks down from some superior height and placidly watches the fish trap, for though knightly it is not above accepting tribute, for it likes fish though it hates fishing.

The great osprey seldom crosses the bay without a challenge from its stealthy foe, the white-belly ... The osprey, with steady beat of outstretched wing, flies "squaking" from its agile enemy, who endeavours to alight on the osprey's back. Just as white-belly stretches its talons for a grip among the osprey's feathers, the osprey turns — and turns without a tremor in its long, sweeping wings — to shake hands with white-belly. For a moment the huge bird rests on its back, silhouetted against the luminous sky, to interlock talons with its nimble foe. But white-belly is fully alive to the risk of getting "into hoults" with so heavy a weight, for on the

instant it swoops up with a harsh cry of rage or disappointment. With but a single flap and no quiver of wing the osprey rights itself and sails away (a methodic, unflurried flight) with fleeter white-belly in pursuit, which when within striking distance swoops again, to be faced by the grim, outstretched talons of the osprey, who has turned in flight with machine-like precision. So swift and sudden is the discreet upward swoop of the white-belly that it almost appears to be a rebound after contact with the bigger bird. So the scrimmage, or, to be exact, screamage, proceeds, for each party to it tells the whole Island of its valour, and business stands still as the series of most graceful, yet savage, aerial evolutions is repeated until the rivals are blotted out by distance ...

For all its laborious fishing, the red-backed sea-eagle is sometimes deprived of its spoil by a bird much inferior in size and weight and which has not the slightest pretensions to the art. An eagle had captured a "mainsail" fish (banded dory) which loomed black against its snowy breast as in strenuous spirals it sought to gain sufficient height whence to soar over the spur of the hill to its eyrie. The fish, though not weighty, was awkward to carry ... Low over the water, close to the fringe of jungle the eagle flew, when a grey falcon dashed out, snatched from its talons the wriggling fish, and with one swoop disappeared under a yellow-flowered hibiscus bush overhanging the tideway. The falcon is no match for the eagle; but, most subtle of birds of prey, it had watched the perplexity of its lord and master, and with audacious courage taken advantage of a moment's embarrassment.

The subserviency of fish to the osprey was noted by the ancients, who attributed a fabulous power of fascination to the bird ...

SMART SCRUB FOWL

The cackle and call of the scrub fowl are nocturnal as well as sounds of the day, being repeated at intervals all through the night. Rarely venturing out of the shades of the jungle, the eyesight of this bird is, no doubt, specially adjusted to darkness and subdued lights, and is thus enabled to detect and prey upon insects which during the day lurk under leaves and decayed wood, or bury themselves in the surface of the ever moist soil . . . In common with "Elia" (and others) the scrub fowl has no ear for music. It seems to have been practising "cock-a-doodle-doo" all its life in the solitary corners and undergrowth, and to have not yet arrived within quavers of it. It "abhors the measured malice of music" . . .

Long before the astute Chinese practised the artificial incubation of hens' and ducks' eggs, these sage birds of ours had mastered it. Several birds seem to co-operate in the building of a mound, which may contain many cartloads of material, but each bird appears to have a particular area in which to deposit her eggs. The chicks apparently earn their own living immediately they emerge fully fledged from the mound, and are so far independent of maternal care that they are sometimes found long distances from the nearest possible birthplace, scratching away vigorously and flying when frightened with remarkable vigour and speed, though but a few hours old. I come gladly to the conclusion that the scrub fowl is a sagacious bird, not only in the avoidance of the dismal duty of incubation, but in respect of the making of those great mounds of decaying vegetable matter and earth which perform the function so effectively . . .

The scrub fowl seems to delight in flying in the face of laws to which ordinary fowls are obedient. While making a law unto herself for the incubation of eggs, she scandalously violates that which provides that the size of the egg shall be in proportion to the size of the bird. Though much less in weight than an average domestic fowl, the egg that she lays equals nearly three of the fowl's. Comparisons between the egg of the cassowary (one of the giants among birds) and of the common fowl with that of the scrub fowl, are highly complimentary to the latter . . . The egg of the cassowary represents 1 per cent of the weight of the bird, the domestic fowl's 3⅛ per cent, and that of the scrub fowl no less than 11½ per cent of its weight.

When these facts are considered, we realise why the horny head of the great cassowary, the layer of the largest of Australian eggs, is carried so low as she bursts through the jungle; why the pair converse in such humble tones, and why, on the other hand, the scrub fowl exults so loudly, so coarsely and in such shocking intervals, careless of the sentiments and of the sense of melody of every other bird . . .

Are the actions of birds due to automatic impulses or hereditary traits? Is instinct merely "lapsed intelligence", or do birds actually reflect? Are they capable of applying the results of habit and observations in respect of one set of circumstances to other and different conditions? John Burroughs expresses the opinion that birds have perceptions, but not conceptions; that they recognise a certain fact, but are incapable of applying the fact to another case. I am almost convinced that some birds are capable of logical actions under circumstances absolutely new to them . . . Two cases in which scrub fowl are concerned may be cited . . .

1. On a remote spot in a very rough and rugged locality, hemmed in by immense blocks of granite, is a large incubating mound. Save at one point it is encompassed by rocks, but the opening does not grant facilities for the accumulation of vegetable debris, yet the mound continually increases in dimensions. At first glance there seems no means by which such a large heap could have been accumulated, for the birds do not carry their materials, but kick and scratch them to the site. A hasty survey shows that the birds have taken advantage of the junction of two impending rocks which form a fortuitous shoot down which to send the

rubbish with the least possible exertion on their part. The shoot is always in use, for the efficacy of the mound depends upon the heat generated by actually decaying vegetation. Did the birds think out this simple labour-saving method before deciding on the site for the mound, or was it a gracious afterthought — one of those automatic impulses by which Nature confronts difficulties?

2. As I wandered on the hilltops far from home I was astonished when Tom, the cutest of black boys, dropped on his knees to investigate a crevice between two horizontal slabs of granite filled with dead leaves and loam. The spot, bare of grass, was about twenty yards from the edge of a fairly thick, low-growing scrub where scrub fowls are plentiful. I was inclined to smile when he said, "Might be hegg belonga scrub hen sit down!" He scooped out some of the rubbish — the crevice was so narrow that it barely admitted his arm — and finally dug a hole with his fingers fully fourteen inches deep, revealing an egg, pink with freshness.

A more unlikely spot for a scrub fowl to lay could hardly be imagined. There was no mound, the crevice being merely filled flush, and the vegetable rubbish packed between the flat rocks did not appear to be sufficient in quantity to generate in its decay the temperature necessary to bring about incubation. Yet the egg was warm, and upon reflecting that the sun's rays keep the granite slabs in the locality hot during the day, so hot, indeed, that there is no sitting down on them with comfort, I perceived that here was evidence on which to maintain an argument of rare sagacity on the part of the bird, and that the hypothesis might be thus stated: This cool-footed cultivator of the jungle floor had during the casual rambling on sunlit spaces become conscious of the heat of the rocks. Being impressed, she surveyed the locality, and of her deliberate purpose selected a spot for the completion of her next ensuing maternal duties which, while it scandalised the traditions of her tribe, presented unrealised facilities ...

None but a mound-builder who, of course, must have general knowledge on the subject of temperatures and the maintenance thereof, could conceive that these heated rocks would obviate the labour of raking together a mass of rubbish. Further, her inherent perception that moist heat due to the fermentation was vital towards the fulfilment of her hopes of posterity would avert the blunder of trusting to the dry rocks alone. The hot rocks and a small quantity of decaying leaves stood in her case for a huge mound, innocent of extraneous heat. Having therefore more time to scratch for her living, she would naturally become a more robust bird, more attractive to the males, and the better qualified to transmit her exceptional mental qualities to her more numerous offspring ...

Let those who believe that birds are capable of taking the step from the fact to the principle continue the trains of thought into which they inevitably lead. Will this particular scrub fowl by force of her accidental discovery start a revolutionary change in the life-history of mound-builders generally?

Nutmeg Pigeons

No birds of the air which frequent these parts attract more attention than the white nutmeg or Torres Straits pigeons, which resort to the islands during the incubating season. White with part of each flight feather black, and with down of pale buff, it is a handsome bird, strong and firm of flesh, and possesses remarkable powers on the wing. Half of the year is spent with us. They come from the north in their thousands during the first week of September, and depart during March. While in this quarter they seek rest and recreation, and increase and multiply on the islands, resorting to the mainland during the day for food. Their flights to and from are made in companies varying from four to five to as many as a hundred — but the average is between thirty and forty. Purpose and instinct guide them to certain islands, and to these the companies set flight. Towards the end of the breeding season, when the multitude has almost doubled its strength by lusty young recruits, for an hour and more before sunset until a few minutes after, there is a never-ending procession from the mainland to the favoured islands — a great, almost uncountable host. Soon some of the tree-tops are swaying under the weight of the masses of white birds, the whirr and rush of flight, the clacking and slapping of wings, the domineering "coo-hoo-oo" of the male birds and the responsive notes of the hens; the tumult when in alarm all take wing simultaneously and wheel and circle and settle again with rustling and creaking branches, the sudden swoop with whistling wings of single birds close overhead, create a perpetual din. Then as darkness follows hard upon the down-sinking of the sun, the birds hustle among the thick foliage of the jungle, with querulous, inquiring notes and much ado. Gradually the sounds subside, and the subdued monotonous rhythm of the sea alone is heard . . .

. . . as darkness follows . . . the birds hustle among the thick foliage of the jungle . . .

TERNS

Twice during lengthy intervals have I been perturbed by the conduct of the sea-swallows (terns) which breed in this neighbourhood. They select for their nurseries coral banks, depositing large numbers of eggs beyond the limit of high tides. In obedience to some law, the joyful white birds began to lay in September, five or six weeks earlier than usual. It seemed to be a half-hearted effort to maintain the strength of the colony, the unanimous and general purpose being postponed for three months, when numerous clutches and marvellously variegated eggs embellished the coral. But that which was a perfectly safe and wise undertaking in September was a foolish and dangerous experiment in December. The tides then approach their maximum, flooding areas denied three months previously. Wholesale tragedy was inevitable. The full moon brought bereavement to many parents, for the sea overwhelmed the nurseries, or the best part of them. Many wise birds had laid their eggs above the limit of the highest tide. Others screamed in protest against the cruelty of the sea, for eggs and fluffy chicks do not surely represent legitimate tribute to Neptune. Several fledglings were found half buried in sand and coral chips, some with merely the head with bright and apprehensive eyes obtruding. Why were not the whole of the parents of the colony prudent when in default the penalty was inevitable? Five score were wise, five hundred were foolish, and the natural increase from the second brood must have been seriously diminished. Several of the parent birds had brooded over their eggs until overwhelmed by the surges and drowned. Some on the tide limit squatted buried to the eyes in sand and seaweed. Of one the tip of a wing only protruded. It was alive, fostering unbroken eggs.

A Drongo — in Name and Deed

Wild birds play, and in their pastimes show all their beauty and gracefulness to advantage; the airs often assumed in their ecstasy are evidence almost of pride in the effect that their antics and feats produce on the mind of the beholder. In many parts of the coastal tract of North Queensland a singularly important little bird — a member of the crow family — is fairly plentiful. To him I would appeal as witness in support of the opinion that birds gloat over their superiority to man in respect of flight.

The spangled drongo is black, but not so black that a shade of greenish purple is absent from his shoulders. He has a decidedly crowish head and bill, brownish-red eyes, and a long, fish-like, forked tail, which he has the habit of twitching or flicking to emphasise the meek, clinking tones of his staid and sober moments. Though a bird of the forest, the drongo chooses resorts adjacent to the jungle ...

In many ways and attributes the drongo is a character. Conspicuous, noisy, self-assertive, fussy, and inconsequent, it might be thought that his duties in the harmony of nature were of little concern to others. But, as a fact, he is so useful and so brave that the lives of many others would be attended with greater risks and be less comfortable and happy if his species were exterminated. Many other birds he bullies most impudently, for he has a voice "like Mars, to threaten and command"; but his office is peaceful; for he is head of the detective department. He owns no deputy. He glories in his work, which he performs with the utmost vigilance. The chief enemy of other birds — domestic as well as wild — in this locality is the grey falcon. Whensoever the falcon comes, the drongo makes proclamation and follows him, using language calculated to provoke a breach of the peace. Domestic fowls understand enough of the drongo's dialect to take up the alarm when he sounds it, and my dogs, well acquainted with the language of the fowls, fuss in response, so that I am almost instantly informed of the presence of the falcon. Of the ruddy-backed sea-eagle, and of the osprey, neither the drongo nor the much-petted fowls take the slightest notice; but a falcon cannot escape detection, and, when three or four drongos make common cause against him, flies away with a sulky air, followed by volleys of such wrathful, feather-ruffling language that two or three days may elapse ere the black detective has another case on his hands ...

When he takes his pleasure, he throws his whole soul into it. His delight is triumphant, his ecstasy transcendent. Yet one is inclined to the belief that he "shows off", conscious of the admiration that is his due. Since few of the antics of wild creatures so vividly express frenzied joy and gladness in life, such utter abandonment to the blissful passion of the moment, an attempt to describe an aerial feat performed almost daily for my special edification cannot be forgone.

All birds save the bloodthirsty, sneaking falcon are privileged, but none understands the rights he enjoys as acutely as the drongo, and none takes such liberties. So when my ears are assailed by a hopelessly discordant jangle, I know that my friend the drongo is ringing his bell as a preliminary advertisement to his superb act. As he jangles, "out of tune and harsh", he impels himself with all his might up into the air almost perpendicularly. At the extreme limit of flight his utterances change, and with stiffened wings, distended to the utmost vertically over his back, he casts himself headlong towards the ground, to the accompaniment of a torrent of twittering, too sharp and rapid and violent for distinct enunciation.

Has the wilful bird gone mad that he should deliriously dash himself to death?

Just as one feels constrained to rouse him to a sense of the danger from his giddy feat by a sharp exclamation, the drongo spreads his wings, and, with an impudent whistle, flies off to a tree, to "chink" and "clink" as he flirts his tail with self-satisfaction over the neat performance of an exciting and incomparable trick.

In the evening, at this season ... in the soil, in the cleared space about the house, are thousands of ivory-white grubs which, when they develop into chubby brown beetles, are regarded as dainties by birds ... Then the drongo comes, and, apologising for his intrusion with a few meek "cheeps", makes the best use of his time. Sport being exciting and the game delicious, he swoops and darts until he is bewildered by the darkness. How intensely human is the drongo! In his distress he sets up a loud and appealing "jangle"; this plaint is immediately answered by his home-keeping consort; off he flutters, guided by her continuous calls, and the upbraidings and the explanations and consolations continue for fully five minutes.

SOCIALISTIC BIRDS

The adult metallic starling is remarkable for the colour and lustre of its eyes, which are ruby-red and glitter gem-like ... a handsome fellow, gleaming black, with purple and green sheen ... A soap bubble, black yet retaining all its changing lights and flashing reflections ...

Where the metallic starlings spend their retreat I know not; but they return with impetuous haste, as if absence had been disciplinary and not for pleasure. They assemble in glittering throngs, shrilly discussing their plans for the season, without reserve debating important concerns of house and home. Shall the tall Moreton Bay ash in the forest be again occupied and the shabby remnants of old nests designedly destroyed before departure last season be renovated, or shall a new settlement be established and the massive milkwood-tree overtopping the jungle be selected as a capital site? Discussion is acidulous and constant. For days the

The adult metallic starling is remarkable for the colour and lustre of its eyes ...

The nests ... are composed of tendrils and pliant twigs elaborately intertwined ...

122

majority of the burnished citizens do little else but talk, while the industrious few begin, some to build nests on the sites of the old, others to lay hasty foundations among the leaves of the milkwood. Each faction wishes to carry its point, for ever and anon both rejoin the main body and proclaim and testify. Then all adjourn to the disputed sites successively and join in frantic commotion until some sage makes an entirely original proposition, and off they all go on a flight of inspection and abruptly end all differences of opinion by favouring a tree which appears to have no distinctive merits . . .

In 1908 the earliest arrivals appeared on August 2nd — eight days before the herald of the nutmeg pigeons. The colony the history of which it is proposed to relate was no doubt an offshoot of the first brood of those which had arrived on that date. Circumstances exist which persuade me that the shining starlings rear two broods during the season . . . Let the diary notes tell of the enterprise as scrutinised through the telescope:

"Nov. 15. Shining calornis (all young birds, mottled grey and black with green sheen on back) busy surveying tree (Moreton Bay ash) on plateau to the north.

"16. Birds seem inclined to build.

"17. Notice that the birds are in pairs; no old, full-plumaged among them.

"18. First beginning of nests. About thirty birds. All seem very excited and full of business.

"20. Several nests well forward. Other parts of the tree now being occupied.

"22. Seventeen nests; some nearly complete.

"23. Eighteen nests; several apparently complete, save for the overhanging entrance. Many quarrels and squabbles in the family, for the nests are in groups and in close quarters.

"27. Three new nests, or rather foundations thereof.

"Dec. 1. Now 25 nests. Those which appeared to be near completion are still being added to. Many have entrances, so that one of the pair works from inside, placing and threading the materials. Sometimes one sits for a long time with the head protruding, as if testing the comfort of the nest. Squabbles are frequent. The backs of some betray a lovely green sheen in the sunshine, with rich purple at the base of the neck.

"4. After two days' heavy rain the birds are as busy as ever. Many flirtations. The great want of the colony seems to be insect powder.

"5. The tree now is in full flower. I watch the birds making feints at bees and butterflies visiting the blooms, but they do not seem to catch insects. Fruit, seeds, and nuts form their diet. The nests, which are composed of tendrils and pliant twigs elaborately intertwined, are domed, and in size somewhat less than a football.

"6. Birds very busy. Most of the nests appear to be fit for habitation. Work is suspended at sundown. They do not roost in the tree. Have not detected their resting-place; but it seems to be some distance in the jungle.

"7. Sunset (6.45). The birds disappeared from vicinity of the tree almost immediately, though twilight lasted half an hour.

"8. Three minutes before sunrise (5.48) birds' voices heard as they approached trees. They were in three or four companies in a bloodwood-tree, where they flirted and fussed and made violent love; then in a trailing mob flew noisily and began work in haste and excitement, one eager bird manipulating a long, slender, partly dry leaf, industriously trying to fit it in various spots. Finding its due place, the limp leaf was thrust in among the compact twigs and tendrils. The leaf was seized close to the stalk, which was deftly inserted, then it was gripped a trifle farther back and pushed and re-gripped, the process being repeated rapidly until nothing but the tip remained visible.

"9. Most of the exterior of the nests is now finished. Work continues briskly on the lining . . .

"In the morning, fuss, fierce purpose, and hurry are shown. As the afternoon wears on, less and less industry prevails. Work is suspended at 6.45 p.m. when the last of the crowd hastily departed. Before sundown all are spent and weary . . .

"15. A more sedate condition prevails in the demeanour of the birds . . .

"17. Egg-laying undoubtedly begins, though improvements to nests, which seemed to be finished over a week ago, occupy odd moments.

"20. Two past days have been dull and showery. Quietude reigns; a tendril or twig is occasionally threaded or poked into the nests. The male muses on the top of the nest, or closely adjacent thereto. The female pops in and out of apparently cosy quarters. Circumstances point to the conclusion that most of the nests contain eggs.

"21. Good deal of rain, which bothers the birds . . .

"22. Heavy rain and never-ceasing squalls. No sign of the birds, though a few notes of passers-by were heard. Finer evening.

"23. Fine and calm. Nests deserted all morning . . .

"26. Full company in possession throughout the day . . .

"27. Serious business of incubation deprives the colony of customary gaiety and impulsiveness . . .

"29. All quiet and industrious. Fancy that the chicks are well forward — rather to my surprise.

"Jan. 2. Very rainy all morning. Did not see any of the birds until the weather cleared. Thought the nests looked sodden, the owners were cheerful and noisy — a tone of pleasure because of the return of the sunshine . . .

"3. Busy all day. At 6.45 a.m. all gathered in a company on the topmost branches, and after two or three preliminary flights to the accompaniment of much commotion and chattering, dashed into the jungle with a unanimous and most acidulous shriek. One of the nests is hanging in shreds.

"4. This morning the birds were engaged for some little time pulling their nests to pieces, strands of tendrils being jerked out and cast away with a contemptuous fling . . .

"5. Before 7 a.m. dismantlement of nests was resumed with enthusiasm and deliberate purpose, shreds being twitched out and cast down. A good deal of chatter. There are a few completely feathered youngsters, the breasts being almost pure white, but not more than one to each nest. Most of the nests have no output, in which case the responsible birds have no assistance in the work of destruction . . .

"7. Demolition very casual. The birds are averse from working in the rain, and to-day several showers have occurred . . .

"10. Very early, the morning being fine and clear, the birds resumed in a playful, lackadaisical way the demolition of the nests; without apparent cause, save the shriek of a passing cockatoo, they fled into the jungle. Did not see them again until late in the afternoon.

"11. Again the birds visited the reserve early. Shortly before sundown I counted sixteen. They were resting silently on the sodden remains of the nests, for there have been heavy showers; some were picking idly at loosened strands as if merely to beguile time . . .

"12. Yesterday's occupations and recreations repeated. The inheritance of parasitic intruders, to cut off which the nests are torn to pieces, now depends on unsubstantialities . . .

"16. No appearance until late in the afternoon, when four, wildly flying, settled for a few minutes and departed shrieking. The tree is not now a home, merely a rendezvous."

And so the history ends. Next August, no doubt, the surviving members of the colony will return, all fully feathered in glossy black, and with eyes aflame, to complete the destruction of the nests — according to habit — and build afresh.

"Dec. 10 (1910). True to attributes, the birds returned yesterday. To-day the one nest which had withstood a year's buffeting was demolished offhand, and twenty-two are now being built with frantic haste."

CALLOO-CALLOO

Among those birds of North Queensland jungles which have marked individualistic characters is that known as the koel cuckoo or Indian Koel which the blacks of some localities have named "calloo-calloo" — a mimetic term imitative of the most frequent notes of the bird. The male is lustrous black, the female mottled brown, and during most parts of the year both are extremely shy, though noisy enough in accustomed and quiet haunts. The principal note of the male is loud, ringing, and most pleasant, but its vocabulary is fairly extensive. Sometimes it yelps loud and long like a puppy complaining of a smart whipping, sometimes in the gloom of the evening it moans and wails pitifully like an evil thing tortured mentally and physically, sometimes it announces the detection of unwelcome intruders upon its haunts with a blending of purr and hiss.

When "calloo-calloo" comes to the islands, resident blacks look to the flowering of the bean-tree, for the events are coincident; while as they understand all its vocal inflections an important secret is often revealed to them by noisy exclamations. Living in flowerland among the tops of the trees, the bird is favourably located for the discovery of snakes, but being strong and lusty there is reason to believe that the presence of slim green and grey arboreal species is ignored. The important office that it holds in the domestic economy of the blacks is in the detection of carpet snakes, which to them form an ever welcome article of diet. Thus when "calloo-calloo" shouts "snake" in excited, chattering phrases they run off in the hope of being able to find the game, and generally one act suffices to rid the bird of a deceitful and implacable enemy and to provide the camp with a substantial meal . . .

The "calloo-calloo" performs such valuable service that . . . under no circumstances will they kill it. Of course, the blacks of North Queensland in native worth have not much art in the killing of birds, but in every case "calloo-calloo" is tabu.

One instance may be quoted. A great outcry was heard on the edge of the jungle, and upon investigation a grey falcon and a "calloo-calloo" were found in such preoccupied "hoults" that both were captured. Here was an opportunity for a meal. The birds were parted, and the falcon given over to the custody of a gin for execution, while the "calloo-calloo", which was dazed, was petted and revived until it at last flew away with a glad call, the blacks assuring a witness, "B'mbi that fella look out snake belong me fella!"

BUTTERFLIES AND LESSER INSECTS

". . . royal blue with black edging to the wings and dandyish swallow-tails, which wanders far and wide and flies high and swiftly, is Ulysses . . ."

LOVERS

... the two most gorgeous butterflies of the land — Ulysses and Cassandra. Science changes its titles so frequently that unless the intellect is to be increasingly burdened it is well to refuse to be divorced from the old and often explicit and fulfilling names. Cassandra is the lovely green and gold-fly which dances in the air so delightfully when he woos his sober, fluttering mate. That of gorgeous royal blue with black edging to the wings and dandyish swallow-tails, which wanders far and wide and flies high and swiftly, is Ulysses ...

Ulysses — first observed in Australia on this very island over half a century ago. It was but a passing gleam, for the visiting scientist lamented that it flew so high over the tree-tops that he failed to obtain the specimen. True to name, the Ulysses still flies high and wide ...

For half an hour the courtship of a perfect Ulysses has interfered with the staid ways of those not in holiday humour. Unlike Cassandra, there is little in appearance to distinguish the sexes, nor in the wooing does the dame exhibit staid demeanour. The object of Ulysses' love is almost, if not quite, as brilliantly decorated as himself. She is not, therefore, to be fascinated

The blue-mantled dandy understands his art.

128

by the display of blue no more lustrous than that of her own proud wings. He may flit and toss about her, but she seems to take scant notice of his affected aerial limpings. Her raiment is just as brave, and she has swallow-tails too. The wider black margin on her wings is no badge of subserviency, but rather an additional charm inciting tremulous fascination. She may soar over the mango-trees with ease as careless as his, and slide down straight to the red flowers with like certainty. She is not to be bewildered by his gyrations, nor thrilled by mock hostile swoops. However sprightly his activities, she has a mood to correspond and power to mimic. Indeed, is she not indifferent? — so much on an equality with him that she might say:

"If thou thinkest I am too easily won,
I'll frown and be perverse, and say thee nay."

Might she not say more at the moment, since her airs are those of independence? Possibly she imagines hers to be the superior sex. Is she to be distinguished from her wooer as she flits from him disdainfully? Can she not imitate his most audacious feats? Ah! but for how long may she restrain primal emotions? The blue-mantled dandy understands his art. His wings beat with the passion of the dominant lover. He tosses himself before her, impeding her flight until she imitates his antics. Tossing is not the privilege of his sex. She exercises her right to toss, and the pair toss in delightful but bewildering confusion, like jewels sent skyward by a conjurer. And thus having established her rights if not her equality, she consents to play the part Nature decrees, and the pair tumble and toss over the mango-trees, while half a dozen others sip contentedly the red flowers.

Pilgrims of the Fence

There are reasons for the belief that green tree-ants understand and respect the laws of neutrality. There are several communities in the mango trees, and since some of the trees overhang the fence, the top wire is used as a highway. When a gate is opened traffic is suspended. In a minute or two of a busy day there will be considerable gatherings on the latch-style, and if the intervening space is narrowed by the swing of the gate the impatient insects begin to make a living bridge across the perilous gap. At one particular gate, which is opened and shut many times a day, it has been noticed that the ants never seem to resent interruptions or to be vexed by them. If they happen to get on the hands or fingers, they submit to be restored to the gate; but go to the formicary on the mango-tree half a dozen yards away and offer a friendly finger, and you will find dozens of pugnacious individuals ready to defend their home. Do they recognise that they are but pilgrims of the fence, enjoying certain rights on sufferance, that it is a path of peace on which belligerents must not intrude, a neutral tract under the custody of the law of nations, which ants, as well as men, must respect? Whatsoever the reason, the deportment of the truculent ant on the highway is that of an upholder of peace at any price. It is to be doubted if the animal world holds more illustrious examples of heroism than a green tree-ants' nest. Two or three individuals may be despised as long as their assaults are confined to the less sensitive parts of the body; but let a huge colony up among the branches of an orange-tree be disturbed, and the first army corps instantly mobilises, and it will not be cowardly hastily to retreat. So eager for the fray are the warriors, so well organised, so completely devoted to the self-sacrificing duty of protecting the community, that two distinct methods of advance and attack are exercised forthwith in the midst of what appears to be calamitous confusion. Swarming on the extremity of the branches among which the formicary is constructed, the defenders, projecting their terminal segments as far into space as possible, eject formic acid in the direction of the enemy. Like shrapnel from machine guns, the liquid missile sweeps a considerable area. Against the sunlight it appears as a continuous spray, and should one infinitesimal drop descend into the eye the stoutest mortal will blink. Attacks are made singly and in detachments. Heroes actually hurl themselves from the branches, and, failing to reach the enemy, run along the ground and scaling his legs, inflict punishment on the first convenient patch of unprotected skin. Detachments muster in blobs, fall in a mass to the ground, and charge. If one of these forlorn hopes happens to be successful, the observant man will retire with little of his dignity remaining.

It is to be doubted if the animal world holds more illustrious examples of heroism than a green tree-ant's nest.

Green-Ant Cordial

White ants, black ants, red ants, brown ants, grey ants, green ants; ants large, ants small; ants slothful, ants brisk; meat-eating ants, grain-eating ants, fruit-eating ants, nectar-imbibing ants; ants that fight, ants that run away; ants that live under coldest stone, ants that dwell among the tree-tops; silent ants, ants that literally "kick up" a row; good ants, bad ants, ants that are merely so so — we have them all and would not part with any — not even the stinging green ants, which are among the most singular of the tribe, nor even the "white ant" (which is not an ant), that would literally eat us out of house and home if not rigorously excluded and warred against with poison, for they are the great scavengers of woodeny debris.

Green ants do disfigure orange and mango trees with their "nests", and they have the temper of furies; but they wage war on many of the insects which bother plants, and clear away insect carrion, and carrion, in fact, of all sorts. This ant, to which has been given the official title of "emerald-coloured leaf dweller", constructs a pocket with leaves of living trees (and, very rarely, of the blades of living grass), and dwelling therein establishes populous colonies. The queen or mother ant sets up her separate establishment by curling a small leaf or the corner of a large one, joining the edges with a white cottony fabric, and forthwith begins to raise a family. She is a portly creature — unlike her slim, semi-transparent workers and warriors — and most prolific, and her family increases marvellously. As it multiplies, ingenious additions of living leaves are made to the pocket or purse, until it may assume the size of a football and be the home of millions of alert, pugnacious, inquisitive, foraging insects, whose bites are dreaded by individuals whose skin is extra sensitive.

Is it not astonishing that insects, possessing even in combination such trivial muscular power as the green tree-ant, should be able to cause leaves twelve inches long by eight inches wide to curl up so that the apex shall almost touch the base, or that the parallel borders shall be brought together with the nicest apposition? ...

The process by which a leaf is curled extends over several days, and but few take part in it. Half a dozen ants may be seen perpetually engaged in, apparently, an unmethodical but extremely minute and critical inspection of the rhachis and the nerves or ribs of the leaf. Days pass. The ants are there all the time, examining the leaf and communicating with each other whensoever they meet. Imperceptibly the leaf begins to curl. The ants continue to make mesmeric passes over the nerves with ever-waving antennae.

In accordance with the will and the design of the architects, who merely stand by and gesticulate, the opposite margins approach, or the apex curls towards the base, or towards one of the sides to form a miniature funnel. When the extremities are so close that the intervening space may be spanned, threads of white gossamer are laced across, and the slack being taken up by degrees, in a few days a cosy pocket with closely-fitting seams is completed.

How is this folding of the leaf accomplished? A theory which presents itself is that the ants eject some active chemical principle into certain of the cells of the leaf tissue, and that the stimulus is transmitted by excitation from cell to cell, bringing about a general and uniform contraction without destroying the vitality of the leaf. Further, by the application of the injection to specific cells the ants convey impulses to specific nerves, causing the leaf to curl longitudinally or laterally, or at any angle they design. The poison that a single ant injects into the neck of a brawny man so affects his nervous system that he twists and writhes and stamps his feet with energy sufficient to destroy millions of the species. Maybe a slightly different compound is reserved for vegetable substances, which can offer only a flabby sort of remonstrance ... Immense and concentrated exertion is necessary to draw far-flung

Spaces between leaves and twigs four and five inches wide are bridged by chains of ants ...

branchlets and leaves together, and the feverish host accomplishes a seemingly impossible feat by an organised combination of engineering with cooperative labour. Spaces between leaves and twigs four and five inches wide are bridged by chains of ants — each individual clasping with its mandibles above the abdominal segment its immediate companion; occasionally the ant grips its fellow by the posterior legs, and is so held by the next in order. In the construction of these chains ants hastily mass at each side of the gulf to be spanned, and crawling, or rather running over each other, form pendant strands, each ant a living link. The chains sway until the terminal links engage, when they are immediately shortened up. Several of these chains are swung across parallel to each other with astonishing rapidity; and in addition to the constant strain of the hauling workers at each end they are used as bridges by innumerable other workers and fussy superintendents, the traffic on them being almost as voluminous and bustling as that of a Thames thoroughfare. Gradually the most obstinate branchlet with its spray of leaves is drawn into juxtaposition with the main part of the mansion. Then the living spans become more numerous, presenting the appearance of great stitches. As the edges of the leaves are brought together they are fastened with white gossamer while the tireless workers strain themselves, heroically holding the edges in apposition. The gossamer seems to be obtained in part from the pupae, which, borne in the mandibles of workers, are passed to and fro as weavers' shuttles. As a rule, insects which house themselves in leaves are vegetarian, but the green ant is demonstratively carnivorous, using leaves solely for shelter.

An Aboriginal — to repeat perhaps a needless observation — regards the most of things of this earth from a dietetic standpoint. He does not so regard the green tree-ant in vain. He knows when the pocket is packed with white larvae and white helpless infant ants, or with helpless green ones big of abdomen, and consenting to the assaults of the adults, cuts away the supporting branch and shakes off the furious citizens, or expels them with the smoke and fire of paper-bark torches, or, maybe, casts the pocket into water so that the adult ants may swim ashore, abandoning those that cannot, on account of immaturity or incompetence, to their fate.

Eaten raw, the larvae are pungent morsels, or macerated in water in company with relatives distended to the degree of helplessness, form a cordial that is sharp to the palate, scarifying to the throat, and consoling to the stomach replete with the cold and sodden foods with which blacks often have to be content.

AN ACTOR

Few insects repay observation better than the mantis and the stick insect, which generally, of most voracious habits themselves, resort to all manner of disguises and devices to elude their enemies and lure their prey. Nearly all furnish striking examples of colour protection. One variety of the mantis here is black and rugged, and is to be found only on charred wood. The wing-cases present the characteristic grain and glint of fresh charcoal, distinctly showing the influence of the condition of its environment. Another is grey, to match its groundwork of dead wood; another brown and slightly hairy, to coincide with the bark of the particular eucalyptus upon which it lurks. Another, and the most graceful, resembles two bright green leaves, the midrib and the nerve system being imitated perfectly.

Among the most singular is one of the stick insects. A fair specimen may be a foot and more long. The body presents the general appearance of a dry stick; the posterior legs, held at different and erratic angles to the grey and brown body, are as sunburnt twigs; the intermediary pair seem to be used primarily as supports. The anterior are stretched out to their fullest extent parallel to each other, and so close together as to resemble one tapering termination, with the head closely packed between the thighs, in each of which is a complementary depression for its accommodation. When the insect is motionless it is difficult to detect. By its long posterior legs, stiffly held aloft, it proclaims to every bird — "Do not be so absurd as to imagine these dry twigs to be legs, belonging to a body good to eat." And if the bird does not take the resemblance for granted and is inquisitive and approaches too familiarly, it finds that instead of a dinner it has discovered a snake. The insect seems to say — "I am a stick! Look at the twigs. No, I am a snake! Long live the serpent!"

The long, slender anterior legs — used more frequently as arms than as legs — form the tapering tail; the other end is the head with mouth open, ready for action — eyes and jaws and protruding tongue complete. This end sways as does the head of an excited snake, and curves round as if to strike, and the boldest of little birds fly off with a note of apprehension and alarm. I have had these strange creatures under observation many weeks, and invariably found that when one was interfered with in any way it used its snake-like aft end as a bogey, curving it round towards the molesting hand. A fowl that will attack an eight-inch centipede without hesitation, makes a sensational fuss and clatter when it detects a stick insect, especially when the stick insect feints, however ineffectually, with its perfectly harmless tail. If it is capable of imposing upon a sagacious fowl, the effect of its terrifying aspect upon an unsophisticated little bird can well be understood.

A Spider and a Bat

At dawn a bat flew into a spider's web spun during the night, the extremities of the wings being so entangled that struggling was almost impossible. A big spider pounced on it. Not a minute elapsed from the entanglement until the bat was released, but the venom of the spider had done its work. There was not a sign of life. The spider is dark grey in colour, bloated of body, slothful, and of most retiring disposition. Huddled up into almost spherical form, it lurks in dark places, which it soon makes insanitary. In the open it crouches among dead leaves which have gathered in the fork of a tree, and will construct a web which spans the coconut avenue with its stays. From one aspect its rotund body invites a good-humoured smile, for the marking exactly simulates the features of a tabby cat, well fed, sleepy, and in placid mood. Venom of virulence to kill a bat almost instantly would be severe enough to a human being. This dirty, obese spider deserves little consideration at the hand of man.

Venom of virulence to kill a bat . . .

A Reasoning Wasp

This morning (October 6, 1909) the soda siphon (which had not been used for a couple of days) refused duty, owing to a plug of terra-cotta-coloured clay. Upon the spout being probed the gush of gas expelled a quantity of clay and thirty-five small spiders, representative of about six different species. The spout had been converted into a nursery and larder by a carnivorous wasp, for in addition to the moribund spiders stored for the sustenance of future grubs were several unhatched eggs. Such wasps are exceedingly common, some building "nests" as large as a tea-cup, the last compartment being fitted with an elegantly fashioned funnel, the purpose of which is not obvious. If these nests are broken up after the hatching out, the grubs are found — several in each compartment — feasting on the comatose spiders or caterpillars stored for their refreshment. Others of the species build a series of nests, detached or semi-detached, and shaped in resemblance to Greek amphorae. Another species selects hollows in wood in which the eggs and insects are sealed. The larger wasps are not fearful of attacking so-called tarantulas, one sting rendering them paralytic . . . an instance of what seems to be the reasoned act of a wasp may be cited. The insect had selected a dead log of soft wood as a site for its egg-shaft. It was at a spot to which the occupations of the season took me daily, so that the boring operations were watched from beginning to end. The work was done rapidly and neatly, and when all was ready for the deposit of the eggs the insect constructed from papier-mâché-like material a disc-shaped lid exactly fitting the mouth of the excavation, to which it was attached on its upper edge by a hinge. Then round and about the disc similar stuff was plastered, so as to form an irregular splash, imitative of a bird's droppings to the degree of perfect deception. In the centre was the lid with the hinge, and whensoever the insect visited its nursery the lid swung up, closing behind it. On departure it fell into position. Unless the insect by its presence betrayed its secret, the shrewdest observer at close quarters would have been misled.

Such wasps are exceedingly common . . .

137

Oo-boo-boo the Tarantula

A few months ago I read in a text-book a dogmatic assertion to the effect that the so-called tarantulas were perfectly innocent of venom, and formidable only to the insects on which they prey. The great, good-tempered fellow, as uncouth in its hairiness as Nebuchadnezzar during his lamentable but salutary attack of boanthropy, is regarded with a good deal of suspicion, if not dread, though it pays for its lodging by reason of its large appetite, which latter statement seems self-contradictory. To satisfy its pangs of hunger it captures numbers of small insects which, willy nilly, tenant our homes.

In well-ordered establishments the aid of a tarantula or two in the suppression of insignificant undesirable creatures should, it might be argued, be unnecessary. Indeed, does not the presence of a fat, flat fellow lurking behind a rafter or in some gloomy corner, ever ready to seize cockroach or beetle, imply lack of order? Yet I have known homes where the tarantula was an honoured, if not a petted, lodger. When it had cleared one room it was coaxed on to a card and thereon transported to the next, and so it went the rounds. The children were wont to say that it knew its carriage, and would sidle on it whenever it was presented. To those of us who live in the bush, and who suffer fresh incursions almost every hour of the day, the help of a long-limbed, obese-bodied spider whose docility is beyond question, whose non-poisonous character is vouched for by high authorities, is by no means unwelcome.

But in spite of negative knowledge I have had my suspicions that the tarantula was not altogether wholesome in his anger, and now I have proof in support of my doubts. In a cool,

Yet I have known homes where the tarantula was an honoured, if not a petted, lodger.

dark cavity under a log in the bush were two huge representatives of the race. Each had its own compartment, a smooth, worn gallery, and they appear to have been on good terms until the moment of disturbance, for which each seemed to blame the other. They fought. It was a very brief, casual, and unentertaining encounter; but in less than half a minute one was dead — shrivelled and shrunk as though fire had passed over it. As no dismemberment or wound was apparent, I was fairly well satisfied that poison, very rapid in its effect, was at the service of the tarantula when its anger was aroused.

The next fact settled the point. Tom, the black boy, felt a nip on the arm as he put on a clean shirt an evening or two ago, and, reversing the sleeve, found a tarantula. Blood was oozing from two tiny incisions, the space between which was slightly raised. For two days Tom suffered pain in the arm, which became slightly swollen, headache, and great uneasiness.

Reading my text-book, I found that the original tarantula spider (from which the Australian species are misnamed) is so called from the town of Tarentum, in Italy. Among the inhabitants of the town and neighbourhood it was a deeply-rooted belief that if any one was bitten by a tarantula he would be instantly inflicted with a singular disease known as tarantismus, which exhibited itself in two extremes, the one being a profound and silent melancholy and the other a continual convulsive movement of the whole body. It was thought that this disease could only be cured by music, and that a certain tune was needful in each particular case. This was the legend.

It will be remembered that among the tales told by "a great traveller" to Pepys was one on the subject of the tarantula. He says that all the harvest long (about which time they are most busy) there are fiddlers go up and down the fields everywhere in expectation of being hired by those who are stung.

As it was all too heavy to fly away with, the wasp dragged it along the ground with much labour and incessant fuss . . .

Of the disease there is no doubt, and that it could be cured by dancing stimulated by music is a natural conclusion. Each patient indulged in long and violent exercise, which produced profuse perspiration; he then fell exhausted, slept calmly, and awoke cured.

For the best part of a day Tom lay stretched on his face in the sun. Like David the psalmist, he refused to be comforted. A profound and silent melancholy subdued the wandering spirit which invariably manifests itself on Sunday. He just "sweated out" the day he usually devotes to hunting, and on Monday was himself again, save for a greyish blue tinge encircling each of the little wounds on his arm . . .

The local name of the house-haunting "tarantula", though befitting and unique, imposes a singularly slight strain upon the resources of the alphabet. What combination of eight letters could be softer and more coaxing? And yet the startled Eves of Dunk Island were wont not only to specialise the spider but to shriek out affright at its unexpected presence by the exclamation "Oo-boo-boo!"

To prove that the "oo-boo-boo" is not always victorious in the fights which take place in the dark, let me tell of a combat between a giant and a slim-waisted orange and black wasp. The latter buzzed about angrily, and, following up a feint, stung the "oo-boo-boo", which became nerveless on the instant and fell. As it was all too heavy to fly away with, the wasp dragged it along the ground with much labour and incessant fuss. The terra-cotta larder was in a hollow log, and only after immense exertions and many failures was the limp carcass tugged to the spot. Then there was more buzzing than ever, for the wasp discovered that its prey was many sizes too large for the clay compartment prepared for it. No amount of trampling and shoving of the limp tarantula was of any avail. Several minutes elapsed before the obvious fact dawned upon the baffled insect. Then it abandoned its efforts at compression, and with many loads of moist clay moulded a special compartment in which the tarantula, still in a state of suspended animation, was snugly stowed.

Just one more. A wasp dropped on the bench a few inches from my nose — a tiny wasp with a rollicking gait. Closer inspection showed half a wasp only. It had been neatly severed at the delicate waist, and on the thatch above was an "oo-boo-boo" — a big "oo-boo-boo" — and it seemed to me to be beaming with that broad, self-satisfied expression that the cat wears when it has eaten the canary.

OF FROGS, SNAKES AND FOUR-FOOTED CREATURES

" . . . a death adder was seen gliding among thickly strewn brown leaves with a limp bird between its jaws . . ."

MUSICAL FROGS

A marked feature of the wet season is the varied chant of happy frogs. During the day silence is the rule. A low gurgle of content at the sounding rain is occasionally heard on the part of a flabby, moist creature unable to restrain its sentiments until the approach of evening. But as the sun sets, each of the countless host utters a song of thankfulness and pleasure. To the unappreciative it may appear merely an inharmonious vocal go-as-you-please, in which each frog is the embodiment of the idea that upon its jubilant efforts the honour and reputation of the race as vocalists depend. But to one class of listener the opera is decently if not scientifically constituted. There is the loud and cheerful, if not shrill, bleating of the soprano, the strenuous booming of the bass, the velvety softness and depth of the contralto and the thin high tenor. Hordes of the alert, sharp-featured, far-leaping grass frog represent the chorus, and they have a perfectly rehearsed theme. Down on the flat along the edge of the pandanus grove the preliminary chords are uttered — a merry, unreflective, chirrupy strain, gay as "the Fishermen's Chorus". The motif is taken up nearer among the coconuts, and is in full swing in the pools below the terrace. Thence the sound passes on through the wattles and bloodwoods to the narrow tea-tree swamp lined with dwarf bamboos and dies in echoes in the distance. A brief interlude, and the pandanus choir gives voice again, stronger and resonant; the companions of the coconuts join lustily, the strain reverberates from the wet lands below, resounds through the forest, and is lost in the mellow distance of the tea-trees. And so the sound rises and falls, swells and dwindles away in chords and harmonies, until presently every amphibian is alert and tremulous with emotion and emulation . . .

There is the loud and cheerful, if not shrill, bleating of the soprano . . .

A Death Adder and a Bird

It may be edifying to confess a particular interest in man's first enemy — not such interest as the man of science displays when he seeks to add to the knowledge of the world, but a kind of social concern. None of us is likely to forget that on the authority of Holy Writ the serpent became familiar with mankind very shortly after his appearance on earth, and whispered injurious secrets into guileless ears. Ever since the scene in the Garden of Eden, war between man and the serpent has prevailed, and now, if we are to credit the sayings of the wise, the end of all reptiles, if not actually in view, cannot be long postponed. Is it not meet, therefore, to take fair opportunity of studying the characteristics and qualities of an animal, closely associated with us by fable and in fact, which is doomed to extinction by the ruthless strides of civilisation, which is regarded by some as cleanly and decent, and by others as repulsive and direful? . . .

Occasionally quite casual happenings and bare and slight matters of fact show that those who study natural history first-hand acquire information not to be obtained from authoritative works. Let one instance concerning the varied diet of the death adder be quoted, since it confounds the experience of one of the most learned men in Australia on the subject. On the beach just at high-water mark, beneath an overhanging shrub, several birds sounded an alarm, notifying by peculiar and persistent screeching the presence of an enemy. After a few minutes' search, for the strained attitudes of the birds indicated the direction, a death adder was seen gliding among thickly strewn brown leaves with a limp bird between its jaws . . . a dusky honey-eater . . . Dusky honey-eaters generally spend their days among the topmost sprays of flowering trees and shrubs, while death adders habitually seek the seclusion of the shadiest places on the surface of the soil. In this case the adder was small, so small that it seemed to be a vain if not impossible feat for it to swallow the bird.

Hitherto the food of the adder had been deemed to be frogs, lizards, beetles, and such game of the ground. Was it curiosity which brought the sun-loving bird within reach of the shade-loving snake?

FIGHT TO A FINISH

With logic as absolute as that of the grape that can "the two-and-twenty jarring sects confute", Nature sets at naught the most ancient of axioms. How obvious is it that the lesser cannot contain the greater! Yet that Nature under certain circumstances blandly puts her thumb unto her nose and spreads her fingers out even at that irrefragable postulate, let this plain statement of fact stand proof.

Where the grass was comparatively sparse a little lizard, upon whose bronze head the sunlight glistened, sighted on a chip a lumbering "March" fly dreaming of blood, and with a dash that almost eluded observation seized and shook it. With many sore gulps and excessive straining — for the lizard was young and tender — the tough old fly was swallowed. While the lizard licked its jaws and twirled its tail with an air of foppish self-concern and haughty pride, a withered leaf not three inches away stirred without apparent cause, and in a flash a tiny death adder grappled the lizard by the waist. The grey leaf had screened its approach.

Both rolled over and over, struggling violently. For a minute or two there was such an intertwining and confusion of sinuous bodies that it was impossible to distinguish one from the other. The grip of the death adder was not to be lightly shaken off. When "time" was called, the truce lasted several minutes. Then the wrestling was continued in a miniature cyclone of sand and grass-chips. All the energy was on the part of the lizard. The death adder kept on doing nothing in a dreadfully determined way. In fighting weight the combatants seemed to be fairly equally matched, but in length the lizard had the advantage by at least two inches. The adder was slightly the bulkier. At times the lizard, full of pluck, would scamper away a few inches, dragging the adder, or would claw the sand into tiny, ineffectual furrows in vain efforts. The adder was never able to shake the lizard; it merely maintained its grip. All the wit and sprightliness of the fight was on the part of the lizard, which lashed its foe with its pliant tail, and endeavoured so to swerve as to bite. Both were light weights. One was all dash and sportive agileness; the other played a dull waiting game with admirable finesse.

In spite of the greater activity and muscular power of the lizard, the combat seemed unfair, for in the cunning persistency of the frail but determined little snake there was something uncanny and nerve-shaking. For fully ten minutes the fight continued. The violent antics of the lizard became less and less frequent. Obviously the tactics of the snake were wearing it down. Though the lizard seemed to have lost none of its spirit, the flesh was becoming weak. While it panted, its eyes twinkled with inane ferocity, and the snake, with that peculiar fearsome, gliding movement — neither wriggle nor squirm — typical of the species, slowly edged its victim under the shadow of a tussock. There both reposed, the snake calm in craft and design, the lizard waiting for the one chance of its life. Swallowing the lizard under any circumstances seemed an impossible feat. To begin the act in the middle of the body was absolutely beyond accomplishment. There would come a time when the death adder must release its hold to re-seize its prey by the head or tail, and if the soul of the lizard could possess itself in patience until that moment, and take advantage of it, all might be well.

Now, it seemed to me, the only witness to this fateful fray, that both parties to it knew that the crisis had yet to come. The lizard reserved all its energy for a supreme effort — for one leap to liberty and life — while its impassive foe stolidly concentrated its powers in the direction of an instantaneous release and a fresh grip at a convenient part. Thus they lay. A thrill of excitement possessed me as I watched. The flashing alertness of a fly-catching lizard, is it not proverbial? Which was to be the master — the more muscular creature with four legs, the whole previous existence of which had depended upon its agility, or the subtle, slow snake, which moves under ordinary circumstances not very much faster than a clammy worm? As I watched with all possible keenness a grey blur followed by bewildering wrigglings and contortions

144

indicated a new manoeuvre. Then instead of two reptiles at right angles, there appeared to be but one, and with a tail at each end! The head of the lizard was in the jaws of the death adder. The fatal quickness of the snake had decided the combat.

But the lizard was not yet resigned to its fate. It rolled and reared and wriggled, tossing and tumbling the adder; but all in vain.

Alas! light-hearted lizard, servant and trustful companion of man, thou art joined in woeful issue! There can be no deliverance for thy jewelled head from that slow, all-absorbing chancery! No striving, no pushing with frenzied fingers, no lashing with that whip-like tail may now avail. Never more may you bask and blink in the glare, or doze in the knife-edged shadows, or pounce upon gauze-winged flies. Thou hast learned too late that snakes, like democracy, never restore anything.

I waited for the finish, which came with painful slowness. The sides of the victim heaved and quivered even as they slowly disappeared, and the end of that once foppish tail twitched sadly as it hung limply from the jaws of the gorged snake.

Although it had practically demonstrated that the lesser can contain the greater, the snake was but triflingly increased in girth. It was just in that phenomenal condition which entitled it to the honour of preservation in a solution of formalin.

Swallowing the lizard under any circumstances seemed an impossible feat.

COOM-BEE-YAN THE ECHIDNA

While the bird life of our island is plentiful and varied, mammalian is insignificant in number. The echidna, two species of rats, a flying fox, and two bats, comprise the list. Although across a narrow channel marsupials are plentiful, there is no representative of that typical Australian order here, and the Dunk Island blacks have no legends of the existence of either kangaroos, wallabies, kangaroo rats or bandicoots in times past . . .

Though the drawings in caves depict lizards, echidna, turtle and men, there is no representation of kangaroo or wallaby. It is highly probable that if such had been common, the black artists would have chosen them as subjects, since nearly all their studies are from Nature.

The largest and heaviest four-footed creature now existent on Dunk Island is the so-called porcupine (spiny ant-eater or echidna). An animal which possesses some of the features of the hedgehog of old England, and resembles in others that distinctly Australian paradox, the platypus, which has a mouth which it cannot open — a mere tube through which the tongue is thrust, which in the production of its young combines the hatching of an egg as of a bird, with the suckling of a mammal, and which also has some of the characteristics of a reptile, cannot fail to be an interesting object to every student of the marvels of Nature. When disturbed, the echidna resolves itself into a ball, tucking its long snout between its forelegs, and packing its barely perceptible tail close between the hind ones, presenting an array of menacing prickles whencesoever attacked. While in this ball-like posture, the animal, as chance affords, digs with its short strong legs and steel-like claws, tearing asunder roots, and casting aside stones, and the ease and rapidity with which it disappears in soft soil are astonishing . . .

By the blacks the echidna, which is known as "coom-bee-yan", is placed on the very top of the list of those dainties which the crafty old men reserve for themselves under awe-inspiring penalties.

. . . the ease and rapidity with which it disappears in soft soil are astonishing . . .

FRUGIVOROUS RATS

Next in size to the echidna is the white-tipped rat, water-loving, nocturnal in its habits, fierce and destructive . . . A collateral circumstance revealed absolute proof of its existence, which had previously depended upon vague statements of the blacks. Cutting firewood in the forest one morning, I came across a carpet snake, twelve feet long, laid out and asleep in a series of easy curves, with the sun revealing unexpected beauty in the tints and in the patterns of the skin. Midway of its length was a tell-tale bulge, and before the axe shortened it by a head, I was convinced that here was a serpent that had waylaid and surprised or beguiled a fowl. Post-mortem examination, however, proved once more the unreliability of uncorroborated circumstantial evidence. The snake . . . had swallowed a white-tailed rat . . .

Next comes the little frugivorous rat of russet brown, with a glint of gold on its fur tips. A delicate, graceful creature, nice in its habits, with a plaintive call like the cheep of a chicken; preferring ripe bananas and pineapple, but consenting to nibble at other fruits, as well as

. . . inspection at close quarters showed how she had converted herself into a novel perambulator.

grain. The mother carries her young crouched on her haunches, clinging to her fur apparently with teeth as well as claws, and she manages to scuttle along fairly fast, in spite of her encumbrances. The first that I saw bearing away her family to a place of refuge was deemed to be troubled with some hideous deformity aft, but inspection at close quarters showed how she had converted herself into a novel perambulator. I am told that no other rodent has been observed to carry its young in this fashion. Perhaps the habit has been acquired as a result of insular peculiarities, the animal, unconscious of the way of its kind on the mainland, having invented a style of its own, "ages ahead of the fashion".

Mr C. W. de Vis, M.A., of the Queensland Museum, who has considerately examined specimens of this rat, pronounces it to be extraordinary, in that it combines types of three genera — the teeth of the mus, the mammae of the mastacomys and the scales on the tail of the genus *Uromys*. In the bestowal of a name he has favoured the latter genus. The animal has been introduced to the scientific world under the title *Uromys banfieldi* . . .

LIFE OF THE SEA

"A coral reef is gorged with a population of varied elements viciously disposed towards each other."

NATURE'S CRUEL BATTLEFIELD

We talk of the strenuous life of men in cities. Go to a coral reef and see what the struggle for existence really means . . . In these fervid and fecund waters life is real, life is earnest. Here, are elaborately armoured crayfish, upon which the most gaudy colours are lavished; grotesque crabs, fish brilliant in hue as humming-birds. Life, darting and dashing, active and alert, crawling and slithering, slow and stationary, swarms in these marine groves.

A coral reef is gorged with a population of varied elements viciously disposed towards each other. It is one of Nature's most cruel battlefields, for it is the brood of the sea that "plots mutual slaughter, hungering to live". Molluscs are murderers and the most shameless of cannibals. No creature at all conspicuous is safe, unless it is agile and alert, or of horrific aspect, or endowed with giant's strength, or is encased in armour. A perfectly inoffensive crab, incapable of inflicting injury to anything save creatures of almost microscopic dimensions, assumes the style and demeanour of a ferocious monster, ready at a moment's notice to cry havoc, and let loose the dogs of war. Another hides itself as a rugged nodule of moss-covered stone; its limbs so artfully stowed away that detection would be impossible did it not occasionally betray itself by a stealthy movement . . . Under the loose rocks and detached lumps of coral for one live there will be scores of dead shells. The whole field is strewn with the relics of perpetual conflict, resolving and being resolved into original elements . . . The very bulwarks of limestone are honeycombed by tunnelling shells. A glossy black, torpedo-shaped creature cuts a tomb for itself in the hard lime. Though it may burrow inches deep with no readily visible inlet, cutting and grinding its cavity as it develops in size and strength, yet it is not safe. Fate follows in insignificant guise, drills a tiny hole through its shell, and the toilsomely excavated refuge becomes a sepulchre. Even in the fastness of the coral "that grim sergeant death is strict in his arrest". All is strife — war to the death. If eternal vigilance is the price of liberty among men, what quality shall avert destruction where insatiable cannibalism is the rule. There is but one creature that seems to make use of the debris of the battlefield — the hermit crab, which but half armoured must to avert extermination fit itself into an empty shell, discarding as it grows each narrow habitation for a size larger. Disconsolate is the condition of the hermit crab who has outgrown his quarters, or has been enticed from them or "drawn" by a cousin stronger than he, or who has had the fortune to be ejected without dismemberment. The full face of the red blue-spotted variety is an effective menace to any ordinary foe, and that honourable part is presented at the front door when the tenant is at home. For safety's sake the flabby gelatinous, inert rear end must be tucked and hooked into the convolutions of the shell, deprived of which he is at the mercy of foes very much his inferior in fighting weight and truculent appearance. The disinterested spectator may smile at the vain, yet frantically serious efforts of the hermit to coax his flabby rear into a shell obviously a flattering misfit. But it is not a smiling matter to him. Not until he has exhausted a programme of ingenious attitudes and comic contortions is the attempt to stow away a No. 8 tail into a No. 5 shell abandoned. When a shell of respectable dimensions is presented, and the grateful hermit backs in, settles comfortably, arrays all his weapons against intruders, and peers out with an expression of ferocious content, smiles may come, and will be out of place only when the aches of still increasing bulk force him to hustle again for still more commodious lodgings . . .

The congested state of a coral reef, and the inevitable result thereof — perpetual war of species and shocking cannibalism . . . Another result of the overcrowding . . . Possibly there may be those who are disinclined to credit the statement that some of the denizens take in lodgers. But the fact remains. Having ample room and to spare within their own walls, they offer hospitality to homeless and unprotected strangers, whom graceless Nature has not equipped to take part in the rough-and-tumble struggle for existence outside. A tender-hearted pinna mollusc accepts the company of a beautiful form of mantis-shrimp — tender, delicate and affectionate — which dies quickly when removed from its asylum, as well as a singular creature which has no charm of character, and must be the dullest sort of lodger possible to imagine. It is a miniature eel, which looks as if it had been drawn out of rock crystal or perfectly clear glass. There is no apparent difference between the head and the tail, save that one end tapers more gradually than the other. Very limited power of motion has been bestowed upon it. It cannot wriggle. It merely squirms in the extremity of laziness or lassitude. These two keep the pinna company — the lively shrimp, pinkish brown and green with pin-point black eyes, and the little eel as bright and as transparent yet as dull and insipid as glass. One of the oysters attracts the patronage of a rotund crab, which in some respects resembles a tick, and a great anemone a brilliant fish — scarlet and silver defined with purple hair lines — which on alarm retires within the ample folds of its host.

The flowers of a coral reef live. A bouquet of lavender-coloured, tender, orderly spikes has a gentle rhythmical, swaying movement. A touch, and by magic the colour is gone — naught remains but a dingy brown lump on the rock, whence water oozes. Another form of plant-like life takes the colour of rich green — the green of parsley — and faints at the touch, as does the sensitive plant of the land. Another strange creature, roughly saucer-shaped, but deep grey mottled with white and brown, continuously waves its serrated edges and pulsates at the centre. It starts and stops, contracts and withdraws steadily into the sand upon interference.

One of the shrimps, (*Gonodactylus chiragra*), in my experience found only far out on the reef

For safety's sake the flabby, gelatinous, inert rear end must be tucked . . . into the convolutions of the shell . . .

at dead low-water winter spring-tides, might be taken as a display collection in miniature of those gems of purest ray serene which the dark unfathomed caves of ocean bear. The emerald-green tail is fringed with transparent golden lace; the malachite body has the sheen of gold; the chief legs are of emerald with ruby joints, and silvery claws; the minor as of amber, while over all is a general sheen of ornamentation of points and blotches of sapphire blue. Long white antennae, delicate and opaque, spring from the head. The decorative hues are not laid on flat, but are coarsely powdered and sprinkled as in the case of one of the rarest of Brazilian butter-flies, and they live. Picture a moss-rose with the "moss" all the colours of the rainbow, on which the light plays and sparkles, and you have an idea of the effect of the jewellery of this lustrous crustacean. Yet it is not for human admiration. Its glints speedily dim in the air. To be gobbled up by some hungry fish is the ordinary fate of the species. Possibly splendour is bestowed upon the shrimp as a means by which certain fish distinguish a particularly choice dainty, and the fish show the very acme of admiration by "wolfing" it. Thus are the examples of high art in Nature remorselessly ravished.

Quite distinct is the unconscious genius which now demands brief reference to its perfections. Though a brilliant example of the employment of unattractive deceptive features, it has no individual comeliness — not an atom of grace, no style of its own. Every feature, attitude and movement is subordinate to the part it plays. Death being the penalty, it may not blunder. Behold, among acres of similar growth, a trivial collection of rough, short weeds of the sea — grey, green and mud-coloured. This microcosm glides and stops. The movement is barely perceptible; the intervals of rest long and frequent. An untimely slide as the chance

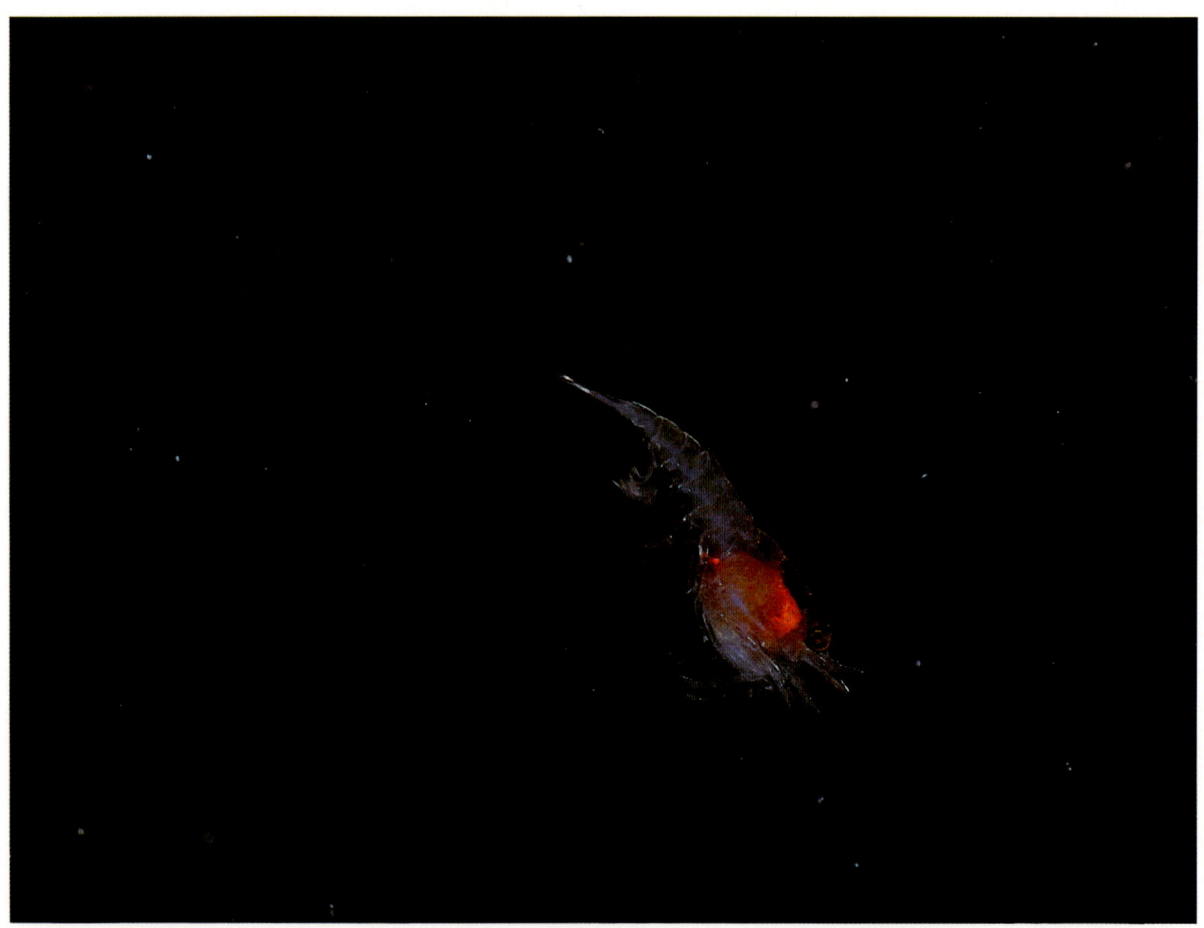

Possibly splendour is bestowed . . . as a means by which certain fish distinguish a particularly choice dainty . . .

gaze of the observer is directed to the spot, betrays that here is the centre of independent life and motive. The dwarf, unkempt weeds cloak a meek, weak, shrinking crab, whose frail claws and tufted legs are breeched with muddy moss, and whose oddly-shaped body is obscured by parasitic vegetation and realistic counterfeits thereof. Inspection, however critical, makes no satisfactory definition between the real and the artificial algae, so perfectly do the details of the moving marine garden blend with the fringes and fur of the animal's rugged and misshapen figure and deformed limbs. As an artistic finish to a marvellous piece of mummery, in one of the crude green claws is carried a fragment of coral, green with the mould of the sea. It and the claw are indistinguishable until, in the faintest spasm of fright, the crab abandons the coral, and shrinking within itself becomes inanimate — as steadfast a patch of weeds as any other of the reef. Recovering slowly from its fright, and conscious of the necessity for each detail of its equipment and insignia, the lowly crustacean timidly re-grips the coral, and holding it aloft, glides discreetly on its way, invisible when stationary, most difficult to detect when it moves.

To see the coral garden to advantage you must pass over it — not through it. Drifting idly in a boat in a calm clear day, when the tips of the tallest shrubs are submerged but a foot or so, and all the delicate filaments, which are invisible or lie flat and flaccid when the tide is out, are waving, twisting and twining, then the spectacle is at its best. Tiny fish, glowing like jewels, flash and dart among the intricate interlacing branches, or quiveringly poise about some slender point — humming-birds of the sea, sipping their nectar. A pink translucent fish no greater than a leadpencil wriggles in and out of the lemon-coloured coral. Another of the John Dory shape, but scarcely an inch long, blue as a sapphire with gold fins and gold-tipped tail, hovers over a miniature blue-black cave. A shoal darts out, some all old-gold, some green with yellow damascene tracery and long yellow filaments floating from the lower lip. A slender form, half coral pink, half grey, that might swim in a walnut shell, displays its transparent charms . . . Another handsome creature of olive green with blue wavy stripes and spots has the shape of a garfish, and to counterbalance a long tubular snout, a slender filament resembling the bare feather shaft of some bird of paradise extending from the tail.

With all its fantastic beauty a coral reef is cruel. Nearer the shore the stony blocks are overspread by masses of that singular skeleton-less coral, known as alcyonaria — partaking of the nature of rubber and of leather — an ugly, repulsive, tyrannous growth, overrunning and killing other and more delicate corals, as undesirable pests crowd out useful and becoming vegetation. It occurs in varying colours and forms — sickly green and grey, bronze and yellow, brown and pink. Loathsome, resembling offal in some aspects as the receding tide lays it bare, it becomes pretty and interesting when covered with calm, limpid water, and its dull life flourishes with star-like, living flowers.

WATERY METEORS

A moonless, cloudless night. The little praam takes the ground in the bay a few yards from the beach, and in the midst of a constellation of "jelly-fishes" spherical in form and varying in size. The larger are so many pale blue orbs floating lazily in a luminous mist, the only visible manifestation of life being a delicate but rhythmical deepening of the central hue. The wash of my wading seems not to affect them. I become conscious of the sudden appearance and swift disappearance of lesser spheres of startling brilliance. They emerge from nothingness, pause for a moment, and shoot towards me with extraordinary impulse. Each is a mere globule, resplendently blue. The tint intensifies as with accelerated velocity the atom flies until of its own excessive energy it explodes with a shell-like flash, leaving a sinuous trail of golden light. To burst into sight, gather force, to flash and slowly vanish — such is the sum of life of a speck of sea-jelly. To be the centre towards which scores of the watery meteors gravitate, to witness their apparently spontaneous beginning, their swift, brief, but ineffectual career and lingering end, delights this night of darkness. How many of the race of man are there whose post-mortem glory outshines life tenfold?

. . . of its own excessive energy it explodes with a shell-like flash . . .

Each is a mere globule . . .

154

PRIMORDIAL LIFE

From the tinted tips of fragile corals to the ooze on the edge of the beach sand there is seething life. Exposed by the ebb tide, the sun-caressed slime glitters and shimmers, so that if the observer is content to stand still for a few moments he shall see myriads of obscure activities, graceful and uncouth, of the existence of which he has not previously dreamt and among which his footsteps make a desolating track. Perhaps in no other earthly scene do the gradations of life blend so obviously in form and appearance. This mud is primal, fertile with primitives, for similitude of environment checks variations.

In such tepid slime primordial life began, and in it even in these latter days the far beginning of superior things may be discovered actively pursuing their craft and purpose in the order of the universe. Worms are abundant, and among them certain genera which might be taken as apt illustrations of the more significant facts of evolution. Studying them, the parting of the ways between two distinct orders, each having a conspicuous feature in common while differing in appearance and habits generally, is made strangely plain, and I propose in my unversed way to demonstrate the line of upward development in a few examples.

Accepting as a primitive form that deplorably thin, phantasmal worm which excavates in the ooze an appropriately narrow shaft indicated by a dimple, or, in some cases, a swelling mound with a well-defined crater and circular pipe, the ascent of the genealogical tree is not beset with any great difficulty. These worms are grey in colour and shoddy in texture, merely a tough description of slime with a crude head and long, simple filaments. The sides of the shafts are smooth, and on the least alarm the nervous inhabitant retracts with surprising alertness. Slightly superior in grade, but in uninterrupted succession, is a similar worm which solidifies its shaft with a kind of mortar and carries it up above the level of the ooze about an inch or so — a crude effort in the direction of the acquirement of some ease of circumstance. These fluelike projections are more frequent on the verge of the sandy beach.

The next in order — still slim, though of a slightly more robust habit of body — has acquired the art of spinning (caterpillar-like) a cocoon, and of causing to adhere to the exterior thereof grains of sand and minute chips of shell. Though this vestlet is very frail and though the sandy outer coat is liable to drop off (when it collapses altogether), it seems to me to indicate distinct progress, a successful accomplishment in the direction of isolation, independence, and security. Does it not signify that the animal has a certain perception of the knowledge of good and evil such as dawned upon Eve as she ate the diverting apple? Eve forthwith took to fig-leaves; the slim worm knitted a shoddy wrapper and reinforced it with grains of sand when it realised that there was something better than slush for a dwelling ...

A still more highly endowed relation spins a similar fabric, upon which are loosely agglutinated numbers of small dead shells, grit, and even opercula a quarter of an inch in diameter ...

The individual worm next to be described typifies such a wonderful advance that it might almost be designated a subsequent and intrusive sport, so marked are the distinctions it exhibits. It is one of the shell-binders, but its mansion of mosaics is unique and beautiful. In the universal struggle for place, self-preservation, and food, the animal has acquired a higher order of intelligence and keener perceptions of safety and of the niceties of life than its fellows. Living in sand and mud, in obedience to some gracious instinct, it gathers numbers of small shells, grit, and fragments of coral wherewith to construct a tube, somewhat similar in shape to the horn of cornucopia, and from three to six inches long. The materials are cemented together in accordance with a symmetrical design, the interior being lined with a transparent substance, which, when dry, is readily separable from the casing. This creature accomplishes by calculation, choice, and dexterity that which a subtle chemical process does unconsciously for the more advanced mollusc, and that it practised the art of the interlocking of atoms ages before the birth of Macadam can scarcely be doubted.

My imagination loves to dwell on the perceptive faculties possessed by this lowly creature, a creature soft and delicate, merely such and such a length of gelatinous substance, slightly stiffened and toughened and graced with a pair of tentacles glittering like tinsel extruded from a marvellously constructed tube.

In certain structural details the animal (which in appearance has greater resemblance to a caterpillar than a worm) is even more remarkable than the ornate dwelling it constructs, for it is an actual though living prototype of the fabled race (catalogued by Othello with the anthropophagi) —

> *"Whose heads*
> *Do grow beneath their shoulders."*

The paradox exists, not as a whim or grimace on the part of Nature but for a definite and vital end. In default the animal would be unable to obey the first law of Nature — self-preservation — for it is soft-bodied and its dwelling has the serious defect of being open at both ends. In such plight lacking special organs it would be at cruel disadvantage in the struggle for existence. The posterior segment of the body is therefore developed into an operculum-like

. . . the slim worm . . . realised that there was something better than slush for a dwelling . . .

organ, smooth and of horny texture, which closes the narrow end of the tube. The other extremity is more elaborately guarded, the anterior segment being fringed with a frontal membrane, while the second segment forms a disc, the minute mouth orifice with the true tentacles and gills being debased to the third segment.

Confronted by danger, the animal closes its front door by retracting until the disc presses immovably against the circumference of the tube, the retraction being so sudden that a frail spurt betrays the whereabouts of an otherwise secret dwelling-place . . .

With what skill and patience does this pectinarian construct its ornate habitation! How artfully does it pick and choose among the tiny shells and grit! . . . And all this laborious neatness and precision absorbed in the construction of a tenement which has no time! Does the inmate possess any sense of duration? Addison (quoting a French authority) says that it is possible some creatures may think half an hour as long as we do a thousand years! The magnificent mind of the modern biologist regards a million of years as a mere fag-end of time. The industrious worm which has built so choice a home may have enjoyed the sense of comfort and security for a period representing an honourable age, while, according to the standards of man, the home was not worth the building for so short a tenancy.

Do we not see in this astonishing example a highly successful effort of a marine worm to improve on the condition and habits of its barbarous ancestors? Analyse a bulk sample of the building material, and you shall find it not dissimilar from the shell of a mollusc, and the interior film — no doubt a secretion of the animal — is to be safely accepted as analogous to the silky smoothness which molluscs (often of rough and rugged exterior) obtain by nacreous deposit and which finds its culmination in the gold-lip mother-of-pearl?

A Pearl in the Making

On a calm and luminous day I waded, disrobed, in shallow water as limpid as the fictitious stream which legend says King Solomon improvised at the foot of his throne when the Queen of Sheba attended his court. Lifting her robes — for she imagined the crossing of the water to be a ceremonial device — the gorgeous Queen displayed her shapely calves. The water resting on the verge of the lovely Isle was as delusively clear, but was not deceptive . . .

In the middle of a clump of brown seaweed, which had fallen apart like the neatly dressed hair of a woman, was a black streak, signifying the gape of a wedge-shaped mollusc known as a pinna. The gape was about as long as the parting of a woman's hair and about thrice as wide. As I crouched to note the functions of the animal, my shadow intervened and the caution of the creature was roused, the valves closing so that no sign of the presence of the shell was distinguishable among the slightly wavering, minute particles of algae. Changing my position, so that the pinna might not be deprived of its share of the rays of the sun, the valves soon furtively opened. A slight movement on my part and they closed again, without having revealed any hidden charms.

After a few minutes, a certain confidence being established between us, the pinna emerged from its retirement, in so far as such creatures are permitted by Nature. The mantle of this particular species is shown as a delicate fringe of lace in old gold and black. It ripples along the upper edges of the confining valves, which are intensely black with a pearly lustre. The pretty movements of the mantle — like the swinging of the skirts of a well-apparelled damsel — attracted admiration, and on peering into the shell a glimpse of something precious was obtained.

Tossed and twirled about just below the old gold fringe was a black pearl about the size of a pea. The prize was safe. Without risk of loss it could be watched in its unceasing revolutions. It seemed as if the animal, with automatic perseverance, attempted to eject the incubus, the weight of which kept it about an inch below the aperture of the valves. Such motion would naturally tend to perfection. Whatsoever its lustre, it would certainly be a sphere. Besides, it was a pearl in the making. As long as it remained within the pinna and it could not be voluntarily rejected, its size would inevitably increase. It was the rolling stone to which time and the secretions of the animal would add weight and, peradventure, beauty . . .

Was it possible for human nature to deny itself so easily gotten and pretty a prize? I confess, though the possibility of the pearl increasing in size and loveliness was obvious, that the fact that pinnas are subject to ills, chances, and mishaps, was also recognised. Left to be slowly tossed about, the pearl would become greater; but size, though an important feature, is not the only desirable quality. And while it grew might not another barefooted beachcomber discover it? Or might not one of the many unintelligent admirers of the pinna itself find entrance by drilling or by the violent crushing of the valves, and, ignoring the treasure, destroy the organs and the substance by and from which it was being delicately elaborated? Suppose, I argued, I remove the gaping shell, I shall no longer be able to enjoy the rare, the unique pleasure of presiding over the gradual perfection of a pearl, an aesthetic advantage to which I alone had been made free. Could present possession of a little sphere of carbonate of lime, polished and sooty black, compensate for the continuance of the chaste joy of watching one of the most covert and intimate processes of Nature? Balancing the immediate material gain against the inevitable moral loss, I was almost persuaded to self-denial, when, with a sudden impulse, begot of the consciousness of rightful acquisition, the pinna was forcibly yet carefully drawn out of the sand in which it was deeply embedded and in which it was anchored by toughened byssus. Directly the valves were prised apart the pearl fell into my hand . . .

A Fantastic Patchwork

For richness of colour and diversity of design some of the lovely corals and sponges, which seem to counterfeit the inventions and contrivances of man, and the algae, and those anomalous "growths" which fixedly adhere to the under surface of stones and blocks of coral debris, are not to be surpassed. These dull stones, partly buried in sand, reveal in blotches, daubs, and smears the crude extravagances of a painter's palette. Can it be that such brilliant colours and tints, so profuse and delicate, are necessary features of animals of such crude organisms that they appear to be merely disembodied splashes and driblets from the brush of the Great Artist? Look at this fantastic patchwork, brightening the obscurity of an upturned stone with glowing orange. In perfectly regular minute dots a pattern of quartered squares, raised slightly in the centre, is being worked out. Many of the squares are finished, but the fabric is rugged at the edges, where, with miraculous precision, the design is being followed, each tiny stitch the counterpart of its fellow. Unless this gross and formless blotch of sage green interferes or this disc of royal blue expands, the whole under surface of the stone may be covered with an orange-coloured quilt as dainty as if wrought by fairy fingers . . .

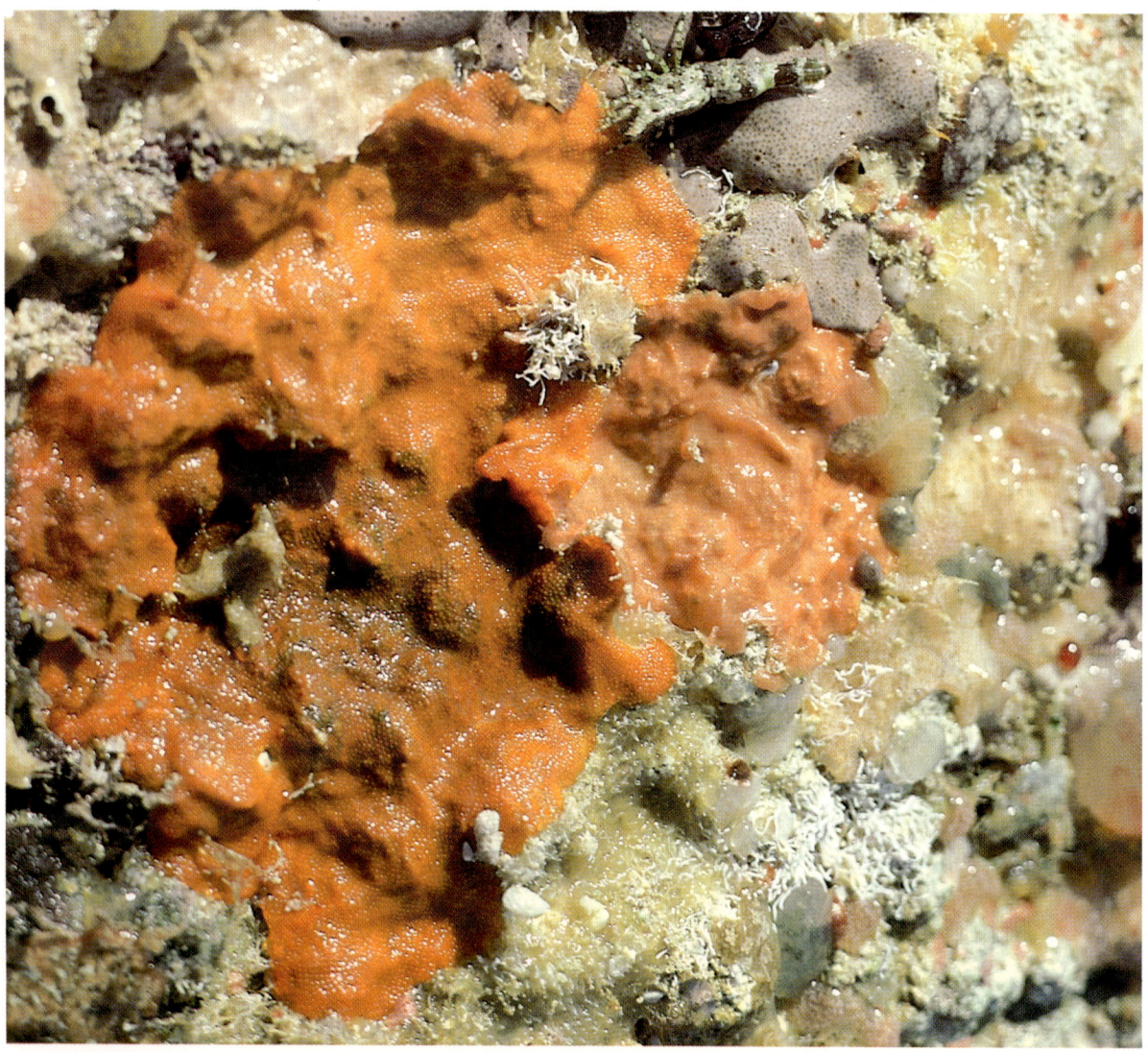

These dull stones . . . reveal . . . the crude extravagances of a painter's palette.

160

THE ANEMONE AND THE FISH

During the cool season the tides on the coast of North Queensland offer peculiar facilities to the observer of the thousand and one marvels of the tropic sea. Spring tides throughout the warm months range low at night and high during the day. In other words, the lowest day spring-tide in winter exposes far more of the reefs than the lowest day tide of summer, while the highest night tide of summer sweeps away the data of the corresponding tide of winter. When, therefore, the far receding water makes available patches of coral reef exposed at other times of the year merely to the cool glimpses of the moon, I am driven to explore them with an eagerness, if not of a treasure-seeker or in the frenzies of naturalistic fervour, at least with the enthusiasm of an ardent student.

It may be that most of the sights which are revealed are of common knowledge among scientific men, and if one is inclined to preach a little sermon on the text of the living stones and polyps and animated jelly, and if such text be trite, let it be granted that the sermon is at least original. Necessarily the sermon will lack commentary and application, and be very imperfect in many other details. If it possesses any virtues, you must apply them personally, for the preacher is not enlightened enough to expound them even to his own, much less to the satisfaction of others.

In many places on this reef little secrets, well kept throughout the rest of the year, are boldly proclaimed when the sea retreats. A fairly common one is a huge anemone of a rich cobalt blue which opens out like a soup-plate with convoluted edges. Another has a form something resembling a hyacinth-glass. The more public parts are not unlike a dwarf growth of that old-fashioned flower the Prince of Wales's feather, save that the colour is a rich brown. Being an animal, it possesses senses in which the most highly specialised vegetable is deficient. It has the power of waving its spikelets, and of the thousand of truncated tentacles which cover the spikelets each seems to possess independent action. Though all, no doubt, contribute to the sustenance of the animal, they, at will, rest from their labours or assume great activity.

It is natural to suppose that the diet of such an animal must be of microscopic proportions. The other day I happened on one which had seized a fish about four inches long, and seemed to be greedily sucking it to death. The fish was still alive, and as it looked up at me with a pathetic gleam in its watery eyes, I released it. It was very languid — indeed, so feeble and faint that it could not swim away. Aid had come too late. The fish was the legitimate prey of the anemone. My interference had been at variance from the laws of property and right. As the vestige of life which remained to the fish was all too fragile for salvation, and as I saw the chance of ascertaining whether the anemone had consciously seized it, or whether it had by mishap blundered against the anemone and had been arrested for its intrusion, I placed the fish close to the enemy. I am certain the anemone made an effort to reach it. There was a decided swing of one of the spikes in the direction of the fish, and decided agitation among the hundreds of minute tentacles. When I, in the interests of remorseless truth, placed the fish in the anemone it was immediately held fast, the activity on the part of the tubes subsiding with an air of satisfaction at the same moment.

It is well known that sea anemones do assimilate such robust and rich diet as living fish. If one's finger is presented the spikelets adhere to it. I cannot describe the sensation as seizure, for it is all too delicate for that; but at least one is conscious of a faint sucking pull. If the finger is rudely withdrawn, some of the tentacles which have taken a firm hold are torn away. Again, the animal is often found apparently asleep, for it is languid and listless, and will not respond to the bait of a finger, however coaxingly presented.

There is another giant anemone known to the blacks as "pootah-pootah", the inner, reflexed, convoluted edges of which are covered with tentacles of brown with yellow terminals. This is friendly to fish — at any rate to one species. It is the landlord or host of one of the prettiest fish of all the wide, wide sea, and seems proud of the company of its guest, and the fish is so dependent upon its host as to be quite helpless apart from it. The fish, (*Amphiprion* species) "intel-intel" of the blacks, is said to be commensal (literally, dining at the same table with its host), as distinguished from the parasite, which lives on its host.

The good-fellowship between the dainty fish — resplendent in carmine, with a broad collar, and waist-band of silvery lavender (or rather silver shot with lavender) and outlined with purple — and the great anemone is apparent . . . the beautiful fish on the least alarm retires within the many folds of its host, entirely disappearing, presently to peep out again shyly at the intruder. It is almost as elusive as a sunbeam, and most difficult to catch, for if the anemone is disturbed it contracts its folds, and shrinks away, offering inviolable sanctuary. If the fish be disassociated from its host, it soon dies . . .

However, it is safe to assert that the association between the stolid anemone and the painted fish — only an inch and a half long — is for their mutual welfare, the fish attracting microscopic food to its host.

. . . the beautiful fish on the least alarm retires within the many folds of its host . . .

A Sea-hare

The sea-hare is . . . the colour of mud and sand and of coral, dead and sea-stained. It reposes, with its back flush with the surface, beside a block of coral or stone defiantly indistinguishable from the ocean floor — a stolid, solid, inert creature, eight or ten inches long, the under part smooth, presenting the appearance of wet chamois-leather, and irresponsive to touch — "the mother tongue of all the senses". Ugly, loathsome, and tough of texture, it is so helpless that if placed on its side in the sand it is extremely doubtful whether of its own volition it could regain its natural position. The surge of the sea might roll it over, and it might then be able to regain the grovelling attitude essential to life. Otherwise, I am inclined to think fatal results would follow the mere placing of the creature sideways on the sand. It seems to possess but the feeblest spark of life, and yet it has its sentiments and love for its kind, for often three or four are huddled together. And how, it may be asked, is this creature, so apt at concealment and so completely disguised, made visible to human eyes?

The answer is that if by chance the animal is disturbed it makes a supreme effort at further concealment, and that impulse — perfect as it may be when set in opposition to the wit of the creature's nervous and apprehensive enemies — reveals it most boldly to man. From a funnel-shaped opening between two obscure flaps on the back — ordinarily invisible — there is emitted a gush of liquid, royal purple in hue, which stains the sea with an impenetrable dye for yards around. The colour, which is delightfully gorgeous, mingles with the water in jets and curling feathery sprays, enchanting the beholder with unique and ever-changing shapes until a glorious cloud is created and he forgets the ugliness and forgives the humility of the originator in the enjoyment of an artistic treat. If the cloud which Jupiter assumed was of the imperial tone and of the fascinating fashion which the groveller in the mud creates, Aegina would have been superfeminine had she not joyously surrendered . . .

And why should this uncouth creature with scarcely more of life than a lump of coral have within it a fountain filled with Tyrian dye? Why? Because it has enemies; and though it seems to be *sans* mouth, *sans* eyes, *sans* ears, *sans* everything, it is instinct with the first law of Nature — self-preservation.

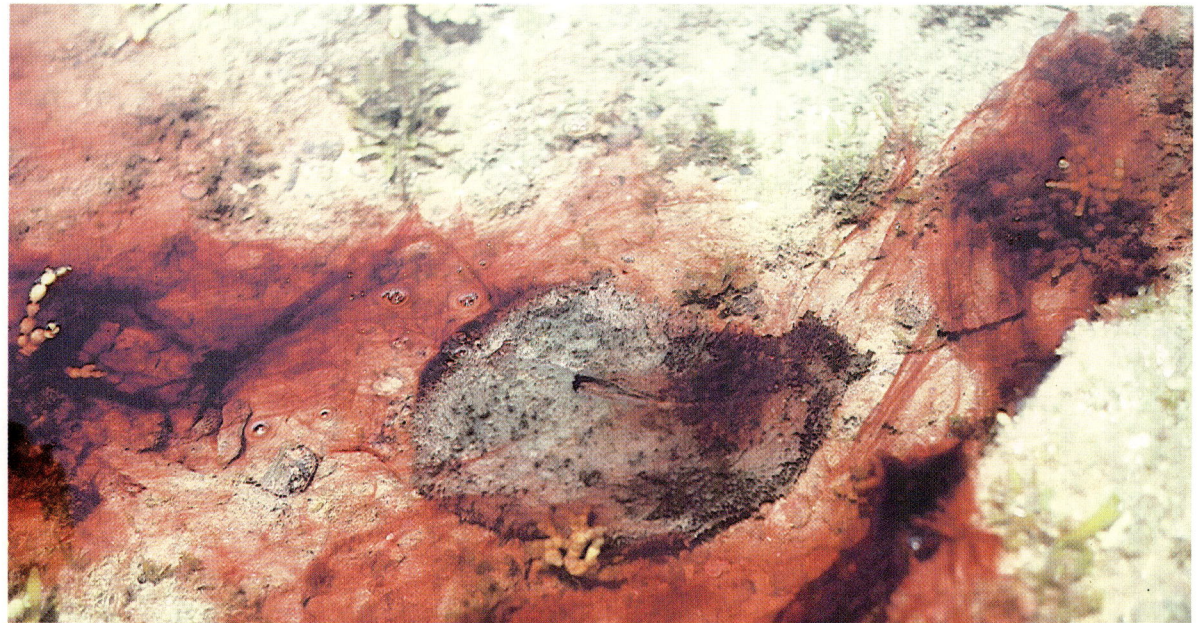

. . . a glorious cloud is created . . .

MASQUERADING AS A SPRAY OF SEAWEED

No one who parades a coral reef can fail to be impressed by the various means adopted by its weaker denizens to evade the consequences of conspicuousness. Among the vast multitude of creatures, mostly hostile to each other, few are more remarkable than the crabs, not only on account of form and habit, but for care of themselves during the periodic casting of their shells. They therefore represent an entertaining study and a never-ending source of pleasure to the observer, who, as he happens on some fantastic member of the family, wonders, remembering his Shakespeare, what impossible matter will Nature make easy next. Dreamy little ripples were laying on the strands sprays of seaweed, torn from the reef which was not quite out of the influence of the easterly swell. The conditions were ordinary, but one fragment made itself noticeable by slight, almost undiscernible, but still distinctive efforts to regain the water, whence it was separated by a few inches. Seaweed alone was visible as it rested on the palm of the hand. Presently it moved hesitatingly and with infinite slowness, and, being reversed, revealed itself as a "watery" crab under living disguise. The specimen was sent to the Australian Museum, Sydney, where it came under the hands of my friend Mr. Allan R. McCulloch, who devotes himself to the phenomena of the sea; and since his references to it are explicit and authoritative, they will be more acceptable than generalities from an uninformed pen: "The crab you sent is the second specimen known of *Zewa banfieldi*, which I described from a dried specimen received from you some years ago. Not only the species, but the genus also, was unknown until you gave me the opportunity of describing this interesting beast. It is one of the spider crabs, most of which have long horns projecting from the rostrum, and are more or less thickly covered with stiff curled setae, to which seaweeds, sponges, and other marine growths — selected according to the taste of the bearer — are attached. When these crabs shed their shells, which they must do periodically to allow of growth, they retire to a dark corner and draw themselves out of a slit between the back and the abdomen, legs and all, which must, I imagine, be a delicate and somewhat painful proceeding" . . .

Masquerading as a spray of seaweed, the crab eludes its enemies, the mask being of such high order that even man, with his perceptions, does not penetrate it unless he exercises his reasoning faculties. Because he knows that a spray of seaweed is not endowed with independent movement, when it does walk about he, at first, is as incredulous as was Macbeth when told of that "moving grove" of Birnam.

No one . . . can fail to be impressed by the various means adopted . . . to evade the consequences of conspicuousness.

A Sand Crab and Bird Policemen

So much of the time of the Beachcomber is spent sweeping with hopeful eyes the breadths of the empty sea, policing the uproarious beaches, overhauling the hordes of roguish reefs, and the medley concealed in cosy coves by waves that storm at the bare mention of the rights of private property, that he cannot avoid casual acquaintance with the scores of animated things which ceaselessly woo him from the pursuit of his calling . . .

Those who know only the great flat, ruddy crabs with ponderous pincers and pugnacious mien, which frequent fishshop windows, can form but a very unflattering opinion of the fancy varieties which people every mile of the Barrier Reef.

The struggle for existence in this vast, crowded, and most cruel of arenas is so appalling that the great crab family has been battered by circumstances into weird and fantastic forms. Only a few come up to the human conception of the beautiful either in figure or colouring. While some shrink from observation, others, though themselves obscure to the vanishing-point, seem to be endowed with a vicious yearning for notoriety.

A certain cute little pursuer of fame is absolutely invisible until you find it stuck fast to one of your toes with a serrated dorsal spur a quarter of an inch long. It is invisible, because Nature sends it into this breathing world masquerading, as she did Richard III, deformed, unfashioned, scarce half made-up. In general appearance it closely resembles a crazy root-stalk of alga — green and not quite opaque, and clinging to such alga it lives, and lives so placidly that it cannot be distinguished from its prototype except by the sense of touch. When you pick it gingerly from between your toes there is a malicious gleam in the pin-point black eyes, and then you understand that it is one of the many inventions designed for the torment of trespassers.

I have often sought specimens of this poor relation of the fishshop window aristocrat, but invariably in vain, until I have found myself suddenly shouting "Eureka!" while balancing myself on one foot eager for the easement of the other, and the giggling demeanour of the imp as it parts company with his spur gives a sort of comic relief to the thrilling sensations of the moment. Upon examination this imp seems to be an example of arrested development. Whimsical fate has played upon it a grim practical joke, flattering it primarily by resemblance to a grotesquely valorous unicorn, and then, having changed her mood to mere pettishness, finished it offhand by adding a section of semi-animate seaweed.

Although among the commonest of the species, the grey sand crab, which burrows bolt-holes in the beaches, is by no means an uninteresting character. Surrounded by enemies, and yet living on the bare, coverless beach, its faculties for self-preservation are exceptionally refined. The eyes are elongated ovals, based on singularly mobile pivots, while the pupils resemble the bubble of a spirit-level. Not only is the range of vision a complete circle, but the crab seems able to concentrate its gaze upon any two given points instantly and automatically. To spite all its skill as a digger, to set at naught its superb visual alertness, the sand crab has a special enemy in the bird policeman which patrols the beach. Vigilant and obnoxiously interfering, the policeman has a long and curiously curved beak, designed for probing into the affairs of crabs, and unless the "hatter" has hastily stopped the mouth of its shaft with a bundle of loose sand — which to the prying bird signifies "Out! Please return after lunch!" — it will be disposed of with scant ceremony and no grace, for the manners of the policeman are shocking.

This quick-footed sand-digger enhances its reputation by the performance of feats of subtlety and skill. Its bolt-hole is sometimes three feet deep, generally on an incline. Piled in a mound the spoil would inevitably betray the site of the operations to the policeman, thus seriously facilitating the duties of that official towards the suppression of the species. From remote depths the crab carries a bundle of sand. You remember the trenchant way in which Pip's sister cut the bread and butter, her left hand jamming the loaf hard and fast against her bib? Just so the crab with its bundle of loose sand, though it has the advantage in the number of limbs which may be pressed into service. The feat of carrying an armful of sliding sand in proportion to bulk about one-third of the body, is far away and beyond the capacities of human beings, but to the crab, which has acquired the trick of temporary consolidation by pressure, it is merely child's play. Arrived at the mouth of the shaft, it elevates its eyes (which in the dark have rested in neatly fitting recesses) for the purpose of a cautious yet sweeping survey. Seeing nothing alarming, it emerges with the alertness of a jack-in-the-box, races several inches, and scatters the load broadcast as the sower of seed who went forth to sow. Then, as suddenly, the crab pauses and flattens itself — its body merging with its surroundings almost to invisibility — preparatory for a spurt for home. During these exertions the intellect of the crab has been concentrated for outwitting the vigilance of enemies, for the plodding policeman is not singular in appreciation. The lordly red-backed sea-eagle occasionally condescends to such humble fare, and the crab must needs be alert to evade the scrutiny with which the eagle searches the sand.

This passing reference to the wit and deftness of the crab would be quite uncomplimentary in default of special notice of the plug of sand with which it stops its burrow. As a rule it is about an inch thick, and in content far more than a crab could carry in a single load. How does the creature, working from below and with such refractory material, so arrange that the plug shall be flush with the surface and sufficiently consolidated to retain its own weight? Of what art in loose masonry has the crab the unique secret? . . .

Unless a crab is a giant in armour, or is endowed with almost supernatural alertness, or is an artist in the art of mimicry, or unless it cultivates some method of rapid disappearance, it has little chance of holding its own in the battle raging unceasingly over the vast areas of the Great Barrier Reef.

. . . the great crab family has been battered by circumstances into weird and fantastic forms.

167

SHARKS AND RAYS

Among the commonest of fish in the shallow waters of the coast are the rays, of which there are many species . . . Some attain enormous size, some display remarkable variations from the accepted type, and at least two are edible though not generally appreciated, for the hunger of the littoral Australian is not as a rule sufficiently speculative to prompt to gastronomic experiment, else food that other nations cherish would not be deemed unclean . . .

The most delicately flavoured of the rays is known as the "blue-spotted". It does not appear to attain a large size, but it is fairly common, and is one of the most comely of the creatures of the coral reefs, the bright blue decorative blotches on a ground of old gold being most effective. It is often found in a few inches of water perfectly motionless, and on being disturbed flutters and glides away swiftly and with little apparent effort. Roasted on an open fire, when a large proportion of the pungent oil escapes, the flesh is pleasant, though possessing the distinctive flavour of the order, which is, however, acceptable at all times to the palate of the black.

One of the formidable sting rays — dark brown in colour, which revels on oysters — has the habit of burying itself in the mud, leaving an angular depression, corresponding to the size of the body, from which the pedestal eyes alone obtrude. In such position it is difficult for the inexperienced to detect the fish until by misadventure it is trodden on, in which circumstance one of two manoeuvres is adopted. Either it flaps and flounders in the slush so that the intruder is startled and jumps clear, or else it lashes out with its whip-like tail in the endeavour to bring into play its serrated weapon, charged with pain, and fearsome on account of the blood-poisoning effect of the mucus with which it is coated.

Ox-rays grow to a great size, their backs being so armoured with thick-set stellate bucklers on a horn-like skin, that to secure them a heavy-hefted weapon and a strong right arm are necessary. But among the largest of the family is that known as the devil fish, which, upon being harpooned, sinks placidly to the bottom, and adhering thereto by suction, defies all ordinary attempts to raise it. This often basks in calm water or swims slowly close to the surface, when the pliant tips of its "wings", appearing at regular intervals above the surface, create the illusion of a couple of large sharks moving along in rhythmic regularity as to speed and muscular movement. Rarely, and apparently only by mischance, does a ray take bait; but when hooked it affords good sport, for its impassive resistance is incomprehensibly great in comparison with its size, and comparable to the pull of a green turtle which in its wanderings has become foul-hooked.

An exciting coursing match entertained me not long since, not only as an exhibition of wonderful speed and agility, but because of the wit with which the weaker creature eluded pursuit. Three hundred yards from the beach the dorsal fin of a huge hammer-head shark obtruded about two feet as it leisurely quartered a favourite hunting-ground. A sudden swirl and splash indicated that game had been sighted, and the next instant an eagle or flying ray leaped out of the sea with prodigious eagerness to reach the beach. In a series of abrupt curves the shark endeavoured to head off the ray, which, as its pursuer gained on it, shot out of the water over the shoulders of the shark, each leap being at least ten feet high. In rising it seemed to switch the shark with its thong-like tail, although apparently in almost despairing fright. After at least a dozen agile and desperate efforts, each timed to just elude the rush of the shark, both came into shallow water in which the quick and regular contours of the shark stirred the mud in a wavy pattern; it became baffled, and in a few seconds the ray slowly, and with infinite caution, "flew" (and that is the correct term to apply to a fish the movements of which in the water are analogous to the flight of a bird) into such meagre depths that the shark would have been stranded had it followed. No ripple indicated its discreet course within a few feet of the water line, and it maintained its way for about two hundred yards parallel with the beach, while the shark furiously quartered the sea off shore.

On the occasion of a similar hunt a ray blundered fatally because of the steeper incline of the beach. When about ten feet off the shore instead of a lateral it took a directly forward "flight", landing six feet up on the dry sand, where it fell an easy victim to a black boy, perhaps not as hungry or as ferocious as the shark, but equally partial to rays as food and incapable of any self-denying act ...

The monstrous grey-striped tiger shark in my experience generally keeps to deep water and hunts singly ... About a hundred yards out from the beach, as we started on a strictly sordid beachcombing expedition to the scene of the squashed wreck of a Chinese sampan, a shark betrayed itself by the dorsal fin quartering the glassy surface of the sea ... Pulling out noiselessly, a trail of oily blood was intersected and the next moment a huge shark appeared, carrying in its jaws a black ray, which it mouthed unceasingly.

Among the commonest of fish in the shallow waters of the coast are the rays ...

DEATH ADDER OF THE SEA

Beware of the stone fish, the death adder of the sea, called also the sea-devil, because of its malice; the warty ghoul because, perhaps, of its repulsiveness; the lion fish, because of its habit of lurking in secret places; the sea scorpion for its venom; and by the blacks "mee-hee". Loathsome, secretive, inert, rough and jagged in outline, wearing tufts and sprays of sea-weed on its back, scarcely to be distinguished from the rocks among which it lurks, it is armed with spines steeped in the cruellest venom. Many fish are capable of inflicting painful and even dangerous wounds, but none is to be more dreaded than the ugly and repulsive "stone fish". Haply, it is comparatively rare. Conceal itself as it may among the swaying seaweed as it lies in ambush ready to seize its prey, or partially bury itself in the mud, it seldom eludes the shrewd observation of the blacks. With a grunt of satisfaction it is impaled with a fish-spear and placed squirming on a rock to be battered to pulp with its prototype — a stone . . .

The stone fish resembles in character and habits the death adder. Its disposition is pacific, it has no frowardness of temper; is never willing to obtrude itself on notice, trusting to immobility and to its similitude to the grey rocks and mud and brown alga to escape detection. Unless it is actually handled or inadvertently trodden upon, it is as innocent and as harmless as a canary. Why then should it be furnished with such dreadful weapons of offence? A full dozen of the keenest of spines, all in a row, extend from the depression at the back of the head towards the tail, each spine hidden in a jagged and uneven fringe, which, when the fish is in its natural element, can scarcely be distinguished from seaweed. Not until the warty ghoul acquires the sagacity which accompanies ripe age and experience, does it encourage deceptive plumes of innocent algae to anchor themselves to its back. Then it is that detection is beyond ordinary skill, and its presence fraught with danger. In a specimen eight inches long, the first spine, counting from the head, can be exposed half an inch, the second and chief fully three-quarters, and the remainder graduate from half to a quarter of an inch. Each spine — clear opal blue — is surrounded by a sac of colourless liquid (presumed to contain the poisonous element), which squirts out as the spine is unsheathed. On the sides, and in lesser numbers on the belly, are irregular rows of miniature craters which on being depressed eject, to a distance of a foot or more, a liquid resembling in colour milk with a tinge of lavender. Fast on the points of a spear the fish gives an occasional and violent spasmodic jerk, when the prettily tinted liquid is ejected from all the little cones. After a pause, during which it seems to concentrate its energies, there is another and another twitch, each the means of sprinkling broadcast what is said to be a corrosive liquid, almost as virulent as vitriol. From almost any part of the body this liquid exudes or can be expelled.

With its upturned cavernous mouth (interiorly a forbidding sickly green), its spines, its cones, its eruptions, its ejecta, its great fan-shaped pectoral fins, and its deformities generally, the stone fish well deserves the specific title of *horrida*. Moreover, has it not a gift which would have brought it to the stake a few score years ago, as a sinful, presumptuous and sacrilegious witch — that of living for an hour or two out of its natural element. It deserves the bad eminence to which it has been raised by the blacks on accounts of looks alone, and if the poisonous qualities are in line with its hideousness, one can but pause and ponder why and wherefore such a creature has existence in "this best of all possible worlds". But it is known that to the Chinese it is dainty. They pay for it with good grace as much as 2s. 6d. per lb., and the flavour is said to resemble crab.

Loathsome, secretive . . . scarcely to be distinguished from the rocks among which it lurks . . .

FOUR THOUSAND LIKE ONE

In the clear water of Brammo Bay, a greenish black object, a yard across by about a yard and a half long, moved slowly along, swaying this way and that, but maintaining a fairly accurate course consistent with the shore. As the boat drifted, it seemed as if an unsophisticated sting-ray had lapsed into the blissfulness of ease, careless alike of mankind and of its enemies in the water. When within reach the boat-hook was used as a spear more to startle the indolent fish than in the vain hope of effecting its capture. The boat-hook passed through what appeared to be the middle of the creature with a splash, and four or five fish, about eight inches long, and of narrow girth, floated away, stunned, killed by the shock. Then it was realised that the apparently solid fish was really a compact mass of little fish, moving along with common impulse and volition, each fish having a sinuous, wriggling motion. So closely were they packed that it was impossible without careful scrutiny to discern individual members of the group, and so intimate their association and so remarkable their mutual sympathy, that they seemed to possess minds with but a single thought, hearts that beat as one. Here were not forty, not four hundred, but more likely four thousand living, moving, and having their being as a single individual . . .

Examining the specimens procured, it was found that they resembled lampreys in shape, olive green in colour, with pale lemon-coloured streaks and marks. Each of the gill cases terminated in a two-edged spur, transparent as glass, and keen as only Nature knows how to make her weapons of defence.

Presently in obedience to some instinct the shoal left the shallow water inshore, and we watched it glide among the brown waving seaweed to the line of dull red, which indicated the outer edge of the coral reef and saw it no more. This, my piscatorial pastor and master says, was no doubt a community of striped cat-fish.

. . . the apparently solid fish was really a compact mass of little fish . . .

DIET OF SLUSH AND GRIT

Another group of worm-like or snaky creatures common on a coral-reef are the sea-cucumbers or bêche-de-mer. In my experience the most singular branch of the family is at once the longest and thinnest, for it resembles a snake so closely that at first sight the observer subconsciously assumes an attitude of hostility. There seem to be two varieties of the species. One is much more ruddy in appearance than the other, and its body is the smoother; but they are much alike in physique and helplessness. The figure of a sausage-skin four or five and even six feet long, and capable of elongation to almost double, containing muddy water in circulation and one end exhibiting a set of ever-waving tentacles, conveys a not unflattering notion of the animal as it lies coiled among the coral, half hidden with algae. Far too feeble to be offensive, it suffers collapse on alarm — that is to say, if such a violent mental and physical ill can befall an animal of such crude organism. At least, the tentacles are withdrawn, nor will they be protruded until some sense — unlikely to be either sight, hearing, taste, or touch, but probably nervous tension acutely susceptible to vibrations — tells that danger is past. Then the tentacles are shyly exhibited and the agitations of the animal are renewed ...

The progress of all species of bêche-de-mer is sedate and cautious, and this, probably the longest and the weakest and limpest of all, surpasses the race in deliberateness. It cannot move

The progress of all species of bêche-de-mer is sedate and cautious ...

as a whole, so it progresses in sections. When the head has been advanced to its utmost, about the middle of the body an independent series of succeedant ripples or wrinkles manifests itself and travels consistently ahead, while farther towards the rear another series follows, and so on, until the lagging tail is enabled to wrinkle itself along ...

The functions of bêche-de-mer are not only interesting, but requisite in the commonwealth of the coral reef ... Some seem to delight in a diet of slush of the consistency of thin gruel; others prefer fine grit; others, again, coarse particles of shell and coral grit and rough gravel ... When submitted to the sun on the dry beach death is speedy, and decomposition in the case of some species complete to obliteration in a few hours ... it melts at the sight of the sun, leaving as a relic of existence its last meal — a handful of grit — covered with a transparent film of varnish, which the first wavelet of the flowing tide dissolves ... Though feeble and of such readily dissolvable texture, bêche-de-mer may be regarded as among the mightiest agents in the conversion of the waste of the coral reef into mud — the sort of mud of which some of the toughest of rocks are compounded.

THE FIRST MEN

"Generation after generation of careless coloured folk must have been born and bred under its branches . . ."

ANCESTRAL SHADE

If it were possible to recall the spirits of the departed of this Isle to solemn session and to exact from them expression of opinion as to the central point of it, the popular, most comfortable and convenient camping-place, there can be no question that the voice of the majority would favour the curve of the bay rendered conspicuous by a bin-gum or coral tree. Within a few yards of permanent fresh water, on sand blackened by the mould of centuries of vegetation, close to an almost inextricable forest merging into jungle, whence a great portion of the necessaries of life were obtained, and but ten paces from the sea, the tree stood as a landmark, not of soaring height, but of bulk and comeliness withal.

Generation after generation of careless coloured folk must have been born and bred under its branches. When the soil became rank because of continuous residence and insects of diabolical activity pestered its occupants, the camp would shift to another site; but there existed proofs that the bin-gum-tree localised the thoughts of those aimless, unstable wanderers to whom a few bushes stuck in the sand as a screen from prevailing winds represent the home of the hour and all that the word signifies and embodies. Many a one was laid to rest beneath its spreading branches, for it was the custom of the pre-white folks days to swathe the dead in frail strips of bark, knees to chin, and place the stiffened corpse in a shallow pit in the humpy which had been in most recent occupation. If the dead during life had possessed exceptional qualities, burial rites would be ceremonious and prolonged. With tear and blood stained faces (for the mourners enforced grief by laceration of the flesh) incidents in the

It offered the hospitality of its shade to man, but little else, save flowers to gladden his eyes . . .

176

admirable career of the departed would be rehearsed in pantomime. The enactment of scenes from the life of the hunter and fighter might occupy hours. The art of the canoe or sword maker would be graphically mimicked. The life of the woman found rehearsal from infancy until she passed from the protection of her father into the arms of her lover. If she had died childless, a protesting infant or an effigy in bark would be placed on her shrunken bosom, so that she might not suffer the reproach of matrons who had preceded her to the mysterious better country.

The ancestral shade was a birthplace, an abiding-place, a cemetery, and the soil grew ever richer, and the thick-trunked tree displayed its ruddy flowers and gave of its best in nectar for birds and butterflies and gauze-winged, ever-flitting creatures.

It was not a comfortable tree to climb, for its grey-green branches were studded with wens each armed with a keen prickle, long and tough. It offered the hospitality of its shade to man, but little else, save flowers to gladden his eyes, though it stood as a perpetual calendar, or rather floral harbinger, of some of the most excellent things in life. At a certain season its big, trilobed, hollow-stalked leaves changed from bright green to pale yellow and lingeringly fell, and often before the last disappeared, flower-buds registered the date with almost almanac exactitude. Then, as the rich red began to glow here and there, and impatient small birds to assemble in anticipation of the annual feast, the old inhabitants of the Isle would comfort one another with reminiscences of the "oo-goo-ju", the nutmeg pigeon, which was wont to congregate in such numbers that adjacent and easily accessible isles were whitened. There would be plenty of eggs then, and in a few weeks squabs quiveringly, helplessly fat.

It was a good tree, for it gave good tidings, and it centralised the shelter of the Isle. Its blooms were delightfully, dashingly red, and they lasted long — that is, if the camp — the soil rectified by sun and rain — happened to be in residence, for then the sulphur-crested cockatoos would be scared. Otherwise the profligate birds would sever the heavy racemes of flower in their eagerness for honey until the ground beneath glowed with a furnace-hued shadow. But there would be still plenty for the gay sun-birds and the honey-eaters, while the grey goshawk would make the site of regular call, for the bibulous lesser birds could not always be on the alert, ready to dart into adjacent tea-trees. The hawk would abide its time, and have occasion, after its kind, to be grateful because of the tree and its seductive nectar which translated artless little songsters into shrill-tongued roysterers, careless of the ills of life, or at least less watchful for the presence of crafty enemies. Flying foxes would swoop into the tree at sundown to squeak and gibber among its repellent branches till dawn, when some, too full for flight, would hang among the lower limbs all day, sleeping with eyes veiled by leathery wings.

For many a long day the bin-gum tolerated no undergrowth. Despotic over its territory, the shade was clean but for a carpet of ferns, and its branches free from the embraces of orchids, save that which bears the ghostly white flowers which set off its own of bold red. But as it passed its maturity shrubs and saplings began to encroach, until it was the centre of a circus of upstart vegetation, though still stretching big, knotty limbs over the slim youths of yesterday. Anterior to this era a neglected fire had scorched a portion of its trunk. Decay set in. A huge cavity gradually appeared, betokening vital injuries. The soft though tough wood does not patiently endure the annihilating fret of time. Far up in a recess of this cavity a toy boomerang was found, placed there by some provident but forgetful piccaninny. At the date of the discovery of the missile the age of the resident blacks had passed away; but still the tree stood, stout of limb, while the encompassing saplings shot up until sun-seeking shoots caressed the branches and familiarised with the blooms, as if taking credit for the seasonal gaiety of the patriarch.

In the prime of life the wood of the bin-gum is of pale straw colour with a faint pinkish tinge, and tough though light. Sapless age makes it tindery, and the decaying fibre descends in dust — glissades of dust which form moraines within the hollow of the base. Then the end is not far off.

The old tree might have been credited with premonition of its fate. However fanciful to ascribe to it power of utterance, some phenomena, perhaps associated with the dusty flux draining its vitals, gave it distinct voice. On silent days it was often heard — a whispering, whimpering sing-song, pitifully weak for so great a tree, but not without appeal. Did it not suggest the sanctuary of some wood-nymph chanting never so faint a death psalm — a monotone which the idlest zephyr might still?

Disdaining to die while consenting to disappear, the great tree, proudly green of head, did not fall headlong, like a giant, in its pride, but subsided silently behind its leafy screen while all the winds were still, and as one who passes away full of years and with untarnished conscience.

Though the saplings and shrubs which fought for its place decently conceal its shattered relics, addressing glossy leaves to the face of the sun, is it quite vain to expect that its graceful proportions — a true and stately dome — will be transmitted to the most worthy of its descendants? Or that they will escape for so long a term the many mischances that befall soft-wooded trees? No; the bin-gum of the bay was unique ... So lovely and conspicuous a feature is not to be reconstituted under a century.

If it be permitted to assume that trees are sentient, that each — since it differs from all others in some material quality and condition — has its individuality, and that one may stand out from the rest as a figure and representative of its age, then was this old monarch which maintained its red robes to the last an exemplar of the race whose births, nuptials, pastimes, deaths and burials it witnessed from the date when the good ship *Endeavour* slowly plodded along the alien coast. The dust of the witness is blending in common decay. A few months and not a trace will be discoverable, and what is left of those who rested in its shade? In the pages of history they will be unchronicled, for were not their lives less beautiful than the life of a tree, and their renown no more durable?

ART STUDIOS

Time and diligent search revealed the location on the island of two art galleries, or rather independent studios, where there are exhibited works of distinct character. Tradition points to the existence of a third, the discovery of which gives zest to each exploratory expedition. Possibly it may also display original exploits in the realms of fancy, and so confirm the opinion that the black artists were not mere copyists of each other, but belonged to different schools, each having his own method and allowing his talent free and untrammelled development.

What may be designated the Lower Studio is on the eastern slope, and is only to be approached from the sea in calm weather, the alternative route being a tiresome climb, a long and tormenting struggle through the jungle, and a descent among a confusion of rocks and boulders. It is situated about a couple of hundred feet above sea-level, quite hidden in the leafy wilderness which covers that aspect of the island from high-water mark to the summit of the ridge. Unless the spot was indicated, one might search for it for years in vain, and though I

Animated nature and still life have been studied and reproduced . . .

179

had made frequent inquiries, its existence was made known only by chance, its importance being considered insignificant compared with the other studio, the glories of which had frequently been descanted upon. Taking the sea-route, there is a natural harbour available, just capacious enough for a small dingy, and up above the rocks, swept bare by the surges, a dense and tangled scrub "whereto the climber upwards turns his face", and taking advantage of such aids as aerial roots, slim saplings, and the reed-like growths of the so-called native ginger, begins the steep ascent. Where the rock does not emerge from the surface, the black soil is loose and kept in perpetual cultivation by scrub fowl, the wonder being that earth reposes at such an angle. But for interlacing and matted roots all must slide down to the sea.

A few minutes' exertion lands one at the portal of the studio, which is of the lean-to order of architecture, a granite boulder having one fairly vertical face being overshadowed by a much higher rock having a dip of about sixty degrees.

Here originally there were five exhibits. Two have weathered away almost to nothingness, some faint streaks and blotches of red earth, in which medium all the pictures have been executed, alone remaining. Those subjects that are readily decipherable are mutilated after the style of certain much-prized antiques.

Of those which have successfully withstood the ravages of time, two apparently represent lizards, and the third seems to portray a monstrosity — a human being with a rudimentary tail. A German philosopher might possibly build upon this embryonic tail a theory to prove that the Australian Aboriginal is indeed and in fact the missing link, and thereby excel in ethnological venture those who merely recognise in him the relic from a prehistoric age of man. Could it not be argued that the picture reveals an act of unconscious cerebration — an instinctive knowledge of ancestors with tails? . . .

Most of the central figure is clearly discernible; but parts of the outline have become blurred and irregular . . . In one case, fact seems to belie tradition, for there exist faint suggestions of a red head — and a red-headed black is as rare as a black with a tail; but the traces are so extremely vague and indeterminate as to render any attempt at restoration hopeless. But does not this obscurity and partial dismemberment lend an air of antiquity, much prized elsewhere, to these savage frescoes?

Of quite a different order are the works in the Upper Studio at the sign of the White Stripe. This lies close to the backbone of the island, in the heart of a bewildering jumble of immense rocks overgrown with jungle . . .

From ships that past to the East may be seen a bold white streak on the face of a huge rock, so sharply defined and accurate in alignment that it might be mistaken for a guide to mariners, or rather a warning, for the floor of the ocean is strewn with patches of coral, and the rocks are singularly forbidding, save on calm days. Opinion current among the blacks asserted that the paintings were on a rock below the disjointed precipice on the top of the ridge made conspicuous by the broad white band. The sign was found to be due to the bleaching of the rock face by the drainage from a mass of stag's horn fern. Possessed of this information, which proved in the long run to be trustworthy, several exploratory trips were undertaken. To reach the locality from Brammo Bay, one must cross the middle of the backbone of the island, and descend some little distance on the Pacific slope.

I scaled and scrambled over and crawled upon huge rocks, peered into gloomy crevices with daylight edges fringed with ferns and orchids, squeezed through narrow tunnels, and groped in dark recesses without finding any evidence of prehistoric art. Blacks do not care to venture into places where twilight always reigns, though they are curious to learn the experiences and sensations of other explorers of the gloom. At last, however, patience was rewarded, and beneath a great granite rock, which on three previous excursions had been overlooked, the paintings were discovered. In their execution the artist must have lain on his back, for the "cave" does not permit one to sit upright in it, except towards the wide and expansive front, and the subjects are on the ceiling, which is fairly flat. The floor, thick with a fine brown dust mingled with shining specks of decomposed granite, and dimpled with hundreds of pitfalls of the ant-lion, slopes upward. It is cool, and a dry, secure spot. Not even the torrential rains of many decades of wet seasons have damped the floor. One feels as though he were disturbing the dust of ages; when sitting back to admire the decorated ceiling, he necessarily imprints patterns which are the replicas of those made by flesh and bone long since numbered among the anonymous dead.

The sea laves the hot rocks 600 feet below, and booms and gobbles in the cool crevices . . . Here, at the entrance, lie a couple of charred sticks, significant of the last fire of the artist, which smouldered out perhaps half a century ago. On the very doorstep is a disc of pearl-shell, the discarded beginning of a fish-hook. These relics give to the scene a pathetic interest. As I looked at them ponderingly, a frog far in the back of the cave gave a discordant, echoing croak, which started the sulky and suspicious black boy who attended me into an abrupt exclamation of semi-fright; while a scrub fowl, scratching for its living overhead, dislodged a chip of granite which went clicking down the rocks. "Tom", at the instant, felt that the spirit of the departed was manifesting, in the hollow tones of a frog and the activity of a bird, resentment at the intrusion of his haunts, and was warning us to begone. But we had come far on a toilsome errand, and were not to be scared away by trifles, though a transient feeling of reluctance to disturb the solemnity of the studio could not be withheld.

Remembering the fervid praises of the treasures by those who had not seen them, a sense of disappointment when they came to be examined was inevitable . . . Apparently the rock surface was slightly smoothed where inequalities existed — in one case the design follows the ridges and hollows — the subjects being worked in in dry earth of a chalky nature, dull red in colour. Animated nature and still life have been studied and reproduced. The turtle is true, and the most conspicuous and sharply-defined study the least convincing . . .

Comparing the works of the two studios, there is little doubt that there were at least two artists native of Dunk Island in times past, and in that respect the island was infinitely superior to its present state. Each appears to have effected a different kind of work — one devoting himself to realistic reptiles and the human form debased, and the other almost solely to the creation of conventional designs, and the representation of the animals and of weapons of his age. One illustrated man, and even gave to one of his reptiles a semi-human shape; the other exercised an exuberant fancy for ornamentation. Each bequeathed to the present day and generation works that are at least free from the subtleties of art.

FRUITS OF THE EARTH

To fare sumptuously every day was not the lot of the natives of Dunk Island. In excessively rainy weather they were often glad of the coarsest and hardest of foods. Certain sharks are eaten with avidity whenever they are secured; but some species are too rank and tough to be endurable under any but extraordinary circumstances. Oysters were always plentiful, but a diet restricted to the most delicate of molluscs palls on the palate even of a black fellow. Ordinarily, food was abundant. For the most part it had only to be picked up and cooked. Frequently it was eaten on the spot, fresh from bountiful Nature's hands; but blacks appreciate changes of diet — even when the change is retrogressive ... When, as sometimes happened, the desire for novelty came, the whole population would paddle away to the mainland or to one or other of the adjacent islands, voyages being undertaken as far away as distant Hinchinbrook. Turtle do not favour the beaches and sandbanks of Dunk Island generally as safe depositories for their innumerable eggs, and when the longing came for these delicacies the inhabitants would with one accord travel to those islands in the security of which turtle still exhibit faith. The drift of the population hither and thither was not due to the scarcity of food but to a wayward impulse. As a rule there was little for the population to do save to eat, drink, laze away the hotter hours of the day, and "corroboree" at night.

Astonishment can scarcely be withheld when an attempt is made to catalogue the available foods of the island, the variety and quantity. No effort was made at cultivation. Blacks took no heed of the morrow, but accepted the fruits of the earth without thought of inciting Nature to produce better or more abundantly, and yet how plenteous were her gifts! ...

The repast might be initiated with a few oysters on the shell (with a choice of three or four varieties); a selection of many fish would be succeeded by real turtle ("padgegal") soup (in the original shell) ... the joint, a huge piece of dugong ("palangul") kummaoried, rich and excellent, with entrees of turtle cutlets and baked grubs ("tamboon"), ivory white with yellow heads, as neat and pretty a dish as could be seen ... When the beetles into which these stolid grubs and fidgety nymphs develop, are chopped out of decayed wood, they have the odour of truffles, and emit two distinct squeaky notes from the throat and the abdominal segments respectively. Each maintains a duet with itself until the hot embers impose silence and convert them into dainty nutty morsels. Roast scrub fowl eggs would be no novelty, and baked crayfish ("toolac"), bluey-white and leathery ... might lend a decorative effect. Raw echinus ("kierbang"), saline and tonic, would clear the palate for succeeding delicacies.

The tough sweet yam ("pundinoo"), the heart of the Alexandra palm ("koobinkarra"), the hard rhizome of *Bowenia spectabilis* ("moonah") after being allowed weeks to decompose, the core of the tree fern ("kalojoo"), the long root-stock of *Curculigo ensifolia* ("harpee") crisp and slightly bitter, the broad beans of the white mangrove ("kumooroo"), would stand as vegetables.

Sweets would be the weakest part of the menu. One pudding might certainly be included, vermicelli (shredded bean-tree nuts — "tindaburra") with honey and orange-coloured balsamic custard, scraped from the outside of the drupes of the *Pandanus tectorius* ("pimnar").

Dessert, on the other hand, might be plentiful and varied. "Bedyewrie" (*Ximenia americana*), thirst-allaying and palate-sharpening, "topkie" (Herbert River cherry), resembling red currants in flavour; "poolboonong" (finger cherry), sweet, soft and appeasing; "panga-panga", raspberry; "koobadgaroo" (Leichhardt-tree), resembling a strawberry in shape, but brown, spicy and hot; "murkuekee" (snow-white berries of *Syzygium suborbicularis*), vapid, and as insipid as an immature medlar; "raroo" (*Planchonia careya*), mealy and biting. Various figs, ranging in size from a large red currant to a tennis-ball, and in colour from white through all the tints from pale yellow and green to red, purple and black, sweet and generally mawkish.

The banana would be there in the *Musa banksia* ("boogaroo"), although "close-up all bone"; but the Davidsonian plum, plentiful on the mainland, would be absent. The scape of the *Hornstedia scottiana*, oozing viscid nectar, might stand as a sweetmeat.

Then, dallying with tomahawks and flat stones with the tough nuts of the "moojee" (*Terminalia melanocarpa*), and the drupes of the "cankee" (*Pandanus aquaticus*) to extract the narrow sweet kernels, and sipping the while cordial compounded of the larvae of green tree-ants ("bookgruin"), acidulous and nippy, the men might indulge in after-dinner stories and reminiscences, as the gins and piccaninnies drink heartily of water sweetened with sugar-bag (honey-comb), and chew the seeds contained in the china-blue pericarp of the native-ginger — "oolpun".

THE SOUL WITHIN THE STONE

Not more than a hundred yards from its mud-besmeared mouth the convenient mangroves disappear and the little creek assumes becoming airs. Huge tea-trees, with cushiony bark, straddle it, and ferns grow strongly in all its nooks and bends. When the big trees blossom in watery yellow, yellow-eared honey-eaters, blue-bibbed sun-birds, and screeching parrots in accordant colours, assemble joyously, for the aroma, as of burnt honey, spreads far and wide, bidding all, butterflies and jewel-backed beetles which buzz and hum, to the feast, until the aerial anthem is harmonic to the rustle of the sea.

The sturdy feet of the trees stand in black peat, through which the water from the wholesome hills oozes and dribbles, and the russet stain from discarded leaves is on their white bases . . .

. . . there is one tree which, if not superior to the rest in broadness of base, height, fairness of bark, and fullness of bloom, has especial endowment. It stands at the spot where generation after generation of the original owners of the soil have crossed the creek, wearing a waving path upon which ferns ever encroach and which every flood amends. In a recess in its massive roots reposes "Kidj-o-bang", the restless stone — a boulder, man's-head size, stained with a rim of sober brown.

This is its accustomed seat. It roves the locality, returning, swallow-like, to the close-fitting hollow of the root. The embraces of the root are sometimes so strong that the dingy stone may not be moved. But the floods of the wet season maintain an unceasing cataract to its dislodgment, and then, according to the legends of the blacks, it begins to "walk about". It may rest a month just out of reach of the disturbing water among the ferns. It has been known to appear mysteriously on the sandy beach two hundred yards away, to which spot it is said to travel by way of the grass lands, avoiding the slur of the muddy creek.

Whether it seeks change of scene beyond the ripple of dead leaves and spoil of the flood, or whether it ventures out on to the open beach, where the breezes from the Pacific play upon it, the round white stone returns, independent of the agency of man, to the sanctuary which time, ever-flowing water, and the hospitable roots of the tree, have combined to afford. It is there this day . . . nestling cosily in the grotto in which the dyed slime smears it as with pale blood.

To the ordinary investigator of the whimsicalities of "Kidj-o-bang" the blacks betray no secret . . . Discreetly pursue the subject and peradventure you may be told precisely why the stone may not always rest in the one spot in the whole world which it fits as a kernel its shell. It has been, they assert, associated with an evil deed of which it is now the emblem . . .

Musing on the spot, the legend of the roving stone usurped my thoughts. The trivial and uncertain notions of the black boy who was the first to tell it, and by theatrical gestures to illustrate its verities, became more and more indistinct. The soothsayers of the long past had been forbidden by Nature to doubt that which was the lore of the camp. Was it that Nature reasserted her influence — that the essences of the scene, subtle and pervasive, had recurred, creating a receptive spirit, so deep a religion of assent that shadow and substance intermingled to my bewilderment? I was permitted to be a sensitive percipient in the midst of the ashes of shiftless folk who had passed away, catching but a casual and deceptive glimpse of the coming of the desolating white man.

Piln-goi, the black boy, had wandered up the creek. A thrilling silence prevailed. Stooping down, I laved my hands in the softly flowing water, idly intent on lifting the stone. The tawny slime defeated irresolute efforts, and my slipping hands bestowed a baptismal splash.

Instantly I became conscious of a strange presence, and, glancing over my shoulder, saw an unfamiliar black boy lurking behind a glistening-fronded cycad.

The whole scene had undergone wishful transformation. The white-barked trees, purified of smears from the sooty fingers of fire, stood out in splendid contrast to a richer, thicker, a flowery undergrowth. Tall fern-trees spread green cobwebs to entrap sunbeams. The cycad under which the boy crouched was slim-shaped, and its foliage resembled that of one of the most beautiful of ferns, with languorous, dolorous fronds, while it was crowned with a huge fruit of golden-brown. All the scene had been wondrously transfigured. Time's treacheries had been defeated. A garden-like age had been restored. The sword-leaved orchid dangled yard-long sprays of brilliant yellow flowers, which saturated the air with delicate perfume. Fearless birds fluttered among and hovered over the pendant blooms, whistling and calling. Water-rats sported in the lily-bespangled stream, and a platypus basked on the bank.

From the strained and expectant attitude of the boy, it was apparent that he was hunting. He stepped cautiously out of cover, and, using a woomera of dark wood with oval clutches of white shell, threw a spear into the long grass. A kangaroo, mad with fear and pain, staggered forward, knowing not whence fate had struck it, and, lurching helplessly, sank among the ferns on the margin of the water. Ignoring my presence, the boy, having completed the hunter's office with a blow from a nulla-nulla, called in a thin, shrill voice:

"Yano-lee!" (We go this way.)

In a few seconds a young girl of his own race stepped through the leafy screen. She cast casual glances at the dead kangaroo, and without saying a word to her companion came to the pool, stooped down beside me, and drank eagerly and noisily, using a scoop improvised from a leaf. Her back glistened with perspiration, and her coarse, fuzzy, uncleanly hair ceased in tufts on her neck. It was a slim and shapely little figure. The plumes of the orchid, golden and syrupy, swayed over her heedless head and seemed to caress it. Her eyes, round, large, and brimful of the bewildering eagerness of youth, relieved the unobtrusive expansiveness of her nose and almost atoned for her savage lips. Though almost touching me, the most shy, wild creature of the bush seemed unconscious of my presence . . .

"Kidj-o-bang" had vanished. There was its cell. A full and stainless stream, in a gurgling cataract, sparkled over the big root, while high among the blossoms birds clambered incessantly for nectar. The primitive pair were at home, but not at ease, in this Garden of Eden. They spoke in mumbling tones, of which I could catch but stray phrases, though I listened eagerly . . .

Swarms of green ants, in a scramble for food, almost obscured the blood-stains on the fur of the kangaroo, and, brushing them away, the boy made and enlarged with his fingers an opening in the body, and having torn out the heart, liver, and kidneys, made a fire, scarce a hand's-breadth wide and smokeless, on which the meat was singed prior to being munched with grim deliberation. They ate largely, some of the flesh from the hind quarters being also eaten, scrap by scrap.

Were they fugitives? Tall and strong, the boy was as alert and suspicious as a dingo. Every sense was strained. He seemed intent upon subduing the very noises in his head as he slowly crushed his food and gulped.

A forlorn cry, half appeal, half gurgle, filtered through the leafage as from the beach, and on the instant the jungle had soundlessly absorbed the affrighted pair. The handful of fire and the mutilated kangaroo remained as the only evidences of the handiwork of man . . . Something in the tone of the voice told of a member of my own race in sore distress. Yet I could not respond to his appeal or move to his aid.

Half an hour of intense silence passed, and then a lusty shout startled the air. Surely, I thought, the wayfarer who makes such outcry in this unpeopled wilderness is an uncouth fellow who has lost his way and thinks to dialogue with echoes for relief of loneliness. Presently the cracking of branchlets and a rumble of discontented phrases told of someone blundering along through the mangroves . . . a big, aggressive, weather-scored man, his only clothing a pair of short pants of canvas, stained with wear and stiff and whitened with frost like sea-salt. The ocean had but an hour ago cast him like its scum on the beach.

He burst on the scene to plunge his broken lips into the water at my feet. Like the natives, he drank long and noisily, and when his thirst was allayed called to an imaginary mate — "Pietro, Pietro!" cursed freely when no answer came, and whimpered like a babe.

Huge of body, strong of limb, bully and brute stamped on his coarse features, yet did his dread of loneliness piteously overcome him. His bald pate, hung about with scant reddish ringlets, had been roasted by the tropic sun until it glowed, and eyes and nose strove for supremacy of inflammation. An unkempt moustache did not hide teeth of disreputable tint; chin and jowl were covered with a fortnight's growth of streaky hair.

Turning from the water, he saw the dismembered kangaroo, and, seizing one of the legs, tore the flesh from the bones and with ravenous greed began an uncleanly feast. The impure drank of the pure water and gulped the strong flesh until his gorged stomach swelled cask-shape, and then he slept as noisily as he had eaten and drank.

A leathern belt, cracked and whitened, furrowed his distended girth, and as he lay stretched with the sun scrutinising his face, flies and mosquitoes and carnivorous green ants feasted on his blood at will . . . What could the assaults and stings of myriads of insects avail against fatigue so formidable? . . .

The strong man fidgeted under the persistent blaze. Perspiration poured from his skin; he snarled; his eyelids twitched and quivered; the veins of neck and forehead throbbed ominously. The sun does not tolerate disobedience. A thin trickle of blood issued from the grimy nose, and with a snort the man awoke, his flame-red eyes swilled with enforced tears. Dazedly he plunged his head into the water and drank greedily, and, sitting up, spat sullenly and with signs of disgust and contempt. What comfort could cold water afford so repleted a stomach?

Having disdainfully spurned the remnants of the kangaroo, he sat head between knees, grumbling against fate. To him the fruitful and pleasant land was disconsolate. A castaway, he had drifted on to its welcome shores, and all that it could offer was loneliness, cold water, the raw flesh of a strange animal, and denial of the solace of sleep. Out of the depths of his misery and dejection he called imperatively on his God, and taking from the lining of his belt a thumb-sized purse of netted silver, displayed a glorious pearl, which he held aloft, and with an admixture of supplication and imprecation proffered it to the Most High as grudging ransom from a God-abandoned country . . .

Steamy heat distilled strong aromatic odours from the myriad leaves; languid flowers gave copiously and of the best of their fragrance; ferns and lotus did obeisance to high noon. The birds had ceased to whistle, and the droning of bees gave to the upper air slumbering rhythm of its own.

Again the intruder slept. Again the sun commanded and he woke raging. Standing, he cursed both loud and long, eyes protuberant, face purpling under the strain of vindictive oaths.

What an unflattering contrast to the unclad natives who had dominated yet blended with the scene — the girl the prototype of a swaying palm, the boy that of a tough young blood-wood beside the creek, among the topmost branches of which a crimson-flowered mistletoe made a splash of colour in harmony with the single red feather from the wing of a black cockatoo which the soft-tongued youth had entangled in his hair.

This gross, profane, sun-smitten, sea-rejected herald of civilisation, disowned by his fellows, disinherited of the world, defiled the spot, and his voice created an inaugural discord.

With arms uplifted, he muttered ineffectual curses against his fellows, upbraided his saints, and defied his deity. But while his lips frothed with the passion of a stuttering tongue, the provoked but just genius of the spot passed sentence, and swiftly and silently the messengers of

All the scene had been wondrously transfigured . . . A garden-like age had been restored.

Death came. Four slender spears penetrated his shaggy chest, as with a scream which ended in a gulp he splashed back into the water. His struggles and splutterings soon ceased. Silence resumed its fascination.

Blood welled from the mouth and nose and spear wounds, which the eager water carried off in wavy, independent streams, while the dead face whitened.

Many minutes elapsed before a dozen wild-eyed natives cautiously oozed through the jungle, stimulating each other's nervousness by reassuring gestures. Certain that the trespasser on their dominion was incapable of mischief, they began to chatter, showing fidgety interest in the body, which they touched and poked fearsomely with spears.

Dead eyes stared unblinkingly at the sun through a curtain of water, which had already cleaned them of heat and passion, and wisps of red hair drifted over the forehead.

The untimely yelp of a dingo some few yards in the jungle inspired a similar response from one of the men, and without shyness or reserve the boy and girl joined the throng, and all began to talk excitedly. Some of the men assumed threatening attitudes towards the girl, who stood submissively, while the boy talked in a rage of excitement. He had chosen his mate, and would not, even on pain of summary death, abandon her.

So trivial an incident as the love affairs of boy and girl could not compare with the phenomenon in the water. The crisis was momentary. Amazement was pictured in every face, and not a man but subjected the bleeding body to gross contempt and what passed among them for ridicule. They mimicked the high stomach as they stood, as the dead man had stood, with arms aloft in rebellion against his lot, and fell back, as he had fallen, screaming, to kick and wallow on the ground. Here was plot and matter for ludicrous corroboree, the first rehearsal of which took place on the scene.

Soon curiosity took possession of the unstable actors. The belt was removed, and on the purse being fumbled with, several small pearls fell out. They were disregarded; but the strong man of the party looped the belt about his own inadequate waist, the girl hid the purse (which had been passed from hand to hand) in her hair, while the men tore the bone buttons from the pants and fitted them into their ears as they strutted foppishly.

The dead eyes stared defiantly up into the sky, the face whitened, and the stains of blood seemed to settle on it.

A harsh sound came as an electric shock, and I heard as from afar off Piln-goi shout:

"You bin sleep long time, boss! Big low water. We fella look out pearl-shell!"

The scene had resumed everyday aspects. The sun concentrated its rays on my head through a rift in the jungle, and the stone, stained dull red, lay in its cell, while rootlets fringed with tawny slime wavered over it . . .

To Paradise and Back

A gaunt old man with grizzled head, shrunk shanks, and a crooked arm was the most timid of the strange mob of blacks who, under the guidance of some semi-civilised friends, visited the clearing of a settler on one of the rivers flowing into Rockingham Bay. Shy and suspicious, his friends had difficulty in reassuring him of the peace-loving character of the settler, whose hut stood in the midst of an orange-grove. In a few days, for no disturbing element existed, the nervousness of the old man in the presence of his host ceased, and it was then noticed that those who had accompanied him from the jungle-covered mountains, as well as the friends he had picked up near the home of the white man, paid him the rare compliment of deference. Well they might, for he was a man of importance, though he lacked clothing and the elements of decency. The old man's friends — perhaps because of his semi-helplessness, due to the twisted limb — performed various friendly offices for him, and never thought of the spice of any dread avowal, for he was far superior to them all, and righteously was he honoured. The lean Old Man had visited that "undiscovered country from whose bourne no traveller returns". There was no doubt of his actual presence in this. There were his young wife and several companions, male and female, ready to corroborate his story; and was not his crippled arm painful but unimpeachable testimony to the reality of his experiences?

In the telling of the history of a too brief sojourn in the paradise of the blacks the old man took but little part, for his English was *nil*. The members of the party knew it by rote, and some of them could make themselves understood. Pieced together — for the story came out bit by bit — it ran thus:

A very long time ago, when the Old Man was young and lusty and the "King" of the tribe, an evil-minded "boy" made great rains. All the rivers overflowed their banks, the plain and tea-tree swamps became impassable, the hollows between the hills were filled with water. Week after week it rained continuously, the floods gradually hemming in the camp and restricting the wanderings of the men to one long ridge of forest country. Soon all the food obtainable within such narrow limits was eaten. Every one became hungry, for the camp was large and its daily necessities considerable. Patiently they waited for the subsidence of the waters, but more rain came and the camp grew hungrier than ever. Many sat in their shelters and drank water copiously, thereby creating a temporary sensation of satisfaction.

In the midst of the adversity the Old Man remembered having seen a "bees' nest" up a gigantic tree some distance away. He had not climbed the tree offhand because the feat seemed to be impossible. What might have been just possible on a well-filled stomach was worth hazarding now that he was famishing. So, wading and swimming, he gained the little dry knoll in the centre of which stood an enormous bean-tree, and there, a long way up, was the "bees' nest". With a piece of cane from a creeping palm and a stone tomahawk he slowly ascended the tree, for he was weak and his nerves unstrung. But he joyed when he reached the "bees' nest", for it was large and full of honey and brood comb — a feast in prospect for the whole camp. Then, as he set to work to chop out the comb, he heard, to his astonishment, voices below, and peering down, saw not only a wife who had departed to the land of spirits a year or so before, but his own mother, who had died when he was a youth. Greeting him in glad tones, they told him to come down, and that they would show him a big camp in good dry country where there was abundance of food.

Descending the tree with the cane loop, he saw that his previous wife was well favoured and fat, that his mother, too, was portly, that they had dilly-bags crammed with tokens of material wealth. They were overjoyed to see him, but expressed wonder that he was so weak when so much good food was available. Saying but little, they struck out for the big camp. The Old Man noticed, as they walked, that a track through the thickest part of the jungle opened up —

a beaten, straight track, which he, for all his wanderings, had never before seen. The country was dry, too. Scrub hens and scrub turkeys, cassowaries, wallabies, huge carpet snakes, pigeons, fruits and nuts, bees' nests, and decayed trees full of great white grubs were there in plenty.

Silently and swiftly the three passed along the track through a country which, at every step, became more desirable, and at last emerged on an immense pocket where there was a concourse of gunyahs from which the smoke curled up, and in every gunyah was abundance . . .

The cup of happiness overflowed when, conducted through merry throngs to a particular spot, the Old Man was greeted by relations and friends for whom he had once duly mourned, plastering his face with ceremonious charcoal and clay, and denying himself needed food . . .

For three days he dwelt in the good land with content, lionised by his relatives, taking part in the hunts, the feasts, the corroborees, and being urged never to return to the camp of floods and hunger. Here was bliss. Every wish amply gratified, who would willingly depart from so entrancing a place? And with fervent promises on his lips never to go away he was conscious of a sharp pain in his wrist and found himself crumpled up, stiff, sore, hungry, and helpless, at the foot of the big tree.

Reluctantly back in the land of stress and distress, so woefully weak that he could not stand without swaying, while his right hand dangled helplessly, confused sounds of Paradise still rang in his ears, verifying all that had recently befallen.

He gazed around, dismayed to see no trace of his wife or mother; no clean-cut, straight path leading to the land of pure delight. Far up the tree hung the cane loop; beside him lay the stone tomahawk. All present realities were of pain and hunger. Bewildered, slowly and with much difficulty, he made his way to the flooded camp, noticing as he went that water-courses he had been compelled to swim were now fordable — proof of the lapse of time.

Eyes starved to impassiveness stared at the gaunt, crippled creature, complaining mutely, for no food had been brought. Some muttered that he had eaten it all during his unaccounted absence.

Silently the old man bound up his wrist excruciatingly tight with strips of bark, and then in detail told of his glad sojourn in Paradise.

Then the faces of the famishing lit up with joyous expectancy and — impatient, reckless, heedless of floods, forgetful of weakness born of hunger — one and all hastened to the scene whence began the straight path to the enchanting land. But keen as the best trackers might be, not the least sign in proof of the Old Man's experiences could be found . . .

Years have elapsed, but the Old Man and his friends have not lost faith in the existence locally of the Happy Land. Had he not been hither, led by wife and mother, and did he not remain there three days — the only days of unimpeded joy in his long life? No such rich privilege had ever befallen any one else; but without questioning or envy all verify his words and delight to do him honour.

All the rivers overflowed their banks, the plain and tea-tree swamps became impassable . . .

PHOTOGRAPHIC CREDITS

Aquavisuals, Townsville
   11
Bay Picture Library
   89, 95, 106, 154, 162, 169, 173, 176
Isobel Bennett
   35, 157, 160, 163
Densey Clyne
   133, 137
Neville Coleman
   151, 172
Gary Hansen
   46, 186
Bill and Betty Hinton
   10, 45, 65, 122, 128, 136, 138, 147
The International Photographic Library
   22, 41, 43, 99, 131, 155, 179
Ralph and Daphne Keller
   23, 69, 73, 81, 91, 93, 111, 114, 123, 139, 142, 145, 146
The Photographic Library of Australia
   2, 3, 7, 15, 27, 31, 48, 60, 64, 86, 90, 118
G. R. Roberts
   103
Robin Smith
   14, 19, 36, 49, 77, 83, 167, 191
Bill Wood
   52, 61, 152, 165, 171